"This book is timely and smart. It handles a particularly significant economic/ social change, the study of which is still relatively under-developed. I particularly liked the mix of national accounts of new labor institutions with cross-national accounts of the impact of flexible labor in the workplace, especially as it discusses issues of integration and compatibility with 'stable' labor forces inside the firms. This poly-focus is a strength, and a novelty with respect to other books in the field."

—*Michael Blim, City University of New York*

Management and Organization of Temporary Agency Work

Over the past two decades, the use of flexible employment relations has increased in most developed countries. The growth of temporary agency work constitutes a significant component of this development. Organizations are now facing the challenges of managing a "blended workforce" (i.e., a workforce consisting of both direct hires and contractors). At a time when Europe, as well as the rest of the world, is facing enhanced global competition and a severe labour market crisis, an understanding of temporary employment practices has become all the more acute. In view of the evolution of agency work in the Western world over the past decade, the chapters in this volume focus on the management and organization of temporary agency work in order to highlight possibilities and pitfalls for the use of temporary employment in the wake of changed employment practices and challenges to labour market stability and welfare structures.

Together, the new case studies presented in this volume provide a wide scope of analysis of the organization and management of temporary agency work, offering a much-needed contribution to the discussion of issues and priorities that guide and shape organizational practices today. The particular uniqueness of this volume lies in the empirical richness and variety of local case studies and the way in which these are related to wider policy aims, ideological shifts, and the dynamics of organizational practice, with a particular focus on the organization and management of "blended workforces."

Bas Koene is Assistant Professor of Organization and Human Resource Management at Rotterdam School of Management, Erasmus University Rotterdam in the Netherlands. He studies human agency and leadership in processes of institutional change and organizational development, especially regarding the organization of work and the management of temporary employment. He has published in journals such as *Leadership Quarterly, Human Resource Management Journal, Journal of Organizational Change Management, Personnel Review, Human Relations,* and *Accounting Organizations and Society.* Bas Koene is also director of the RSM Case Development Centre.

Christina Garsten is Professor of Social Anthropology at Stockholm University and of Globalization and Organization at Copenhagen Business School. She is Chair of the Executive Board of Score (Stockholm Centre for Organizational Research, Stockholm University, and Stockholm School of Economics). Her research interests focus on flexible forms of employment, subjectivity, and identity (*Workplace Vagabonds*). More recent research engages with transparency and accountability in global organizations (*Transparency in a New Global Order*, co-edited with M. Lindh de Montoya; *Organizing Transnational Accountability*, co-edited with M. Boström), corporate ethics (*Ethical Dilemmas in Management*, co-edited with T. Hernes), and the role of think tanks in influencing policy agendas.

Nathalie Galais is Senior Lecturer at the Department of Organizational and Social Psychology at the University of Erlangen-Nuremberg, Germany. Her main research interests include worker-organization relationship in non-standard work arrangements, effects of contingent work status on team climate, and workers' identity formation. She has conducted research on skill development and health outcomes of different groups of contingent workers for federal institutes such as the Federal Institute for Vocational Education and Training, the Federal Institute for Occupational Safety and Health, and the Ministry of Education and Research. She has published the results of this research in *Human Relations* and the *International Journal of Selection and Assessment.*

Routledge Studies in Management, Organizations, and Society

For a full list of titles in this series, please visit www.routledge.com

This series presents innovative work grounded in new realities, addressing issues crucial to an understanding of the contemporary world. This is the world of organized societies, where boundaries between formal and informal, public and private, local and global organizations have been displaced or have vanished, along with other nineteenth-century dichotomies and oppositions. Management, apart from becoming a specialized profession for a growing number of people, is an everyday activity for most members of modern societies.

Similarly, at the level of enquiry, culture and technology, and literature and economics, can no longer be conceived of as isolated intellectual fields; conventional canons and established mainstreams are contested. Management, Organizations, and Society addresses these contemporary dynamics of transformation in a manner that transcends disciplinary boundaries, with books that will appeal to researchers, students, and practitioners alike.

Other titles in this series

Management and Organization of Temporary Agency Work

Edited by Bas Koene, Christina Garsten, and Nathalie Galais

Routledge
Taylor & Francis Group

NEW YORK AND LONDON

First published 2014
by Routledge
711 Third Avenue, New York, NY 10017

and by Routledge
2 Park Square, Milton Park, Abingdon, Oxon OX14 4RN

*Routledge is an imprint of the Taylor & Francis Group,
an informa business*

© 2014 Taylor & Francis

Library of Congress Cataloging-in-Publication Data

Management and organization of temporary agency work / edited by
   Bas Koene, Christina Garsten, and Nathalie Galais.
      pages cm. — (Routledge studies in management, organizations, and
society ; 27)
      Includes bibliographical references and index.
   1. Temporary employment.   2. Temporary employment—Europe.
3. Temporary help services.   4. Temporary employees.   I. Koene, Bas,
1966–   II. Garsten, Christina.   III. Galais, N. (Nathalie)
      HD5854.M36 2014
      331.12'8068—dc23
      2013035114

ISBN: 978-0-415-89581-1 (hbk)
ISBN: 978-1-315-81583-1 (ebk)

Typeset in Sabon
by Apex CoVantage, LLC

Contents

PART III
Managing the Temporary Workforce

PART IV
Variety in the Development and the Organization of
Temporary Agency Work

Foreword

This book is the reflection of a long-term research interaction and many discussions about the influence of employment flexibility on the management and organization of work. The discussions were stimulated by research done in the context of two EU projects investigating contingent work from an organizational (NUEWO) and a psychological perspective (PSYCONES) in the early 2000s. The two projects reflected a growing experience with contingent employment in European labour markets and also triggered a broader academic interest in its management and organization.

The basis for cooperation that led to the chapters in this volume was laid at a much later stage during a small academic conference at ERIM, the Rotterdam School of Management research institute, in June 2008 on 'International Developments in Management and Organization of Temporary Agency Work.' At that time, many of the researchers involved had been meeting each other at academic conferences worldwide for a number of years, discussing the consequences and challenges of contingent employment and especially temporary agency work. After challenging representatives of the temporary work agency industry that a better understanding of management and organization of temporary employment—and agency work more specifically—was warranted given the growing proliferation and acceptance of the phenomenon, Randstad and the European association of temporary work agencies Eurociett graciously agreed to facilitate an international academic event bringing together academics specifically around the theme of management and organization of temporary agency work. The event was organized as an academic conference with explicitly no influence of practitioners on the program, but their promise to attend the conference with key policy makers from the field.

The conference led to creative debates, surprising and challenging both academics and practitioners. It strengthened the attitude of engaged scholarship with the academics and triggered curiosity and reflection on the part of the involved practitioners, leading to further events in the following years bringing together academics and practitioners. It also led to this volume showcasing the important academic and practical themes around the management and organization of a new world of work with temporary and mediated employment relationships that fundamentally change the organizational and managerial challenges in Human Resources Management. We hope that the present volume will trigger you the same way that the topic has gripped us, and that the kaleidoscope of perspectives presented will elicit the same kind of fascination with the field that has captivated all contributors to this volume when considering the challenges, opportunities and responsibilities of the temporary and mediated organization of work.

Rotterdam, Nuremberg, Stockholm,
Bas Koene, Nathalie Galais, Christina Garsten

1 Management and Organization of Temporary Work

Bas Koene, Christina Garsten, and Nathalie Galais

REGULAR EMPLOYMENT REVISITED

Over the past two decades, the concept of "regular employment" has been challenged and changed rapidly and fundamentally. We have seen a growth of short-term employment. Increasingly, organizations make use of contingent employees (Bergström and Storrie 2003) and contract work (Barley and Kunda 2004). From the beginning of the 1990s onwards, the growth of these "non-standard work arrangements" has attracted scholarly attention (e.g., Casey 1991; Delsen 1995; Purcell and Purcell 1998; Kalleberg 2000). Along with these developments, temporary work and the temporary work agency industry have both grown rapidly. In the United States, temporary agency work (TAW) grew at an annual rate of 11 per cent between 1972 and 1998, against 2 per cent annual growth for regular non-farm employment (Kalleberg 2000). During the 1990s, temporary work agencies were legalized and regulated in many European countries (Bergström and Storrie 2003), reflecting a growing sociocultural readiness for temporary employment and supporting its proliferation (Koene, Paauwe, and Groenewegen 2004). Critics voiced concern about the risks of bringing contingency back in and of undermining work conditions and workplace community (e.g., Benner, Leete, and Pastor 2007; Kalleberg 2009). Still, during the 1990s, temporary contracts in Europe grew by 25 per cent (Kalleberg 2000), and in the first decade of the new millennium, we saw a steep growth of agency work in Europe from 2,605 million to 3,924 full-time equivalents between 2002 and 2007 when it peaked, a growth of 51 per cent (Ciett 2011).

The use of agency work is but a small component of the total amount of temporary work. In 2009, the temporary work agency industry reported penetration rates of 2.5 per cent in the Netherlands, 1.6 per cent in Germany, 1 per cent in Sweden, and 0.7 per cent in Italy in 2009; whereas estimates of temporary work in these countries were approximately 20 per cent in the Netherlands, 15 per cent in Germany and Sweden, and just over 12 per cent in Italy (Ciett 2011). However, there is more to small figures than meets the eye. The growth of the temporary work agency industry reflects a structural acceptance of temporary work that seems to reflect a substantive change in our conception of "regular" employment. Developments over the past 20 years have fundamentally changed the employment landscape and our understanding of a "regular" job. In employment studies, often with roots in economics or sociology, these developments have been scrutinized with respect to the societal and legal consequences of TAW (e.g., Peck and Theodore 1998; Kvasnicka 2009). This research has stimulated debates on the nature and desirability of TAW and ways to contain its negative side effects (Viebrock and Clasen 2009; Pruijt and Dérogée 2010; Crouch 2012). In the meantime, a multinational industry has emerged providing professional employment services, and in most developed economies, the use of temporary agency workers has developed into a regular, if not respectable, employment solution.

After many decades of debate and discussion about the effects of TAW on precariousness, its basic desirability, and its socio-economic effects, by now most agree that employment flexibility seems to be an irreversible trend. The use of temporary employment and the associated employment intermediation industry have grown rapidly, and TAW has been legalized and regulated in many countries (International Labour Office 2009). This reflects a broader trend of specialization and modularization that is moving beyond the old bureaucratic mode of organizing of the twentieth century (Barley and Kunda 2004, 2006; Anand and Daft 2007).

However, research on the organization of temporary work has only partly kept up with the rapid growth of the phenomenon and the changing nature of questions and debate, experience and challenges around it. In terms of our present academic vocabulary, we still label temporary work as "non-standard" employment (Kalleberg 2000; Ashford, George, and Blatt 2007). As a consequence, much research to date has mostly compared temporary work to traditional ("regular") forms of employment, and most studies of the contributions of temporary work agencies have emphasized their labour market contributions, rather than how they reflect and contribute to a new way of organizing and understanding employment. In their review of the literature to date, Ashford, George, Blatt (2007) argue that the changing employment practices raise important theoretical issues about the nature of work, relationships between individuals and organizations, and the interaction between individuals. Reviewing the literature on labour market intermediaries (LMIs), Bonet, Cappelli, and Hamori (2013) revert to a categorization of LMIs that reflects the labour market contribution of LMIs (information provider, matchmaker, and administrator) and with it note a paucity of research addressing the substantive changes in the organization of work. We need to start answering basic questions related to these new ways of organizing employment: how can we understand career development, and what are short- and longer-term effects of engaging temporary work agencies in core human resources (HR) processes? The developments create new challenges *and* opportunities for the organization and management of employment. This book addresses these developments from different social science perspectives. The contributors represent the emerging body of research that investigates the management and organization of TAW and provide new insights that complement the rich body of research that documents and discusses the socio-economic effects of employment flexibility and agency work. In many organizations, the use of agency work mirrors the changing views on the role of non-standard and temporary employment in the organization. Especially in Europe, where the use of TAW has been relatively contested, the developments in organization and professionalization of the use of temporary labour are noteworthy. National differences highlight different aspects of the management and organization of temporary employment. The chapters in this volume present a kaleidoscope of the challenges of management and organization of temporary employment from various national contexts, as well as transnational trends and broader developments. Together, they provide an overview of key themes for the management and organization of temporary work in the years to come. Furthermore, they exemplify themes and issues relevant in specific national labour markets depending on the local experience with and attitude towards agency-mediated temporary employment.

The chapters are organized around four key themes. Part I addresses how the changing nature of work affects our understanding of temporariness and flexibility and the challenges it poses for the relationship between workers and organizations (Garsten and Haunschild, Chapter 2), introducing the particularly European notion of "flexicurity" (Dekker and Wilthagen, Chapter 3). Part II subsequently investigates the organization of the triangular employment relationship, documenting strategic choices on the part of agencies and client organizations to structure temporary employment in the organization (Goudswaard and De Leede, Chapter 4), the challenges of operating high-skill contingent workers in key positions (Nesheim, Fahle, and Tobiassen, Chapter 5), and investigating the conditions for successful development of sustainable regional inter-organizational flexicurity practices (Xhauflair and Pichault, Chapter 6). Part III presents research that investigates the challenges of managing the temporary workforce when it becomes a significant part of the total workforce. It addresses issues of worker identity and commitment (De Gilder, Chapter 8), attitudinal spillover effects (Connelly, Gallagher, and Wilkin, Chapter 7), and complexities in the development of multiple psychological contracts (Chambel, Chapter 9). Whereas the first three parts thus document our growing insight into the nature and management of temporary employees, Part IV addresses questions of variety and development in the organization of TAW, thus illuminating different possibilities in the development of the post-industrial organization of (temporary) employment. These developments deepen our insight into the possibilities that temporary work agencies provide in the organization of tailored employment solutions and employment flexibility. Besides broadening the strategic labour-sourcing possibilities, as shown in the chapter by Goudswaard and De Leede (Chapter 4), the chapters in this section describe the development of labour market institutions alongside the development of the temporary work agency industry in Italy (Regalia, Chapter 10), the adaptation of the temporary work agency industry business model within a context of strong job security in Sweden (Walter, Chapter 11), and the organization and competitive positioning of placement of disadvantaged workers in the North American context (Carré, Herranz, and Dorado, Chapter 12).

Together, the chapters in this volume address challenges at the level of labour markets and organizations, where we address both the organization and the management of the changing nature of employment. The changing perspective on agency work articulates more broadly the changing notions of flexibility and flexible employment.

CHANGING NOTIONS OF FLEXIBILITY AND FLEXIBLE EMPLOYMENT

Technological change, global competition, and social change have stimulated the growth of short-term employment relationships and contingent work (Bidwell et al. 2013). During the last half of the twentieth century, temporary employment was mostly understood as an instrument to deal with ad hoc labour shortages and labour market imperfections (Autor 2009). Flexible employment was mostly seen as a temporary state of being, and mostly understood as a temporary solution to fleeting employment problems. At the same time, temporary work—and especially agency work—was seen as societally problematic because opportunistic entrepreneurs used it to avoid employer *and* employee responsibilities (Kalleberg 2009, 2011).

Over time, however, it has become less ad hoc, more structural, less opportunistic, and more widespread. The nature and use of flexible employment and agency work have changed. We see four important drivers for this development: specialization, individualization, rationalization driven by strategic focus and cost reduction, and growing complexity of employment, partly due to increased globalization of labour markets and employment practice.

Over the past decade, many authors have pointed to the growing specialization of labour. Specialization has led organizations to think about core competencies and the active management of their use of specialized labour (e.g., Lepak and Snell 1999; Malone, Laubacher, and Johns 2011), and recently, academics have started to theorize and research the role of specialized contingent staff in organizational learning in knowledge-intensive firms where contingent workers increasingly impact core areas of the firm and where the synergistic interaction between itinerant professionals and organizations is essential for organizational development and competitiveness (Matusik and Hill 1998; Nesheim, Olsen, and Kalleberg 2007). This growth of flexibility reflects organizational differentiation and specialization where organizations do not necessarily control technical knowledge and its sources in the organization (Barley 1996). It changes the role of employment intermediation. It creates triangular employment relationships that can truly benefit the high-skilled temporary employee, shifting the focus of the agency from the user organization to the temp depending on labour market conditions (Koene and Purcell, forthcoming). It also blurs the boundaries between employment intermediaries and specialist employers such as consultancy organizations. Most of all, however, it positions temporary labour as a regular and key type of labour sourcing.

This development coincides with a growing *individualization* in Western labour markets, with a growing independent labour force of self-employed contractors. In the Netherlands, the number of self-employed contractors has grown by 38 per cent over the past decade (Statistics Netherlands, 2012). We see new classes of professionals and experts emerge, different from the traditional professions (e.g., Barley and Kunda 2004, 2006). They operate independently of traditional organizations and aim to organize and maintain their professionalism in novel ways (Furusten and Werr 2005). Actors in these individualized temporary employment relationships have to deal with market uncertainties in other ways than traditional professions. Often the focus is on highly skilled professionals, but independent actors also include skilled truck drivers and craftsmen, as well as the independent mail delivery workers who are paid on piece-rate schemes. In this case, the uncertainties in these new relationships and the imbalance in power between the contracting actors often require novel ways of managing the employment relationships, frequently involving employment intermediaries to make them sustainable. Even in Barley and Kunda's (2004) study of independent information technology contractors in Silicon Valley, all but the most successful individual contractors worked through agencies to stabilize their flow of assignments. Garsten (2008) shows how individualization of work contracts and relationships brings forth new ways of disciplining and "scripting" oneself as a temporary agency worker and undermines a sense of collegiality among the employees.

Besides specialization and individualization, we see two other important developments affecting both the flexibility of employment and the outsourcing of HR services to third parties. These developments have to do with the rationalization and professionalization of labour-sourcing practices. First, the ongoing *rationalization* of businesses has also touched human resources management (HRM) processes in organizations. Furthermore, organizations are more carefully considering their labour-sourcing strategies, creating a "breathing workforce," where numerical flexibility helps to adapt to changing market demands (Brunhes, Rojot, and Wassermann 1989; Davis-Blake and Uzzi 1993; George and Ng 2010). Organizations increasingly outsource operational management of related HR practices to other organizations specialized in matching and managing labour capacity.

Second, especially in Europe (but also worldwide), demographic developments are creating local labour market imbalances (Berkhout et al. 2012).

Here, relatively complex cross-border labour-sourcing practices are developing and are expected to grow (Berkhout and Van den Berg 2010). These developments are often supported by multinational professional employment agencies able to deal efficiently with the *complexity* of organizing and managing cross-border employment relationships (Ciett 2011). At present, much cross-border migration is organized through placements of a temporary nature of "posted workers" (European Union [EU] 2011). Individuals work outside their home country for a limited period with the intention of returning home after some time. At the same time, temporary work agencies provide cross-border placement services that do not provide permanent jobs in the host country but can manage placements of significant duration abroad. Relative to local hiring, these activities require more complex HR activities, which have stimulated the growth of specialized intermediation services in these areas (EU 2011; Ciett 2011).

Whereas the developments in flexible employment are thus driven by a number of underlying variables, one of the consequences is that the role and nature of *non-standard* temporary (agency) employment has changed and has become widely accepted. Governments have incorporated it in legislation, unions in collective agreements, and companies in their labour-sourcing practices. This challenges our understanding of "regular" employment and many of our traditional employment practices.

REPOSITIONING FLEXIBILITY

Part I of this volume investigates how the growing importance of flexible employment forces us to re-evaluate our understanding of temporariness, flexibility, and the relationship between worker and organization. We need to move beyond the traditional bureaucratic mode of organization that draws on the 1950s perspective of the "organization man" (cf. Ashford, George, and Blatt 2007) when defining regular employment. Garsten and Haunschild (Chapter 2, this volume) indicate how the increasingly transient and flexible "world of work" affects workers, redefines their relationship with the work organization, and creates new challenges for durable organization and management of working lives. Reflexivity, they suggest, has become habitual in contemporary, flexible forms of work, as has ways of refashioning oneself to better suit the new demands of work life. Their contribution illuminates key challenges and opportunities for individuals in flexible forms of work and articulates the need for further research that highlights the implications for the management of TAW.

At the level of labour market policy, the changing view of flexibility is exemplified by the European discussions around the notion of "flexicurity" (Wilthagen and Tros 2004), investigating the possibilities of shifting from the regulation of job security to work security. Central issues in the European debate are how to safeguard social security and labour force capabilities in the face of international economic pressures for flexibility and rationalization of employment (European Commission 2012). To recognize the different labour market characteristics of the various EU member states, four different routes towards flexicurity (i.e., flexicurity pathways) have been distinguished, recognizing specific issues and a variety of local solutions to deal with the tensions between flexibility and security and to move towards more flexicure labour markets. The pathways are based on four pillars that support flexicurity: (1) the integration of non-standard employment in labour law through flexible and reliable contractual arrangements; (2) active labour market policy to strengthen transition security, or rather, the movement from job to job; (3) systematic and responsive lifelong learning; and finally, (4) social security contributing to *positive mobility*, where movement between jobs is beneficial for both organizations and workers (EU 2007). The flexicurity debate constitutes a specifically European way of dealing with the challenges of growing flexibility in the labour market. In Chapter 3 of this volume, Dekker and Wilthagen discuss the notion of flexicurity and flexicurity pathways, and their meaning for the organization and management of TAW. They clarify how the shift from job security to work security affects our understanding of efficient and effective employment contracting and also how the different flexicurity pathways provide opportunities for— but also place responsibilities on—the various labour market actors (i.e., employers, employees, and governments).

The chapters in Part I thus clearly show how locating the responsibility for productive work life and careers with individuals rather than organizations requires a different way of organizing employment and social security, regulating the sharing of economic risk between parties in the labour market. Furthermore, it asks for active consideration of the matter of maintaining and developing the quality of the labour force, which does not happen automatically anymore in the context of career development in traditional production organizations. These long-term effects and consequences are difficult to capture and address in traditional short-term market-based employment contracts.

Ultimately, these chapters highlight how the changing nature of work affects our understanding of temporariness, flexibility, and the relationship between workers and organizations.

NEW CHALLENGES FOR ORGANIZATION AND MANAGEMENT OF EMPLOYMENT FLEXIBILITY

Whereas the societal consequences outlined above have received a lot of attention, the impact of flexibility on HRM in organizations has remained relatively under-investigated. How does flexibility affect organizations and their management of their workforce, and what new challenges are they up against? In traditional organizations, we see the heart of the organization formed by a stable core of employees with scarce key skills and experiences that are hard to find in the marketplace. The well-known core-periphery model of Atkinson (1984) exemplifies this thinking, distinguishing a stable organizational core and peripheral layers around it, where workers become less important for the organization and also more loosely connected to the organization. In response, Lepak and Snell's (1999) modelling of the HR architecture implied that organizations have to make strategic choices about their relationships with specific groups of employees based on the value of their human capital for the organization and their uniqueness in the labour market. Unique and high-value human capital is internally developed as core personnel in the organization. It is managed using commitment-based HR practices "encouraging significant mutual investment on the part of employers and employees in developing critical firm skills" (Lepak and Snell 1999, 36). By contrast, peripheral employees are those with generic skills that are of "limited strategic value [that] can be purchased easily on the open labor market [and] can be treated essentially as a commodity" (Lepak and Snell 1999, 39). As such, Lepak and Snell's strategic human resources architecture reinforced the basic distinction between a stable core and a flexible periphery, as introduced by Atkinson.

However, with the growing use of flexible labour, careful management of this group of peripheral employees becomes more and more important. In a study of flexible contracting in the Netherlands, Goudswaard et al. (2008) reported a flexible periphery in regular production organizations of approximately 20 per cent, with companies expecting this to grow to 25 per cent of their labour force in the years to come. In Europe, the average share of temporary contracts in 2009 was 12 per cent, with Poland, Spain, Portugal, and the Netherlands leading the charts with shares between 20 and 30 per cent (Ciett 2011). Besides this growing number, the use of temporary employees in organizations has also changed. Matusik and Hill (1998) pointed to the possible role of temporary specialists to strengthen core processes. In a study of Norwegian organizations, Nesheim, Olsen, and Kalleberg (2007) reported how organizations in dynamic markets use employment intermediaries to staff core activities. According to Anand and Daft (2007), this is part of a broader trend of hollowing out of organizations.

With external staff fulfilling more and more significant and core tasks in the organization, management faces new challenges. Core and periphery become harder to distinguish from one another. In effect, the core may be partly constituted by externals performing key functions alongside more stable, internal core employees. Furthermore, the development and maintenance of unique skills and experience for core processes becomes more complicated when these are partly developed by temporary staff. When organizations increase the flexibility of their core and differentiate their labour-sourcing strategy, they need to deal with two key challenges: (1) actively manage an increasingly differentiated workforce and (2) seek ways to stabilize consistent performance and to safeguard access to the relevant (human) resources at all times.

ORGANIZING EMPLOYMENT FLEXIBILITY

In view of organizing flexibility and creating a reliable periphery, research to date has mostly focused on behavioural effects of temporary employment and the dynamics of a blended workforce in otherwise traditional organizational arrangements. Only recently have organizations started to recognize that a substantive reliance on a non-standard temporary workforce also requires a different organization of employment and HRM. The challenge places novel demands on managers. They need to develop mechanisms for collaboration, build lateral relationships, and seek clarity rather than control (Anand and Daft 2007). In traditional thinking, the need for flexibility is, to some degree, at odds with the need to build relationships and develop mechanisms for collaboration. Discussing the possibilities of a differentiated HRM architecture, Lepak and Snell (1999) suggested that agency work, which is not unique and of relatively low value, should be treated as a commodity and traded ad hoc in the marketplace. Organizations should only form alliances with actors who provide peripheral human capital that is, at the same time, of relatively low value to the organization and that is unique. Their example was that of legal advice, which benefits from specific experience with the company but may be too expensive and too far from a company's core business to maintain in-house. However, the use of temporary agency workers in significant numbers, on a structural basis (Goudswaard et al. 2008; Ciett 2011), and in core processes of the organization (e.g., Nesheim, Olsen, and Kalleberg 2007) sets new challenges for the organization. Research on the strategic and organizational HR choices regarding the management of the temporary workforce is still scarce. In a comparative study of operational HR management of temporary agency workers, Koene and Van Riemsdijk (2005) found significantly better HR outcomes (e.g., sick leave, average tenure, and turnover) in cases where HR organization and management acknowledged the different requirements and possibilities of the temporary employees. Part II of this volume presents three studies addressing the organization of employment flexibility, dealing professionally with the competing demands of multiple stakeholders. In Chapter 4 of this volume, Goudswaard and De Leede present a study of different forms of strategic cooperation of agencies with client organizations. They investigate the possibilities for sustainable cooperation between agencies and client organizations where "the highest degree of work flexibility has to be delivered at the lowest possible price." Considering Dutch best-practice cases, they found three types of improvement goals that lead to sustainable cooperative relationships between employment agencies and client organizations: efficiency improvement (reducing costs in HR processes), enhancing organizational flexibility (i.e., functional adaptability), and improving labour market position (enhancing labour market position and quality and skills of personnel). Their findings show that strategic cooperation—reflected in new ways of organizing and managing employment—can be beneficial for the hiring company, but that it needs to be carefully organized. Their findings, however, also show that these forms of cooperation require significant commitment of both agency and client organization in a number of areas.

In Chapter 5 of this volume, Nesheim, Fahle, and Tobiassen document the challenges of working with high-skill contingent workers in key positions. It requires sharing employment responsibilities between organizations, blurring organizational boundaries, and diminishing the possibilities of simple linear hierarchical coordination. It requires new ways to secure the availability of employees with the right qualifications at the time required, but it also offers new possibilities. Matusik and Hill (1998) sketched a mutually beneficial market dynamic between high-skill specialist contractors and client organizations, where both benefit from short-term relationships and where each assignment serves to extend the knowledge and skill base of the itinerant specialist. Although theoretically beautiful, in practice, this kind of cooperation presents the management of hiring firms with clear dilemmas. Nesheim, Fahle, and Tobiassen (Chapter 5, this volume) investigated how these tensions become resolved inside organizations. Studying the management of external professionals operating in core processes in companies in the Norwegian oil industry, they identified four key management challenges: dependence on external consultants, having a high proportion of externals in projects, balancing integration versus separation of consultants, and dealing with social comparisons.

Organizing flexibility does not only lead to clear dilemmas inside organizations. Xhauflair and Pichault's (Chapter 6, this volume) argument in this volume is that coming up with good flexicurity solutions is not a matter of defining the best solution because these situations are highly specific and are constantly developing. Through action research in a Francophone industrialized area in Belgium, Xhauflair and Pichault studied the process of arriving at balanced flexicurity solutions and defined the key characteristics of a process of developing inter-organizational employment schemes that deal effectively with the tensions inherent in flexicurity solutions.

MANAGING A BLENDED WORKFORCE

Besides organizational issues, reliance on temporary staff also presents challenges in daily management of the workforce. More and more of the work in organizations is done by blended teams. Tasks and duties of the core workers and the externals are interwoven, and the differentiation between internal and external workers is becoming more complicated. Furthermore, in the context of TAW, the involvement of multiple organizations increases the complexity of relationships. The dynamics of the resulting interactions require careful management. This includes individual- and team-focused measures, as well as the coordination and communication between organizations.

However, management attention for this issue is not self-evident. Measures of HRM are tailored for the core workers of the organization, and specific concepts for the integration and the development of temporary agency workers are still missing. Moreover, the relationship between the client organization and the agency usually does not go beyond that of customer–supplier (Goudswaard and De Leede, Chapter 4 in this volume). Research shows that objectives for flexibility in organizations are often related to short-term cost reduction and rationalization (George and Ng 2011) and are not accompanied by an adequate personnel policy.

In these cases, temporary employees are often treated as expendable (Koene and Van Riemsdijk 2005) and are reported to be subject to devalued treatment (Boyce et al. 2007) and as experiencing low job quality (Nienhüser and Matiaske 2006; Olsen 2006). In terms of management of employees, the 1950s company-man perspective still dominates our theorizing, and the study of non-standard and temporary employees, as well as the related new managerial challenges and possibilities, is still in its infancy (Ashford, George, and Blatt 2007).

Research also shows the need to better understand the complex behavioural dynamics in blended workforces and the determinants affecting attitudinal variables, such as employee commitment, identification, and the psychological contract implications (Connelly and Gallagher 2004). The scarce findings on the effects of the use of external workers on core workers suggest rather negative effects on core workers' attitudes (Von Hippel et al. 1997) and also suggest further difficulties when managing growing proportions of non-standard employees (Broschak and Davis-Blake 2006). This is especially the case when temps are perceived as a threat (Kraimer et al. 2005) or as an inhibitor of the career mobility of the core workers (George, Chattopadhyay, and Zhang 2012).

With regard to attitudinal outcomes of the temporary agency workers, research on organizational commitment is predominant. In the case of temporary agency workers, organizational commitment can be displayed towards the client as well as to the agency. Findings suggest that there is a positive relation between the two variables (Liden et al. 2003), but that temporary workers generally seem to be more committed to the client than to the agency (Felfe et al. 2008). Furthermore, temporary agency workers especially display a high commitment towards the core workers in the client organization (De Gilder 2003).

Comparisons between core workers' and temporary agency workers' level of commitment have produced mixed results (George and Ng 2011). Findings in the field of TAW suggest that temporary agency workers may similarly be as committed to the client organization as core workers are (Broschak, Davis-Blake, and Block 2008), and that they may even display higher job satisfaction than the core workers (Sodenkamp and Schmidt 2001). By contrast, other findings suggest that temporary workers may be less committed towards the client organization than permanent workers (Biggs and Swailes

2006). The comparative approach concerning the level of organizational commitment and job satisfaction of core workers and external workers is methodologically problematic because the findings depend on the characteristics of the population that is under investigation, the underlying selection processes in the groups, group-related standards of comparison, and contextual factors (e.g., organization, country, etc.). All these uncontrollable and confounding factors reduce the interpretability and generalizability of comparative findings.

Research that focuses more on the determinants has found that HR practices are crucial for the attitudes and the organizational behaviour of temporary agency workers. Findings indicate that perceived organizational support by the client as well as the agency has positive effects on workers' commitment (Liden et al. 2003; Van Breugel, Van Olffen, and Olie 2005) and on their job satisfaction (Druker and Stanworth 2004). Findings also show that the nature of the relationship between temporary agency workers and their organizations is not only determined by organizational practices, but also by the initial motives for temping, the perception of voluntariness, and the instrumental value of temping (De Cuyper and De Witte 2008). The motivational background further determines the nature of the psychological contract that connects workers with the client organization as well as with the agency (Felfe et al. 2008).

There is evidence that workers who voluntarily chose TAW are more committed to the agency than those who temp involuntarily (Chambel and Castanheira 2007; De Cuyper and De Witte 2008; Van Dyne and Ang 1998) and that they are more satisfied with their jobs (Ellingson, Gruys, and Sackett 1998; Feldman, Doerpinghaus, and Turnley 1995; Tan and Tan 2002). Involuntary temps seem to be more committed to the client, especially when they are seeking a permanent position in the client organization (Felfe et al. 2008). Furthermore, the stepping-stone motive was positively related to extra-role behaviour in the client organization, and workers who worked as temporary agency workers voluntarily showed higher extra-role behaviour towards the agency (George et al. 2010).

This may sound all good, if research findings had not suggested that those who are highly committed to the client—but do not get a permanent position—suffer most and show increased health complaints (Galais and Moser 2009). Also, whereas motives play an important role in the attitudes of the temporary workers, the few findings on performance outcomes suggest that initial motives for temping have no effects on individual performance (Ellingson, Gruys, and Sackett 1998), and that involuntary temporary workers do not perform less well than those who pursue TAW voluntarily (Tan and Tan 2002).

Generally, most studies in the context of TAW have either adopted a comparative perspective between permanent workers (i.e., those with an open-ended contract) and temporary agency workers or have focused on particularities related to TAW. These approaches are similar in that they concentrate on the effects of the formal work status, and that permanent workers are implicitly or explicitly seen as the reference group. This perspective has limited potential to uncover the dynamics and the complexity of the relationships that emerge in the triangular work constellation.

MANAGING COMPLEX ATTITUDINAL DYNAMICS

The chapters of Part III of this book present a broadened perspective on the attitudinal and behavioural dynamics resulting from the triangular work arrangement. This includes the consideration of the interdependences between attitudes and behaviours that manifest themselves in spillover effects, in changed relationships between individuals and organizations, and in the social identity formation of workers. In Chapter 7, Connelly, Gallagher, and Wilkin introduce the paradigm of spillover effects into the context of TAW and highlight the interdependence of intra-individual and inter-individual behaviours and attitudes. The authors outline that the multiple organizational affiliations have their own dynamics, and that the attitudes and behaviours towards the involved organizations and between temporary agency and core workers can affect each other. It becomes clear that there is a dramatic change of the relationships between workers and organizations in the process of personnel flexibility. De Gilder shows in Chapter 8 how the social identity formation of temporary workers underlies these changes in relationships and affiliations that result from the triangular work constellation. Finally, in Chapter 9, Chambel focuses on the exchange mechanisms between workers and organizations in the context of dual employment relationships. In Part III of the book, it becomes clear that the investigation and the management of temporary agency workers require unique approaches.

THE ROLE OF PROFESSIONAL EMPLOYMENT INTERMEDIARIES

The first nine chapters thus show how changes in employment flexibility have clear consequences for individual careers and also for the organization and management of employment. Their conclusions reflect the growing awareness that there is much to gain from a careful, appreciative, and (pro)active management of temporary employees and the dynamics of blended workforces. Transient careers require new ways of development, maintenance, and support. Furthermore, flexibility of the core requires management to deal with the challenge of developing a reliable labour supply, where employees with the right qualifications and career experience will be available for the organization when needed.

With these challenges in mind, we turn to developments in employment intermediation and, more specifically, the role of temporary work agencies. The development and growth of the temporary work agency industry is closely connected to the flexibilization of employment. Whereas some blame the growing employment intermediation industry for the problems arising with employment flexibilization, a dispassionate analysis of the work of employment intermediaries reveals that, although they are definitely not disinterested actors, the work of agencies is to provide solutions to (some of the) challenges of employment flexibilization (Koene and Purcell, forthcoming). The fact is, however, that the developments in labour markets and organizations have coincided with the emergence and quick growth of the private employment intermediation industry that organizes employment flexibility outside traditional production organizations. Some argue that temporary work agencies have become the most widespread form of labour market intermediation (e.g., Benner, Leete, and Pastor 2007). Studies on the role of employment intermediaries and the development and possibilities of triangular employment relationships still hold a lot of promise. In practice, we see much variation in practices of temporary work agencies, providing rich empirical data on the challenges and possibilities of their role in the organization of work.

A significant body of evidence has developed that addresses the historical development of the agency industry in the United States and in Europe (Hatton 2011; Smith and Neuwirth 2008; Van Driel and Koene 2011). These historical studies describe the evolving institutional positioning of the temporary work agency industry and the active debates on the desirability of agency work over time. They also describe the development of an industry that has come to play very different roles in the labour market over time. The development in the Western economies shows a development where the role of the industry developed from illegal and opportunistic ad hoc labour sourcing, emerging from the margin of the labour market, to an industry seeking to establish its societal relevance and legitimacy in dealing with temporary flexibility and provision of work arrangements for non-standard employees at the fringes of the labour market, to an industry that now needs to provide employment solutions that serve a growing share of the labour force and that needs to compete in an environment where organizational flexibility and project work are becoming the norm rather than the exception. In many of these developments, we see a co-evolution of the industry and the labour market institutions that over time transforms both the industry and the societal understanding of agency work (e.g., Koene 2006). In-depth studies of the organization and management of TAW are needed to help us understand the limits, possibilities, and transformational effects of intermediated temporary employment on the organization of work.

In her chapter on Italy (Chapter 10, this volume), Regalia describes how the legalization of agency work in Italy has triggered the co-evolution of institutional innovations in the labour market intended to offset its negative side effects. The chapter sketches the process of legalization and regulation of agency work and shows how acceptance of agency work was only possible in an environment where all parties trusted the government to take the necessary measures to contain the negative side effects of agency work and could only be sustained with the development of new labour market institutions that secured dedicated forms of protection and welfare for agency workers.

Studies of the role of the agency industry itself initially mostly followed the debate on the desirability of agency work. Peck and Theodore (1998) studied the strategic positioning of temporary work agencies in the labour market, distinguished high-road and low-road strategies in the context of the U.S. labour markets, and considered the impact of temporary work agencies on labour markets and the quality of employment relationships. They showed how the difference between high-road strategies, where agencies focus on skilled employees, and low-road strategies, where agencies "restructure down" into "the lowest paid and most exploitative niches of the labor market" (Peck and Theodore 1998, 655), resulted in an increased polarization of the labour market.

Rather than distinguishing agencies by their specific focus on segments of the labour market, recent studies in, for example, the Dutch context show that agencies can increasingly differentiate themselves through the professionalization of their HR practices, which is reflected in the active management of *all* segments of temporary agency workers (Koene and Van Riemsdijk 2005) and in the strategic organization of employment services (Goudswaard and De Leede, Chapter 4 in this volume). These differences can greatly affect the impact that temporary work agencies can have in the labour market.

The chapters by Walter (Chapter 11) and Carré, Herranz, and Dorado (Chapter 12), in this volume, specifically investigate the possibilities of the temporary work agency model. Comparing the developments in Europe and the United States, we see that the role employment intermediaries come to play in labour markets is very much dependent on the institutional context in which they operate. At the same time, the different contexts present quasi-experimental differences that highlight specific possibilities of the agency model. In Chapter 11, Walter shows how in Sweden, where temporary work agencies have to employ temps through open-ended employment contracts, an agency industry has evolved that employs rather high-skilled temps on permanent contracts that can be placed in client organizations flexibly.

In Chapter 12, Carré, Herranz, and Dorado investigate the developments on the opposite side of the spectrum, describing the development of alternative staffing organizations in the United States. Alternative staffing organizations provide job placement and support services to disadvantaged workers. They are non-profit organizations founded and supported by community-based organizations or other types of non-profit organizations. The chapter by Carré, Herranz, and Dorado describes the possibilities and limitations of these organizations in the regular labour market. They show how the stigma of disadvantaged workers is dealt with by providing professional employment services that support the management of these workers in the workplace, sometimes even giving them an advantage over regular low-skilled workers who are placed through regular agencies with much less placement services and on-site management.

CONCLUSION

In all, the studies in this volume show that the challenges of managing a temporary workforce are significant. A growing share of the workforce operates in some kind of temporary relationship to the organization, a situation that challenges the view of temporary employment as ad hoc, and highlights the need to manage it professionally. Proactive and strategic organization of the temporary workforce leads to better performance on a number of HR outcome variables. However, the incongruence between short-term and long-term outcomes, and the related issues of market pressure, complexity, and uncertainty, often lead to a rather opportunistic and unambitious organization of the flexible workforce. The research indicates the need for significant commitment of the different parties in organizing triangular flexible employment solutions and the need for a well-developed and supportive institutional environment to establish good flexicurity solutions for specific and concrete situations.

At the same time, the studies show how, over the past decade, agencies have been extending their activities, in the process broadening the arsenal of organizational solutions for managing employment flexibility sustainably. Looking into the future, we may expect this development to become mainstream in organizational practice and new opportunities for employment matching to surface. Talent exchanges on the Web are already starting to transform the landscape of job marketplaces and the organization of temporary job placement. New business models for online staffing solutions are developing. Furthermore, outsourcing and modularization provide new avenues for organizational resource flexibilization, changing both the competition for and the role of employment agencies. These transformations warrant much more research on the organization and management of labour sourcing, as well as on the development of the temporary work agency industry and how it does, can, and should contribute to the societal organization of employment flexibility. After all, work—in all its shapes—constitutes a significant dimension of our lives, individually and collectively.

REFERENCES

Anand, Narasimhan, and Richard L. Daft. 2007. "What Is the Right Organization Design?" *Organizational Dynamics* 36, 4: 329–344.
Ashford, Susan J., Elizabeth George, and Ruth Blatt. 2007. "Old Assumptions, New Work: The Opportunities and Challenges of Research on Nonstandard Employment." *Academy of Management Annals* 1: 65–117.

Atkinson, John. 1984. "Manpower Strategies for Flexible Organisations." *Personnel Management* 16 (8): 28–31.

Autor, David H. 2009. "Studies of Labor Market Intermediation: Introduction." In *Studies of Labor Market Intermediation*, edited by D. Autor, 1–26. Chicago: University of Chicago Press.

Barley, Stephen R. 1996. "Technicians in the Workplace: Ethnographic Evidence for Bringing Work into Organization Studies." *Administrative Science Quarterly* 41: 404–441.

Barley, Stephen R., and Gideon Kunda. 2006. "Contracting: A New Form of Professional Practice." *Academy of Management Perspectives* 20 (1): 45–66.

Barley, Stephen R., and Gideon Kunda. 2004. *Gurus, Hired Guns, and Warm Bodies: Itinerant Experts in a Knowledge Economy*. Princeton, NJ: Princeton University Press.

Benner, Chris, Laura Leete, and Manuel Pastor. 2007. *Staircases or Treadmills? Labor Market Intermediaries and Economic Opportunity in a Changing Economy*. New York: Russell Sage Foundation.

Bergström, Ola, and Donald Storrie. 2003. *Contingent Employment in Europe and the United States*. Cheltenham, Northampton, UK: Edward Elgar.

Berkhout, Ernest, Michael Sattinger, Jules Theeuwes, and Maikel Volkerink. 2012. *Into the Gap, Exploring Skills and Mismatches*. SEO report no. 2011–56. Amsterdam: SEO Economic Research.

Berkhout, Ernest, and Emina van den Berg. 2010. *Bridging the Gap*. Randstad/SEO report 2010-01. Amsterdam: SEO Economic Research.

Bidwell, Matthew, Forrest Briscoe, Isabel Fernandez-Mateo, and Adina Sterling. 2013. "The Employment Relationship and Inequality: How and Why Changes in Employment Practices Are Reshaping Rewards in Organizations." *Academy of Management Annals* 7 (1): 61–121.

Biggs, David, and Stephen Swailes. 2006. "Relations, Commitment and Satisfaction in Agency Workers and Permanent Workers." *Employee Relations* 28 (2): 130–143.

Bonet, Rocio, Peter Cappelli, and Monika Hamori. 2013. "Labor Market Intermediaries and the New Paradigm for Human Resources." *Academy of Management Annals* 7 (1): 341–392.

Boyce, Anthony S., Ann Marie Ryan, Anna L. Imus, and Frederick P. Morgeson. 2007. "Temporary Worker, Permanent Loser? A Model of the Stigmatization of Temporary Workers." *Journal of Management* 33 (1): 5–29.

Broschak, Joseph P., and Alison Davis-Blake. 2006. "Mixing Standard Work and Nonstandard Deals: The Consequences of Heterogeneity in Employment Arrangements." *Academy of Management Journal* 49 (2): 371–393.

Broschak, Joseph P., Alison Davis-Blake, and Emily S. Block. 2008. "Nonstandard, Not Substandard: The Relationship among Work Arrangements, Work Attitudes, and Job Performance." *Work and Occupations* 35 (1): 3–43.

Brunhes, Bernard, Jacques Rojot, and Wolfram Wassermann. 1989. *Labour Market Flexibility: Trends in Enterprises*. Paris: OECD.

Casey, Bernard. 1991. Survey Evidence on Trends in Non-Standard Employment. In *Farewell to Flexibility?* edited by Anna Pollert, 179–199. Oxford: Blackwell.

Chambel, Maria José, and Filipa Castanheira. 2007. "They Don't Want to Be Temporaries: Similarities between Temps and Core Workers." *Journal of Organizational Behavior* 28: 943–959.

Ciett. 2011. *Adapting to Change*. Brussels: Eurociett.

Connelly, Catherine E., and Daniel G. Gallagher. 2004. "Emerging Trends in Contingent Work Research." *Journal of Management* 30 (6): 959–983.

Crouch, Colin. 2012. "Beyond the Flexibility/Security Trade-Off: Reconciling Confident Consumers with Insecure Workers." *British Journal of Industrial Relations* 50 (1): 1–22.

Davis-Blake, Alison, and Brian Uzzi. 1993. "Determinants of Employment Externalization: A Study of Temporary Workers and Independent Contractors." *Administrative Science Quarterly* 38 (2): 195–223.

De Cuyper, Nele, and Hans de Witte. 2008. "Volition and Reasons for Accepting Temporary Employment: Associations with Attitudes, Well-Being, and Behavioural Intentions." *European Journal of Work and Organizational Psychology* 17: 363–387.

De Gilder, Dick. 2003. "Commitment, Trust and Work Behaviour: The Case of Contingent Workers." *Personnel Review* 32 (5): 588–604.

Delsen, Lei. 1995. *Atypical Employment: An International Perspective—Causes, Consequences, and Policy.* Groningen, The Netherlands: Wolters-Noordhoff.

Druker, Janet, and Celia Stanworth. 2004. "Mutual Expectations: A Study of the Three-Way Relationship between Employment Agencies, Their Client Organisations and White-Collar Agency 'Temps.'" *Industrial Relations Journal* 35 (1): 58–75.

Ellingson, Jill E., Melissa L. Gruys, and Paul R. Sackett. 1998. "Factors Related to the Satisfaction and Performance of Temporary Employees." *Journal of Applied Psychology* 83 (6): 913–921.

European Commission (EC). 2012. *New Skills and Jobs in Europe: Pathways towards Full Employment.* (EC, EUR 25270. Luxembourg: Publications Office of the European Union.

European Union (EU). 2007. *Flexicurity Pathways, Turning Hurdles into Stepping Stones.* Flexicurity Expert Group final report. http://ec.europa.eu/social/BlobServlet?docId=1519&langId=en.

European Union (EU). 2011. *Study on the Economic and Social Effects Associated with the Phenomenon of Posting of Workers in the EU.* Final Report VT/2009/062, March 2011. Idea Consult/Ecorys on Behalf of European Commission Directorate General Employment, Social Affairs and Equal Opportunities, Brussels.

Feldman, Daniel C., Helen I. Doerpinghaus, and William H. Turnley. 1995. "Employee Reactions to Temporary Jobs." *Journal of Managerial Issues* 7 (2): 127–141.

Felfe, Jörg, Renate Schmook, Birgit Schyns, and Bernd Six. 2008. "Does the Form of Employment Make a Difference? Commitment of Traditional, Temporary, and Self-Employed Workers." *Journal of Vocational Behavior* 72 (1): 81–94.

Furusten, Staffan, and Andreas Werr, eds. 2005. *Dealing with Confidence: The Construction of Need and Trust in Management Advisory Services.* Copenhagen: CBS Press.

Galais, Nathalie, and Klaus Moser. 2009. "Organizational Commitment and the Well-Being of Temporary Agency Workers: A Longitudinal Study." *Human Relations* 62 (4): 589–620.

Garsten, Christina. 2008. *Workplace Vagabonds: Career and Community in Changing Worlds of Work.* Basingstoke: Palgrave Macmillan.

George, Elizabeth, Prithviraj Chattopadhyay, and Lida L. Zhang. 2012. "Helping Hand or Competition? The Moderating Influence of Perceived Upward Mobility on the Relationship between Blended Workgroups and Employee Attitudes and Behaviors." *Organization Science* 23 (2): 355–372.

George, Elizabeth, Alec Levenson, David Finegold, and Prithviraj Chattopadhyay. 2010. "Extra-Role Behaviors among Temporary Workers: How Firms Create Relational Wealth in the United States of America." *International Journal of Human Resource Management* 21 (4): 530–550.

George, Elizabeth, and Carmen K. Ng. 2010. "Nonstandard Workers: Work Arrangements and Outcomes." In *APA Handbook of Industrial and Organizational Psychology*, vol. 1, edited by Sheldon Zedeck, 573–596. Washington, DC: American Psychological Association.

Goudswaard, Anneke, Jan de Leede, Madelon van Hooff, Tony Brugman, John Klein Hesselink, Marc de Leeuw, and Gu van Rhijn. 2008. *De toekomst van flexibele arbeid*. Report for ABU. Hoofddorp, The Netherlands: TNO.

Hatton, Erin. 2011. *The Temp Economy: From Kelly Girls to Permatemps in Postwar America*. Philadelphia: Temple University Press.

International Labour Office (ILO). 2009. "Private Employment Agencies, Temporary Agency Workers and Their Contribution to the Labour Market." Issues Paper for Discussion at the Workshop to Promote Ratification of the Private Employment Agencies Convention, 1997 (No. 181), 20–21 October 2009, International Labour Office, Sectoral Activities Programme, Geneva.

Kalleberg, Arne L. 2011. *Good Jobs, Bad Jobs: The Rise of Polarized and Precarious Employment Systems in the United States, 1970s–2000s*. New York: Russell Sage Foundation.

Kalleberg, Arne L. 2000. "Nonstandard Employment Relations: Part-Time, Temporary and Contract Work." *Annual Review of Sociology* 26: 341–365.

Kalleberg, Arne L. 2009. "Precarious Work, Insecure Workers: Employment Relations in Transition." *American Sociological Review* 74 (1): 1–22.

Koene, B.A.S. 2006. "Situated Human Agency, Institutional Entrepreneurship and Institutional Change." *Journal of Organizational Change Management* 19 (3): 365–382.

Koene, B.A.S., Jaap Paauwe, and John Groenewegen. 2004. "Understanding the Development of Temporary Agency Work in Europe." *Human Resource Management Journal* 14 (3): 53–73.

Koene, B.A.S., and Kate Purcell. Forthcoming. "The Value of Relationships in a Transactional Labour Market: Constructing a Market for Temporary Employment." *Revista Latinoamericana de Estudios del Trabajo*.

Koene, B.A.S., and Maarten van Riemsdijk. 2005. "Managing Temporary Workers: Work Identity, Diversity and Operational HR Choices." *Human Resource Management Journal* 15 (1): 76–92.

Kraimer, Maria L., Sandy J. Wayne, Robert C. Liden, and Raymond T. Sparrowe. 2005. "The Role of Job Security in Understanding the Relationship between Employees' Perceptions of Temporary Workers and Employees' Performance." *Journal of Applied Psychology* 90 (2): 389–398.

Kvasnicka, Michael. 2009. "Does Temporary Help Work Provide a Stepping Stone to Regular Employment?" In *Studies of Labor Market Intermediation*, edited by David Autor, 335–372. Chicago: University of Chicago Press.

Lepak, David P., and Scott A. Snell. 1999. "The Human Resource Architecture: Towards a Theory of Human Capital Allocation and Development." *Academy of Management Review* 24 (1): 31–48.

Liden, Robert C., Sandy J. Wayne, Maria L. Kraimer, and Raymond T. Sparrowe. 2003. "The Dual Commitments of Contingent Workers: An Examination of Contingents' Commitment to the Agency and the Organization." *Journal of Organizational Behavior* 24 (5): 609–625.

Malone, Tomas W., Robert J. Laubacher, and Tammy Johns. 2011. "The Age of Hyperspecialization." *Harvard Business Review* 89 (7/8): 56–65.

Matusik, Sharon F., and Charles W. L. Hill. 1998. "The Utilization of Contingent Work, Knowledge Creation, and Competitive Advantage." *Academy of Management Review* 23 (4): 680–697.

Nesheim, Torstein, Karen M. Olsen, and Arne L. Kalleberg. 2007. "Externalizing the Core: Firms' Use of Employment Intermediaries in the Information and Communication Technology Industries." *Human Resource Management* 46 (2): 247–264.

Nienhüser, Werner, and Wenzel Matiaske. 2006. "Effects of the ʔPrinciple of Non-Discrimination' on Temporary Agency Work: Compensation and Working Conditions of Temporary Agency Workers in 15 European Countries." *Industrial Relations Journal* 37: 64–77.

Olsen, Karen M. 2006. "Atypiske ansettelser—dårlige jobber?" [Atypical employment—bad jobs?]. *Tidsskrift for samfunnsforskning* 47 (3): 387–412.

Peck, Jamie, and Nikolas Theodore. 1998. "The Business of Contingent Work: Growth and Restructuring in Chicago's Temporary Employment Industry." *Work Employment and Society* 12: 655–674.

Pruijt, Hans, and Pascal Dérogée. 2010. "Employability and Job Security, Friends or Foes? The Paradoxical Reception of Employacurity in the Netherlands." *Socio-Economic Review* 8: 437–460.

Purcell, Kate, and John Purcell. 1998. "In-Sourcing, Outsourcing and the Growth of the Contingent Labour as Evidence of Flexible Employment Strategies." *European Journal of Work and Organisational Psychology* 7 (1): 39–59.

Smith, Vicki, and Esther B. Neuwirth. 2008. *The Good Temp*. Ithaca, NY: Cornell University/ILR Press.

Sodenkamp, Daniel, and Klaus-Helmut Schmidt. 2001. "Erleben von Rollenambiguität bei Leiharbeitnehmern" [The experience of role ambiguity of temporary agency workers]. *Zeitschrift für Arbeitswissenschaft* 55 (1): 32–38.

Statistics Netherlands, 2012. Webmagazine Centraal Bureau voor de Statistiek, Toename aantal zelfstandigen (growth self-employed). www.cbs.nl/nl-NL/menu/themas/arbeid-sociale-zekerheid/publicaties/artikelen/archief/2012/2012-3611 -wm.htm

Tan, Hwee-Hoon, and Chwee-Peng Tan. 2002. "Temporary Employees in Singapore: What Drives Them?" *Journal of Psychology* 136 (1): 83–102.

Van Breugel, Gerla, Woody van Olffen, and René Olie. 2005. "Temporary Liaisons: The Commitment of 'Temps' towards Their Agencies." *Journal of Management Studies* 42 (3): 539–566.

Van Driel, Hugo, and Bas Koene. 2011. "The Rhetoric of Restraint: The Struggle for Legitimacy in the Dutch Temporary Work Agency Industry, 1961–1996." *Enterprise and Society* 12 (3): 562–600.

Van Dyne, Linn, and Soon Ang. 1998. "Organizational Citizenship Behavior of Contingent Workers in Singapore." *Academy of Management Journal* 41 (6): 692–703.

Viebrock, Elke, and Jochen Clasen. 2009. Flexicurity and Welfare Reform: A Review. *Socio-Economic Review* 7: 305–331.

Von Hippel, Courtney, Stephen L. Mangum, David B. Greenberger, Robert L. Henemann, and Jeffrey D. Skoglind. 1997. "Temporary Employment: Can Organizations and Employees Both Win?" *Academy of Management Executive* 11 (1): 93–104.

Wilthagen, Ton, and Frank Tros. 2004. "The Concept of 'Flexicurity': A New Approach to Regulating Employment and Labor Markets." *Transfer: European Review of Labour and Research* 10 (2): 166–186.

Part I

The Changing Nature of Work

2 Transient and Flexible Work Lives
Liminal Organizations and the Reflexive Habitus

Christina Garsten and Axel Haunschild

TRANSIENT ORGANIZATIONS, FLEXIBLE SELVES

Current accounts of changing forms of work and organization highlight that organizations increasingly integrate market mechanisms and that workers are increasingly required to pursue the ideal of an enterprising self (Storey, Salaman, and Platman 2005). Although the emergence and change of forms of work and organizations as well as individuals' behavioural, perceptual, and cognitive patterns are obviously intertwined, theoretical explanations of this co-evolutionary process are scarce. This chapter aims at making a contribution to fill this gap by using the concept of reflexive habitus (Sweetman 2003) as a way to shed light on how reflexivity itself has become habitual in flexible forms of work and how, with reflexive habitus, processes of self-refashioning are "second nature" rather than difficult to achieve. The focus is to provide an understanding of what living in transient and flexible worlds of work—of which temporary agency work is a prevailing example—means to workers and how we can make sense of it. Such understanding is, in our view, essential for a critical conceptualization of the role that human resources management (HRM) and employment policies play in shaping individuals' (work) lives. Whereas HRM can undoubtedly have a positive effect on temporary agency workers' productivity and well-being, its broader consequences for workers' identities and life courses should be kept in mind, too. What are the implications of temporary assignments and flexible working conditions for individuals? How do people deal with situations of uncertainty and expectations on creativity? What roles do the agency and the client organizations have in facilitating for the individual employee in managing flexible and changing employment conditions? Previous studies of temporary employment have shown, for example, that individuals develop attitudes and skills to deal with the temporal and spatial discontinuity of temporary agency work, involving a moulding of subjectivity (Garsten 2008); that flexible forms of work are conducive to simulated "designer cultures" involving a shift in employee identification (Casey 1996); and that flexible work conditions often require a metacognitive competence characterized as a self-governing competence (Hanson 2004) by which the individual is able to define, structure, and discipline her own performance and, ultimately, her ability to manage and govern herself in a wider, functional sense.

One attempt to link changing forms of work and organization to broader economic and societal changes has been provided by Boltanski and Chiapello (2005) in their book *The New Spirit of Capitalism*. The authors argue that capitalism has been able to integrate the "artistic critique" of "dehumanizing," "alienating," and "exploitative" forms of Taylorist and mass production as well as managerial and bureaucratic organizational structures by increasingly enacting the vision of a *cité par projets*, in which project-focused forms of organization and production become the dominant paradigm. Due to the spread of inter-organizational cooperation, careers, and professional communities, such organizational forms often imply unclear boundaries between organizations and their environment. In this new justificatory regime, *activity* is the principle by which, in last resource, actors qualify their actions. This activity is performed in networks, seen as the *natural* infrastructure of societies (Castells 1996) and mostly in networked projects. In this order, *activity* has features that differ from other forms of capitalistic activity, namely, the *industrial* form (Boltanski and Chiapello 2002, 9):

> Contrary to what happens in the Industrial Cité—where activity means "work" and being active means "holding a steady and wage-earning position"—in the Project-oriented Cité, activity overcomes the oppositions between work and no-work, steady and unsteady, paid and unpaid, profit-sharing and volunteer work, and between that which can be measured in terms of productivity and that which cannot be assessed in terms of accountable performances.

To accomplish this engagement, individuals must be flexible, adaptable, and polyvalent. Such project-based forms of organizing promote (and require) values and attitudes like entrepreneurship, networking, flexibility, and marketability instead of organization-based career aspirations and long-term commitment. Current post-industrial conditions in work and production have rendered problematic some of the primary categories of industrial society, such as the division of labour and occupation, regular and temporary forms of work, and core and periphery forms of employment. The organization-based commitments and prospects are to some degree substituted by trans-organizational ones, involving a flexible mindset and skills in networking and in the marketing of oneself as "employable" and entrepreneurial.

This broader perspective on a move towards project-based and flexible forms of organizing reveals how ways of organizing work are intimately connected to larger societal changes and are predicated on economic and market-related developments (see e.g. Sennett 2006). With globalizing financial flows, forms of production and organizing work are transformed in line with new templates, and labour markets are being re-regulated.

Organizations in flux and transformation may provide lesser degrees of stability than they used to do, in terms of long-term expectations of employment and community. This often entails ambivalence regarding (transient) organizational structures and individuals' positions within these structures, a state we will characterize as organizational *"liminality."* Concomitantly, individuals' relations to work, ways of constructing identity, career, and community from within the realms of work, also change. Especially when work is less tied to place and particular groups of people, and more fluid in relation to place and time, we see a differentiation of ways of relating to work and new sets of attitudes being formed. The workplace continues to be a pre-eminent site for the making, contestation, and reshaping of human identity, individual and collective (Miller and Rose 1995, 428), now fostering enhanced reflexivity.

These altered conditions imply what we may call a "creativity imperative" for both workers and organizations. Organizations are often expected to provide a platform for the development of creativity, and individuals are expected to explore their creative potentials at work. Flexibility in organizational forms and employment contracts thus in a general sense place demands on the creativity of employees not only to be agile and adaptable to varying conditions of work, but also to contribute innovative ideas, perspectives, and solutions. Individuals are often required by organizations to bring in their whole creative potential and to continuously self-market not just their competencies but their person as a whole. Rather than have workers adhere to depersonalizing bureaucratic rules or homogenous cultural norms, Fleming (2009) argues that many large corporations now invite employees to simply "be themselves." Alternative lifestyles, consumption, ethnic identity, sexuality, fun, and even dissent are now celebrated because employees are presumed to be more motivated if they can just be themselves. In situations like these, formerly clear-cut boundaries between "work" and "life" tend to blur. Hence, blurred organizational boundaries go hand in hand with blurred boundaries between work and life: Liminal organizations require liminal subjects (Garsten 1999), motivated to creatively test and transgress boundaries between work and life, organizational identities and personal identities, and old and new ways of doing things. Whereas a demand for creativity is obvious in the case of so-called knowledge or creative workers, we argue that blurring organizational and work–life boundaries requires creative ways of dealing with ambiguities and temporariness from all individuals working in flexible, project-based organizational work contexts. Regardless of their skill or qualification level, temporary agency workers are therefore exposed to the creativity imperative. But how can we conceptually link the described developments towards a project-based production regime, transient organizational forms, and flexible, adaptable, and polyvalent individuals? So far, there is a lack of theoretical explorations of the link between flexible forms of work organization and workers' enactments of and ways of handling work–life boundaries. Such explorations require theoretical approaches that provide an appropriate conceptual framework for linking the social enactment of organizations, individual agency, and how this agency is shaped by societal structures or forces.

One interesting candidate for exploring the link between organizational liminality and work–life boundaries is Bourdieu's habitus concept, which addresses individuals' behavioural, perceptual, and cognitive schemes as a set of (stable) dispositions that are constituted by their position in social space (class and capital endowments). Bourdieu's theory of social practice does not say much about organizations, however. Furthermore, many social scientists have criticized that the habitus concept tends to overemphasize the societal determination of agency. In order to avoid a too one-sided structuralist view, we will refer to recent attempts to loosen Bourdieu's structuralist assumptions, in particular Sweetman's (2003) "reflexive habitus." We will then use two empirical examples, creative workers in the cultural industries and temporary agency workers in administrative positions, to illustrate the demands that transient and flexible work environments put on individuals regarding how to deal with work–life boundaries and what the demands entail for self-reflection. Despite the many differences between agency work (often defined work packages or modules within the client organization) and the cultural industries (intrinsic motivation, self-employment, trans-organizational networks, and projects), there are also significant similarities: Work arrangements are transient, providing organizations with numerical flexibility and bringing about organizational liminality by making membership structures more ambiguous. We will also show that in both cases workers have to creatively develop ways of managing the often blurred boundaries between their work and private lives. The "be creative" imperative, therefore, refers not just to work itself but to the individual's whole life because practices like self-marketing, maintaining employability, managing "boundaryless careers," and a work-dominated life can neither spatially nor temporally nor cognitively be designated to the work sphere alone. Flexible forms of work pose important questions pertaining to the management of flexible workforces. How can we best understand flexible, dynamic, and creative forms of work; how are they to be managed; and which management practices or work arrangements endanger the well-being of individuals by excessively enhancing the pressure on creative self-management?

In the subsequent section, we outline some basic characteristics of project-based forms of organizing, and "liminality" is suggested as a pivotal feature of contemporary organizations. The section "Work–Life Boundaries" gives a brief account of the work–life boundaries debate and argues that blurring work–life boundaries and blurring organizational boundaries have to be seen as intertwined. The central concept with which we seek to analyze these intertwined levels of boundaries, the "reflexive habitus" (Sweetman 2003), is introduced in the section "The Reflexive Habitus," and then, in the section "Temporariness and the Need for Creative Selves," illustrated by two examples, temporary agency work and theatre artists. Some conclusions will be drawn in section "Conclusion: Reflexivity in Practice."

PROJECTS, BOUNDARIES, AND ORGANIZATIONAL LIMINALITY

In the world of organizations, a long-term, permanent employment relation has long been the norm. The long-term contract has provided a base for organizational action as well as a sense of loyalty and community. As new ways of organizing production and managerial trends influence organizations to change, this model relationship is also changing. The idea of "lifelong permanent work" is now increasingly being eroded (Cappelli 1995; Kalleberg 2000; Stone 2012). Standard contracts covered by collective bargaining agreements, the concentration of work in large factories or office sites, and the expectation of permanent employment are being questioned and increasingly dissolved (Allen and Henry 1996; Beck 1992). In its place, ideas like "flexibilization," "employability," and "lifelong learning" appear as key points of reference (Garsten and Jacobsson 2004). Workplaces are increasingly dispersed, and even contingent and employment contracts, working hours, and skills need to be more flexible. Employees are facing new expectations and new contexts within which to construct a sense of identity and community (see, e.g., Garsten and Turtinen 2000; Lindgren and Wåhlin 2001). Although much attention has been paid to flexibilization and the erosion of permanent employment relations for workers in manual trades and services (Elliot and Atkinson 1998; Standing 2009), this is also the case for knowledge workers (Baldry et al. 2007; Brown and Hesketh 2004; Felstead, Burchell, and Green 1998; Rasmussen and Håpnes 2012).

The flexibilization of employment contracts and ways of work involves a challenge to established organizational boundaries and structures (Marchington et al. 2005). The discourse of flexibility invokes notions of a different, alternative kind of labour market and individual disposition, one in which projects are increasingly becoming the standard organizational form, rather than the exception. Project-based organizing is now also somewhat of an ideal in management trends (Boltanski and Chiapello 2005). With the focus on projects, the expectation is that dynamism and entrepreneurial spirit grow, whilst hierarchy and bureaucracy become weaker. For employees, career success is understood to depend more on the results of the projects on which they work, rather than on time spent in a position or on organizational politics. For being successful in such a system, self-management competencies are vital that enable individuals (and teams) to achieve output-related performance criteria, meet project deadlines, and solve conflicts in diverse project teams. The organization is expected to become more agile and to be able to respond quickly to changing customer needs. Thus, project-based organizing, like other late-modern managerial ideals, suggests that organizations are, or should, become more fluid and flexible. This in turn, has some important consequences for the structure of organizations, and for the experience of work among employees.

We want to suggest here that project-based organizations can be characterized as liminal in some important respects. Liminality, as conceptualized by Van Gennep (1960) and later theorized by Victor Turner (1967), implies a state of in-between positions and/or structures. A liminal subject is neither entirely here, nor there, but rather "betwixt and between" given positions and/ or structures. As a subject moves through processual changes in life, the liminal state marks the very stage of transfer between fixed and more stable states. For example, an apprentice may be conceived of as in a liminal state, neither a complete novice nor a full-fledged master. Likewise, the period of working on one's PhD degree is in many ways a liminal phase because one is neither an undergraduate student nor an independent researcher. Elsewhere, Garsten (1999) has argued that temporary employees are liminal employees, in that they are betwixt and between the more stable spatial and temporal structures of the labour market, characterized by long-term contracts and work being confined to one location, which is also the location of one's employer.

Liminality is generally characterized by a degree of ambivalence. The status of a liminal subject is open to contestation, and hence ambivalence. Oftentimes, it involves status reversal, so that the given position of the subject is turned upside down, making him or her open to critique, contestation, or even mockery. At the same time, the liminal position is a privileged one, in which learning is encouraged and prescribed, where new knowledge is being recognized, and hence a position worthy of respect.

There is also often a temporal dimension to liminality, implying that the position is a transient one, through which a subject moves on the way to another, more stable position. In the case of temporary agency workers, the temporary assignment has an end point attached to it. In addition, temping is usually something one does in a certain period in life: after graduating from high school, when returning to the labour markets after parental leave or unemployment, or when looking to move into a different sector of work.

Whilst the concept of liminality was originally used to denote a particular status of an individual, we propose to use it here for purposes of highlighting a particular status at a collective, organizational level. Project-based organizations often involve a break with the established ways of working in more stable forms of organizing. Temporally, they are contingent by nature, dissolving or reorganizing as the project comes to an end. They are populated by contingent workers and consultants, as well as with experts and professionals. Project-based organizations are likewise often looked upon with a degree of ambivalence. They are at once high-risk environments, where performance is continually evaluated and judged, and exciting places where new ideas and products are being crafted. We suggest that such organizations provide little of the stability expected from organizations more generally, in terms of long-term expectations of employment and community. Such liminal organizations tend to be more open in relation to their environment and to other organizations, boundaries being continuously worked on and regularly blurred. They are as well characterized by a degree of indeterminacy as to their future shape and existence. The organizations of the cultural industries are a case in point here because they are dependent on a degree of openness and flexibility in relation to other organizations and to the market, and by living off of the creativity and innovation of their employees (Caves 2000; Hesmondhalgh 2007).

WORK–LIFE BOUNDARIES

In accordance with the emergence of liminal organizations, the relationship between individuals' work and private lives has become a matter of concern among workers, employers, and policy makers. Current debates on work–life balance indicate that there is either a "new" problem workers have with balancing the two spheres of work and life and/or an increased awareness on the part of workers, organizations, and policy makers regarding the relationship between these spheres. Whilst working time has not increased for most workers but, since early industrialisation, has continuously decreased (Roberts 2007), work- and life-related responsibilities (work pressure and work intensification; individualization of care responsibilities) seem to have grown, and the insecurity and instability of work arrangements entails an additional burden. However, it is mainly the skilled middle-class employees who raise their voice in order to articulate their desire for a more balanced work life (Warhurst, Eikhof, and Haunschild 2008). Employers' work–life balance policies can thus be interpreted as responses to these voices and as attempts to help (in particular skilled) workers coping with intensified work demands and a spillover from work to life.

One shortcoming of the work–life balance discourse is that it often narrows down the "life side" to care responsibilities and that it (implicitly) assumes that individuals draw a clear separation between "work" and "life" and also seek to maintain this separation (Eikhof, Warhurst, and Haunschild 2007). However, empirically we observe that different groups of workers enact different boundaries between work and life, ranging from entire fusion (many artists) over a work-dominated life (many knowledge workers such as consultants, information technology workers, architects, designers, etc.) to a clear separation (Warhurst, Eikhof, Haunschild 2008). These patterns of boundaries are often the result of a co-evolution of workers' lifestyles, work arrangements, and human resources practices (Haunschild 2011). Blurred boundaries between life and work can, but do not necessarily have to, be perceived as problematic by individuals. Therefore, typical work–life balance measures address a specific group of workers only.

Nevertheless, it has to be stated that for many employees current developments in the world of work lead to increasing demands from employers to bring their whole personality into work and—fostered by project-based forms of organizing work as well as communication technologies—to be available beyond traditional working hours (see, e.g., Fleming 2009). What has been customary for freelancers and the self-employed is now more and more expected from "regular" employees too—to self-market themselves within intra-organizational customer-supplier relationships and to maintain one's employability not by attending training courses organized by the employer but self-organized and outside paid working hours.

Liminal organizations, that is, organizations with an increased lack of stability and demand on flexibility as well as blurring organizational boundaries, we argue, thus go hand in hand with a shifting of the boundaries between work and life (see also Pongratz and Voß 2003; Henninger and Papouschek 2008). In order to further explore the transient and flexible work lives that result from this co-evolution of blurred organizational and work–life boundaries, we will refer to the concept of *reflexive habitus.*

THE REFLEXIVE HABITUS

Bourdieu's (1984) concept of habitus provides a powerful tool for analyzing the linkage between social structures and (the collective nature of) individual preferences, tastes, perceptions, thinking, and actions. But does this concept help us to understand work lives that are characterized by flexibility, continuous adaption and creative self-marketing in changing work contexts?

With the notion of "habitus," Bourdieu conceptualizes the *incorporated* life conditions, that is, cognitive, perceptual, and behavioural schemes that develop on the basis of embodied milieu-specific endowments with economic, social, and cultural capital (Bourdieu 1984). The habitus provides stable dispositions that constrain the ways in which individuals can act in social fields and thus limit the diversity of possible actions. The pre-reflexive character of habitus and—even more so—its proposed stability have been subject to objections, however (see, e.g., Calhoun 1993; Sweetman 2003; Lahire 2003, plurality of dispositions; see also Mutch 2003). In Bourdieu's notion, habitus does not imply that human actions are not reflexive, but that "the habitus itself is not amenable to reflexive interventions" (Sweetman 2003, 535). The assumed stability and pre-reflexivity of habitus can be criticized fundamentally at a conceptual level by, for example, pointing out that it simply "is possible to change the way we walk and talk" (Sweetman 2003, 536). Sweetman's main argument, however, adds a historical or evolutionary dimension by stating that nowadays "reflexivity itself may have become habitual" (Sweetman 2003, 528) and a "'second nature' for some" (p. 529). As evidence, he refers to examples of shifting patterns of work and employment (flexible work, but also emotional labour), changing forms of community and relationships (reflexive monitoring of relationships; cf. Giddens 1994), and consumer culture (lifestyle choices; continuous self-monitoring and self-improvement through consumer acts; cf. Featherstone 1991).

Whereas in Bourdieu's perspective habitual changes require major crises in which the adjustment of habitus and fields is disrupted, Sweetman (2003, 541) argues that for more and more individuals in contemporary society there is "a more or less permanent disruption of social position, or a more or less constant disjunction between habitus and field." Unstable social conditions regarding changing forms of work, organization, and work–life boundaries, may therefore lead to a constant need to reflect on one's habitus in the light of changing field-related requirements. Sweetman's main point now is that we cannot just observe an increased reflexivity towards the habitus, but that contemporary conditions "may contribute to the development of a *particular type of habitus,* characterized by a pervasive and habitual reflexivity . . ." (Sweetman 2003, 542) making (certain contemporary) individuals become engaged in "reflexive projects of self-(re)construction" (ibid.).

Sweetman regards the increasing reflexive orientation towards the workplace and the demand to adapt to a variety of work contexts, in particular in higher status occupations, as one of the key factors contributing to the emergence of a reflexive habitus (Sweetman 2003, 544). Sweetman thus sees a strong connection between flexibilization and marketization of the workplace and individuals' habitual reflexivity. Such habitual reflexivity is beyond the mere reflection of day-to-day practices and decisions by knowledgeable actors (Giddens 1984) but addresses deeper levels of appearance, taste, perceptions, lifestyle, and identity. Habitual reflexivity requires a considerable degree of creativity because individuals continuously have to identify their position in social space, to react to changing work-related demands without the help of traditional anchors (permanent employment, stable work teams, clearly defined incentives, work processes, and organizational boundaries), and to creatively enact and self-manage the boundaries between work and life. In the following section, we will further explore this creativity imperative and the role of reflexive habitus for the relationship between organizational and work–life boundaries by looking at two groups of workers, temporary agency workers and theatre artists (actors).

TEMPORARINESS AND THE NEED FOR CREATIVE SELVES

Temporary work arrangements, unclear organizational membership, and the need to creatively enact and self-manage the boundaries between work and life can be found in different industries and among different kinds of workers, and temporary agency workers are definitely among them. But the creative or cultural industries (film, music, theatre, dance, fine arts, literature/publishing, media, design, etc.; cf. Caves 2000; Hesmondhalgh 2007) have an even longer tradition of flexible, project-based work arrangements, competitive labour markets (Menger 1999; Haak 2008), inter-organizational mobility, and employment uncertainty—often combined with low incomes. Therefore, it comes as no surprise that the creative industries have—in normative, often neo-liberal discourses—been used as a role model for future workers and flexible forms of organizing. Furthermore, social scientists have become increasingly interested in the labour process in creative industries in order to study individual, organizational, and societal consequences of flexible work arrangements (see, e.g., the compilation of some of these studies in McKinlay and Smith [2009]).

Here, we refer to studies into the German theatrical employment system to explore the reflexive habitus and the relationship between organizational and work–life boundaries (Haunschild 2003; Eikhof and Haunschild 2006). Many theatre actors in Germany are members of resident theatre ensembles and hold temporary contracts of usually one year. Permanent contracts are rare and only apply to actors with 15 years of seniority within one theatre. The labour market is highly competitive, and there is always a large pool of qualified actors seeking to enter the ensemble system. Due to continuous project-related role assignments based on artistic decisions of theatre managers and directors, competition not only takes place in the recruitment process but is omnipresent. Actors are expected to pursue a career that transgresses organizational boundaries, and inter-organizational networks play a decisive role for gaining reputation, maintaining employability, and thus for getting the next job (Haunschild and Eikhof 2009).

Although theatre actors perceive themselves as artists who produce art for art's sake, they have to self-market themselves on a permanent basis in order to become known by influential directors and theatre managers and to make those individuals interested in their artistic capabilities. Because of often diffuse feedback on their performance and capabilities and because work-related skills cannot be separated from their personality and their body (habitus), theatre artists need to constantly reflect on their habitus. What is remarkable is that for theatre artists the boundaries between work and life are often invisible: Life is centred around work, and being an artist (or following an artistic calling) renders a separation between work and other spheres of life irrelevant or even problematic and counterproductive for pursuing an artistic career.

However, what we could observe in an intensive qualitative case study is that a collective lifestyle based on bohemian values helps these artists to anchor the self in a world of continuous demands for flexibility and reflexivity (Eikhof and Haunschild 2006; see also Sweetman 2003, 543) and provides something "to hide behind" (Sweetman 2003, 546). Creative self-reflection is nevertheless essential at two levels: for (self-)constructing oneself as an interesting artist in a volatile work environment and for trying to accommodate non-work-related demands (family, reproduction, and social life) into a work-dominated artistic life.

Temporary agency work, like work in the creative industries, is characterized by a "manufactured uncertainty" (Giddens 1994, 184) in both spatial and temporal terms. Many aspects of working life, such as if and when there will be a next assignment and where one will go for the next one, are undecided until shortly before the current assignment is terminated. The continuity of work is organized only in terms of "scenario thinking," in the way of an as-if construction of possible future outcomes. And because transience has become a more or less permanent condition, individuals have no choice but to reflect critically on their own, individual role in influencing future work trajectories (see Garsten 2008, 116).

Temporary agency managers emphasize the importance of a continuous readiness to learn functional, social, and emotional flexibility, and a creative capacity in order to stay "on the books" and to be "employable." Being creative, in the sense of being open to learn new ways of thinking about the job and of performing the job, finding solutions to problems, and performing above expectations is part and parcel of what makes up "the professional temp." However, the kind of creativity that is fostered in temporary work is by necessity circumscribed by the need for a degree of predictability in performance and behaviour.

For the temp agency, stressing adaptation and creativity is part of the fostering of a continuous and market-driven kind of reflexivity in the employees. Skilled and specialized, as well as unskilled temps, are taught to be alert to changing places and conditions of work, as well as to the varying needs of their clients. Emphasizing adaptation and creativity is also a way for the agency to manage the performance of their dispersed workforce. The reflexive habitus operates as a way of "governing at a distance" (Rose 1999), so to speak, whereby individuals learn to incorporate the expectations and demands of the agency and the client organization alike.

CONCLUSION: REFLEXIVITY IN PRACTICE

Taking Boltanski and Chiapello's (2005) analysis of contemporary capitalism—with its paradigm of project-focused forms of work and organization—as a starting point, we outlined how blurring organizational and work–life boundaries results in a creativity imperative for organizations and workers. We introduced the term *liminal organizations* to characterize organizations in flux and transformation that entail ambivalence regarding (transient) organizational structures and individuals' positions within these structures. Working in or for such organizations requires practices like self-control, self-marketing, maintaining employability, and managing trans-organizational careers—practices that can neither spatially nor temporally nor cognitively be designated to the work sphere alone. Rather, they demand a continuous self-reflective process that enables individuals to define, structure, and discipline their own performance and, ultimately, their ability to manage and govern themselves (Hanson 2004).

With the aim of analyzing what living in transient and flexible worlds of work means to workers, we searched for a theoretical concept that helps to explore the link between project-based forms of work, blurring organizational boundaries, and the resulting demands on individuals' creative self-management. Sweetman's (2003) concept of the reflexive habitus fills this gap. Sweetman argues that reflexivity itself has become habitual in flexible forms of work, and that, with a reflexive habitus, processes of self-refashioning have become "second nature" (ibid.).

A less deterministic conceptualization of habitus not only takes into account that, under current work regimes, individuals reflect on their habitus and creatively try to adapt to changing social contexts, but also allows for considering that the reflexive work-related habitus is mainly influenced by organizational practices and that these practices are—in turn—shaped by organizational members and their habitus. The concept of reflexive habitus, we argue, therefore helps to conceptually link liminal organizations with workers who actively and creatively try to enact and cope with blurred work–life boundaries.

The two examples of a creative reflection of habitus that we used, temporary agency workers and theatre artists, represent distinct groups of workers. However, both groups share common characteristics: They both work under flexible work arrangements and in transient work constellations. Both groups also have to self-market themselves and need to cope with work demands that challenge a clear separation of work and life. The example of temporary agency workers, who can be highly skilled but do not necessarily have to be, shows that Sweetman's claim that the need for a reflexive habitus mainly applies to higher status occupations has to be qualified. The example of artists reveals that a shared lifestyle that incorporates work-related requirements can help workers to cope with uncertainty and flexibility. This includes the acceptance of temporary work arrangements because these entail perceived individual freedom, a high degree of mobility, and often a network of friends that is distributed across the country, also providing accommodation when travelling between different job locations. An artistic self-understanding can thus be seen as a prototype of an "inbuilt" reflexive habitus. Therefore, it can be assumed that temporary agency workers, who represent a larger part of the workforce with respect to work attitudes than artists, face more problems with a creativity imperative challenging their work–life boundaries, bringing about a permanent disruption of their social position, and forcing them into a reflexive habitus.

Efforts to manage temporary agency work(ers) should therefore be accompanied by a reflection of the broader effects on the lives of workers who often do not have an alternative to working in or for liminal organizations. What are the implications at the individual level of working on temporary contracts? What kinds of skills and capacities does it take to balance the needs of different clients? How does one accommodate to changing workplaces and workmates? And what are the implications for the social texture of the work group? Questions such as these invite us to explore the worlds of temporary work more carefully and to ask what the implications for the management of temporary agency work and workers are.

REFERENCES

Allen, John, and Nick Henry. 1996. "Fragments of Industry and Employment: Contract Service Work and the Shift towards Precarious Employment." In *Changing Forms of Employment: Organisations, Skills, and Gender*, edited by Rosemary Crompton, Duncan Gallie, and Kate Purcell, 65–82. London: Sage.

Baldry, Chris, Peter Bain, Phil Taylor, Jeff Hyman, Dora Scholarios, Abigail Marks, AileenWatson, Kay Gilbert, Gregor Gall, and Dirk Bunzel. 2007. *The Meaning of Work in the New Economy.* Basingstoke: Palgrave Macmillan.

Beck, Ulrich. 1992. *Risk Society: Towards a New Modernity.* London: Sage.

Boltanski, Luc, and Eva Chiapello. 2005. *The New Spirit of Capitalism.* London: Verso.

Boltanski, Luc, and Eva Chiapello. 2002. *The New Spirit of Capitalism.* Paper presented at the Conference of Europeanists, 14–16 March, Chicago, IL.

Bourdieu, Pierre. 1984. *Distinction: A Social Critique of the Judgement of Taste.* London: Routledge and Kegan Paul (originally in French 1979).

Brown, Phillip, and Anthony Hesketh. 2004. *The Mismanagement of Talent: Employability and Jobs in the Knowledge Economy.* Oxford: Oxford University Press.

Calhoun, Craig, ed. 1993. *Bourdieu: Critical Perspectives.* Cambridge: Polity.

Cappelli, Peter. 1995. "Rethinking Employment." *British Journal of Industrial Relations* 33 (4): 563–602.

Casey, Catherine. 1996. "Corporate Transformations: Designer Culture, Designer Employees and 'Post-Occupational' Solidarity." *Organization* 3 (3): 319–339.

Castells, Manuel. 1996. *The Rise of the Network Society.* Vol. 1 of *The Information Age: Economy, Society and Culture.* Cambridge, MA: Blackwell.

Caves, Richard E. 2000. *Creative Industries: Contracts between Arts and Business.* Cambridge, MA: Harvard University Press.

Eikhof, Doris, R., and Axel Haunschild. 2006. "Lifestyle Meets Market: Bohemian Entrepreneurs in Creative Industries." *Creativity and Innovation Management* 13 (3): 234–241.

Eikhof, Doris, R., Chris Warhurst, and Axel Haunschild. 2007. "Introduction: What Work? What Life? What Balance? Critical Reflections on the Work-Life Balance Debate." *Employee Relations* 29 (4): 325–333.

Elliot, Larry, and Dan Atkinson. 1998. *The Age of Insecurity.* London: Verso.

Featherstone, Mike. 1991. *Consumer Culture and Postmodernism.* London: Sage.

Felstead, Alan, Brendan Burchell, and Francis Green. 1998. "Insecurity at Work: Is It Getting Worse?" *New Economy* 5 (3): 180–184.

Fleming, Peter. 2009. *Authenticity and the Cultural Politics of Work.* Oxford: Oxford University Press.

Garsten, Christina. 1999. "Betwixt and Between: Temporary Employees as Liminal Subjects in Flexible Organizations." *Organization Studies* 20: 601–617.

Garsten, Christina. 2008. *Workplace Vagabonds: Career and Community in Changing Worlds of Work.* Basingstoke, UK: Palgrave Macmillan.

Garsten, Christina, and Kerstin Jacobsson, eds. 2004. *Learning to Be Employable: New Agendas on Work, Employability and Learning in a Globalizing World.* Basingstoke, UK: Palgrave Macmillan.

Garsten, Christina, and Jan Turtinen. 2000. "'?Angels' and 'Chameleons': The Cultural Construction of the Flexible Temporary Employee in Sweden and the UK." In *After Full Employment: European Discourses on Work and Flexibility*, edited by Bo Stråth, 161–206. Brussels: Peter Lang.

Giddens, Anthony. 1984. *The Constitution of Society Outline of the Theory of Structuration.* Cambridge, MA: Blackwell/Polity Press.

Giddens, Anthony. 1994. "Living in a Post-Traditional Society." In *Reflexive Modernization: Politics, Tradition and Aesthetics in the Modern Social Order*, edited by Ulrich Beck, Anthony Giddens, and Scott Lash, 59–109. Cambridge, UK: Polity.

Haak, Carroll. 2008. *Wirtschaftliche und soziale Risiken auf den Arbeitsmärkten von Künstlern.* Wiesbaden, Germany: VS.

Hanson, Marika. 2004. "Det flexibla arbetets villkor: Om självförvaltandets kompetens." Doctoral thesis, 127, Department of Pedagogy, Stockholm University. Worklife in Transition Series, 8, National Institute for Working Life.

Haunschild, Axel. 2011. "Lifestyles as Social Contracts between Workers and Organizations." *Schmalenbach Business Review* 63: 361–375.

Haunschild, Axel. 2003. "Managing Employment Relationships in Flexible Labour Markets: The Case of German Repertory Theatres." *Human Relations* 56: 899–929.

Haunschild, Axel, and Doris R. Eikhof. 2009. "Bringing Creativity to Market. Theatre Actors as Self-Employed Employees." In *Creative Labour: Working in the Creative Industries*, edited by Alan McKinlay and Chris Smith, 156–173. Basingstoke, UK: Palgrave.

Henninger, Annette, and Ulrike Papouschek. 2008. "Occupation Matters-Blurring Work-Life-Boundaries in Mobile Care and the Media Industry." In *Work Less, Live More? Critical Analysis of the Work-Life Boundary*, edited by Chris Warhurst, Doris R. Eikhof, and Axel Haunschild, 153–172. Basingstoke, UK: Palgrave.

Hesmondhalgh, David. 2007. *The Cultural Industries*. 2nd ed. London: Sage.

Kalleberg, Arne. 2000. "Nonstandard Employment Relations: Part-Time, Temporary and Contract Work." *Annual Review of Sociology* 26: 341–365.

Lahire, Bernard. 2003. "From the Habitus to an Individual Heritage of Dispositions. Towards a Sociology at the Level of the Individual." *Poetics* 31: 329–355.

Lindgren, Monica, and Nils Wåhlin. 2001 "Identity Construction among Boundary-Crossing Individuals." *Scandinavian Journal of Management* 17 (3): 357–377.

Marchington, Mick P., Damian Grimshaw, Jil Rubery, and Hugh Willmott, eds. 2005. *Fragmenting Work: Blurring Organisational Boundaries and Disordering Hierarchies*. Oxford: Oxford University Press.

McKinlay, Alan, and Smith, Chris, eds. 2009. *Creative Labour. Working in the Creative Industries*. Basingstoke, UK: Palgrave.

Menger, Pierre-Michel. 1999. "Artistic Labor Markets and Careers." *Annual Review of Sociology* 25: 541–574.

Miller, Peter, and Nikolas Rose. 1995. "Production, Identity, and Democracy." *Theory and Society* 24 (3): 427–467.

Mutch, Alistair. 2003. "Communities of Practice and Habitus: A Critique." *Organization Studies* 24 (3): 383–401.

Pongratz, Hans J., and Günter G. Voß. 2003. "From Employee to 'Entreployee': Towards a 'Self-Entrepreneurial' Work Force?" *Concepts and Transformation* 8 (3): 239–254.

Rasmussen, Bente, and Tove Håpnes. 2012. "Permanent Temporariness? Changes in Social Contracts in Knowledge Work." *Nordic Journal of Working Life Studies* 2 (1): 5–22.

Roberts, Ken. 2007. "Work-Life Balance—the Sources of the Contemporary Problem and the Probable Outcomes: A Review and Interpretation of the Evidence." *Employee Relations* 29 (4): 334–351.

Rose, Nikolas. 1999. *Powers of Freedom: Reframing Political Thought*. Cambridge: Cambridge University Press.

Sennett, Richard. 2006. *The Culture of the New Capitalism*. New Haven, CT: Yale University Press.

Standing, Guy. 2009. *Work after Globalisation: Building Occupational Citizenship*. Cheltenham, Northampton, UK: Edward Elgar.

Stone, Katherine V. W. 2012. "The Decline in the Standard Employment Contract: Evidence from Ten Advanced Industrial Countries." Law-Econ Research Paper, No. 12–19, UCLA School of Law, Los Angeles.

Storey, John, Graeme Salaman, and Kerry Platman. 2005. "Living with Enterprise in an Enterprise Economy: Freelance and Contract Workers in the Media." *Human Relations* 58 (8): 1033–1054.

Sweetman, Paul. 2003. "Twenty-First Century Dis-Ease? Habitual Reflexivity or the Reflexive Habitus." *Sociological Review* 51 (4): 528–549.

Turner, Victor. 1967. *The Forest of Symbols. Aspects of Ndembu Ritual.* Ithaca, NY: Cornell University Press.
Van Gennep, Arnold. 1960. *The Rites of Passage.* Chicago: University of Chicago Press. Originally published as *Les rites de passage* (1909).
Warhurst, Chris, Doris R. Eikhof, and Axel Haunschild. 2008. "Out of Balance or Just Out of Bounds? Analysing the Relationship between Work and Life." In *Work Less, Live More? Critical Analysis of the Work-Life Boundary*, edited by Chris Warhurst, Doris R. Eikhof, and Axel A. Haunschild. Basingstoke, UK: Palgrave.

3 Temporary Agency Work and the Pathways to Flexicurity

Ronald Dekker and Ton Wilthagen

The issues of labour market flexibility and atypical work, including agency work, are increasingly being discussed from the perspective of flexicurity. As a concept, flexicurity was developed within academia at the end of the 1990s and has recently been taken up by the European Commission as a key objective of the European Employment Strategy. The main thrust of flexicurity as an employment and labour market strategy is that labour market flexibility and employment security should and can indeed be simultaneously enhanced. Whereas labour market flexibilization is typically at odds with the more traditional notion of job security, employment security can be enhanced in the context of a flexible labour market by improving employability and employment opportunities even for those workers who do not enjoy job security.[1]

The "flexicurity claim" is that there is an optimal policy mix that enhances both labour market flexibility and employment security, typically involving a shift from job to employment security. This chapter describes the four general and ideal-typical pathways that have been identified within the European flexicurity debate that should inspire member states to map out their own specific pathways towards flexicurity. This chapter attempts to explore the role that temporary agency work can play within these flexicurity pathways. For this purpose, the chapter presents a theoretical framework in which the employment relationship at the firm level is analyzed, including the triangular employment relationship. This theoretical framework is then used to analyze the challenges posed by the four different pathways to flexicurity and the extent to which the partners in the triangular relationship can deal with these challenges.

Temporary agency work has received considerable attention in labour market literature (economic, sociological, labour law) over the past 20 years. It is often treated as part of the wider trend towards labour market flexibilization (e.g., Delsen 1991; Barker and Christensen 1998; Kalleberg 2000); however, some research deals specifically with temporary agency work (e.g., Storrie 2002; Koene, Paauwe, and Groenewegen 2004). Furthermore, there is a considerable body of "stepping-stone" literature on the "conversion" rate of temporary (agency) workers to permanent employees (e.g.,

De Graaf-Zijl 2006; Dekker 2007; Picchio 2008; Amuedo-Dorantes, Malo, and Munoz-Bullon 2008; Giesecke 2009) and on the training of these workers (Autor, Levy, and Murnane 1999; Autor 2001; Forrier and Sels 2003; Schmidt and Thommes 2007).

It is of interest to couple the flexicurity policy concept with the potential role of temporary agency work in Europe, especially because the employment security aspects of this form of employment have not yet been discussed within this framework. Furthermore, it is of interest to see how the flexicurity concept can be operationalized at the level of the firm and the concrete effects of this for workers, employers, and agencies.

OUTLINE OF THE CHAPTER

We will first introduce the flexicurity concept as adopted by the European Commission as a guideline for labour market policy. Second, we will discuss how the flexicurity concept can be operationalized at the level of the individual firm or organization, where formal labour contracts play an important role at the organizational level. At the level of the firm, labour contracts traditionally involve two contracting partners, the employer and the employee. In recent years, in many labour markets it has become more prevalent to have labour contracts involving three parties, namely, the hiring firm, the employee, and an "intermediary" party, often a temporary work agency (TWA). Third, we will discuss the four flexicurity pathways and the role that temporary agency work has played and can—or must—play when facing the challenges posed by each of these pathways.

EUROPEAN UNION (EU) FLEXICURITY POLICY AND FLEXICURITY PATHWAYS

What is flexicurity? Generally speaking, flexibility and security in labour markets are perceived as opposites, either as inversely proportional, so that more flexibility means less security and vice versa, or at least like oil and water, which can coexist but do not mix properly. Moreover, labour market and social security policies tend to display a "leapfrog" approach. Traditionally, policies aimed at enhancing security are of a reactive nature; they follow, usually with a significant delay, the political recognition and assessment that a lack of security exists or that developments within or outside the labour market are harmful to the security of certain groups. In turn, flexibilization policies are usually launched, also after some delay, to adjust labour market and social security institutions that are considered too "tight," protective, or static and thus are presumed to hamper economic development, dynamism, and competitiveness.

In the early 2000s, a new academic and scientific paradigm labelled "flexicurity" was developed to explore ways to transcend traditional approaches and embark on a quest for a new dynamic equilibrium, facilitating and enhancing adaptability and the capacity to deal with change in both individuals and companies (Wilthagen 1998). The main contribution of this new paradigm is that it shifts away from the mainstream neoclassical economic paradigm in which the sole focus is on flexibility. In this respect, the flexicurity concept's recognition of the need not only for individual workers but also firms to have some level of security is a major improvement. Flexicurity is defined as a policy strategy to enhance—at the same time and in a deliberate way—the flexibility of labour markets, the work organization, and employment relations on the one hand, and security—employment security and income security—on the other (Wilthagen and Tros 2004). From a theoretical point of view, flexicurity policies can be characterized as a form of coalescence and synchronization of economic and social policy (Wynn 2000, 501) or as a post-deregulation strategy (Keller and Seifert 2000, 293).

The flexicurity concept has met with much acclaim and criticism after becoming a key policy concept within the European Employment Strategy, as shown, in particular, by the adoption of the common principles on flexicurity by the European Council on 5 December 2007,[2] the report and resolutions on flexicurity by the European Parliament on 29 November 2007,[3] the joint labour market and flexicurity analysis presented by the European social partners on 18 October 2007,[4] the communication on flexicurity by the European Commission dated 27 June 2007,[5] the much debated green paper on the modernization of labour law issued 22 November 2006,[6] and the recently proposed Europe 2020 integrated guidelines on economic and employment policies, of which guideline 7 calls on the member states to integrate the flexicurity principles into their labour market policies and apply them.[7] Thus, as was the case with the Lisbon Strategy, flexicurity is expected to help achieve the employment goals of the EU's 2020 agenda for smart, sustainable, and inclusive growth.

All in all, a European policy framework has now been established, and it is now up to the EU member states to make flexicurity work in a decent and constructive way at the various levels: national, sectoral, company, and individual. According to the European Commission (2007) and Boeri et al. (2007), current socioeconomic challenges require a more flexible labour market, combined with satisfactory levels of security to respond to the new needs of employers and employees simultaneously. Individuals increasingly require employment security to complement job security, as fewer have a job for life.

As an integrated policy strategy, flexicurity should address many of these issues at the same time. Its objective is thus to combine employment and income security with flexible labour markets, work organizations, and labour relations. As mentioned previously, this approach aims to question the simple trade-off between flexibility and security, where the former is seen to be in the exclusive interest of the employer, and the latter in the interest of the employee. The key principle that underpins a flexicurity strategy is that flexibility and security are not necessarily opposites but can be made mutually supportive. Flexicurity strategies should start with the notion that a win-win situation based on trust and highly developed industrial relations can be achieved.

Considering the wide differences between countries in terms of practices and challenges, the EU does not believe in a one-size-fits-all approach. Moreover, it also has to respect the autonomy of each member state with regard to labour market and social policies. Therefore, the EU proposed (in its communication on flexicurity) a set of flexicurity pathways based on the work of Boeri et al. (2007), addressing the different challenges and possible solutions for member states. The notion of flexicurity pathways suggests that there are different roads that countries can take to improve their labour markets, depending on different challenges, priorities, and possibilities. Flexicurity pathways can be designed and implemented across four policy components defined by the European Commission, (European Commission 2007, p. 12) which need to be taken into account as a whole:

1. Flexible and reliable contractual arrangements
2. Efficient active labour market policies (ALMPs) to strengthen transition security
3. Systematic and responsive lifelong learning (LLL)
4. Modern social security provisions that also contribute to good mobility in the labour market

Moreover, a supportive and productive social dialogue and highly developed trust-based industrial relations serve as a general precondition or process variable to make such a flexicurity system work (see also Xhauflair and Pichault, Chapter 6 in this volume). It is important to note that in the following each pathway emphasizes one of these core policy components, but attention to all four policy components is generally required.

FLEXICURITY AT THE FIRM LEVEL: THE EMPLOYMENT CONTRACT

Distributing Risk, Flexibility, and Security at the Firm Level

At the level of the firm, the employment contract is the institution that defines the nature of the employment relationship. In economic terms, the labour contract can be regarded as a more or less efficient solution to the problem of incomplete information in the labour market, thereby distributing risks across the parties involved. In a majority of employment contracts, there are only two parties involved, the employer and the employee.

Different types of direct employment contracts represent different distributions of flexibility and security between employer and employee. Permanent contracts provide some degree of job security in most countries and leave some scope for flexibility, functional or otherwise. Temporary contracts provide lower levels of job security and leave less scope for flexibility with respect to the content of the work due to the short-lived nature of the contract.

In an environment where the rate of technological change is high, the need for the flexible redefinition of jobs and task allocations is generally perceived to be high. This can be done in many different ways and is associated with the flexibility element of the flexicurity concept. The most relevant forms of flexibility are external numerical flexibility, that is, the flexibility to alter the number of workers in your firm quickly, and functional flexibility, or the flexibility to adapt the tasks assigned to workers.

Depending on the nature of any technological change, or other changes in the competitive environment and the regulatory framework, the emphasis will be on one of these forms of flexibility. In the Anglo-Saxon/Rhineland dichotomy of industrial relations regimes (Freeman 1998), the use of external numerical flexibility and wage flexibility is typically associated with Anglo-Saxon countries, whereas Rhineland countries more often opt for functional flexibility and internal numerical flexibility. Firms in the Anglo-Saxon world more often choose to adapt job content to production techniques, whereas firms in Rhineland regions will make more effort to allocate tasks on the basis of the qualifications of their existing workforce (Marsden 1999), with more emphasis on external numerical flexibility in Anglo-Saxon countries as a result.

The use of external numerical flexibility strategies, and in particular the consequences of being employed on a flexible (temporary or otherwise) contract later in a one's career, are documented quite extensively in the empirical literature (e.g., Booth, Francesconi, and Frank 2002; Scherer 2004; Dekker 2007; Picchio 2008).

Interestingly, relatively few economic studies have focused on explaining why firms use flexible forms of employment. In a relatively recent contribution, Polavieja (2003) formulated an employment-rent model to explain the use of temporary employment contracts, partly based on the work of Sorensen (1994, 2000). In the employment-rent model, temporary contracts function as an "incentive" for temporary workers by presenting them with the potential conversion of the contract into a permanent one. The rate of conversion is positively related to task specificity but leaves some scope for firms to continue to use temporary contracts even with a high degree of task specificity (Polavieja 2003). The employment-rent model also incorporates a so-called buffer effect so that workers on permanent contracts are relatively well protected compared to temporary colleagues in the same firm, the latter functioning as a shield against the risk of unemployment of the former. As a result, the "rents" for permanent workers in such firms will be higher. The higher this "buffer" effect, the higher the reward for a temporary worker to receive a permanent contract. Thus, the "buffer" effect strengthens the "incentive" effect (Polavieja 2003).

ARE THINGS DIFFERENT FOR TWA CONTRACTS?

With temporary agency work, three parties are involved: the worker, the agency, and the firm. This more complicated relationship has resulted in the coinage of the term "triangular employment relation" (Kalleberg 2000). The triangular employment relation has the potential advantage of providing greater degrees of freedom to optimally distribute flexibility and security between three, rather than only two, parties.

This triangular relationship is somewhat more cumbersome to analyze in terms of the "economic rent model" (Polavieja 2003). To some extent, there is an "incentive" effect for the worker because some TWA assignments are converted into contracts (possibly temporary) within the firm. However, temporary agency work is generally more distant from the core, so the incentives are typically lower.

In terms of the "buffer" effect, temporary agency workers provide similar protection against unemployment for permanent workers in the firm as do workers on temporary contracts. Thus, the "buffer" effect is also relative to the proportion of workers on these contracts. In the context of temporary agency work, this "buffer" effect strengthens the smaller "incentive" effect. In the case of agency work, however, there is an additional incentive effect: Temps can get other temporary jobs through the agency. This creates a form of flexible security.

THE ROLE OF FLEXICURITY

The general idea of flexicurity is to create a well-balanced mix between flexibility and security, which can also function at the level of an employment contract with a firm. For both the direct temporary employment relationship and the triangular employment relationship involving a TWA, it is fair to say that flexibility is mainly enjoyed by the employer/hiring firm, and the lack of security is experienced mainly by employees, especially when temporary agency work is their main source of employment. This imbalance is more pronounced when temporary agency work is concentrated at the bottom end of the labour market, as is often the case.

The challenge for flexicurity at the level of the employment contract is to introduce elements of flexibility that are also welcomed by workers and at the same time introduce new forms of security that do not necessarily limit the flexibility enjoyed by the firm. In the flexicurity framework, a central role is played by "employment security," which is defined as "the security of being able to keep, find or create gainful employment based upon one's human capital and well-functioning labour market institutions" (Dekker 2012, p. 7, translated from Dutch). In the triangular employment relationship, there is more scope for flexicurity arrangements because flexibility, security, and the risks can be shared by three parties, one of which (the

TWA) has a greater capacity than individual employers and employees to pool risks, flexibility needs, and security claims. In particular, TWAs might be able to mitigate the lack of job security experienced by the temporary agency workers by providing employment security through new assignments with other hiring firms, whereas at the same time providing flexibility and risk reduction for these hiring firms.

FLEXICURITY PATHWAYS AND THE ROLE OF TWAs

To investigate different ways to enhance flexicurity, the following sections present the four different pathways to flexicurity identified by the EU and analyze to what extent the three parties involved in the triangular employment relationship can contribute to the challenges posed by these pathways.

The ideal-typical flexicurity pathways, which could inspire member states in setting their own flexicurity agenda, are briefly described subsequently. The pathways recognize the differences between individual member states, in particular the different challenges they face on their respective labour markets. Within these pathways, the different policy components have different weights, but member states should not neglect either one of them.

The flexicurity pathways allow different responses to national challenges, while at the same time attaining the goal of increased flexibility and employment security. To give an example, Great Britain does not face any real challenges with regard to labour market flexibility, but it does face an enormous challenge in terms of policy component 3 ("systematic and responsive LLL") because the high degree of flexibility leads to underinvestment in firm-sponsored training caused by the short-lived nature of flexible labour contracts (Picchio and Van Ours 2010). Another example is Spain, where a major issue is the "divide" between workers on temporary contracts versus those on permanent contracts. There is ample flexibility in the form of a high share of temporary contracts, but very little flexibility in permanent contracts. Furthermore, transition security (in particular into permanent employment) is lacking. Therefore, the emphasis for Spain is on policy components 1 ("flexible and reliable contractual arrangements") and 2 ("efficient ALMPs to strengthen transition security").

After a concise characterization of the situation in a country and the determination of the pathway it needs to follow, the challenges posed along these pathways can be addressed in terms of two more concrete questions: (1) What are the challenges in relation to the management and organization of TWAs in this flexicurity pathway? (2) What are the possible roles for TWAs in meeting these challenges on this pathway?

The first question is essentially a policy challenge and deals with integrating TWAs into broader labour market institutions, whereas the second question is more focused on the role that TWAs themselves can play in meeting the challenges of the respective pathways.

FLEXICURITY PATHWAY 1: DEALING WITH FLEXIBILITY ON THE MARGINS

The first pathway addresses the issue of flexibility on the margins of the labour market. It suggests that the asymmetries between standard and non-standard work be reduced by promoting upward transitions in the labour market and by integrating non-standard contracts fully into labour law, collective agreements, social security, and LLL systems. Non-standard contracts would then be treated as equal to standard contracts following the principle of *pro rata temporis* ("in proportion to the duration of the contract"). Alternatively, standard contracts can be made more attractive to companies by introducing an open-ended contract in which specific elements of protection are built up progressively over time until "full" protection is achieved. Such a contract guarantees basic but adequate protection from the start and automatically builds up "full" protection as the working relationship continues. Social partners and governments should negotiate the terms of these arrangements. Examples of countries for which this pathway is relevant include Spain and Portugal.

CHALLENGES FOR PATHWAY 1

Pathway 1 is relevant for countries that have "[b]ifurcated, two-tier labour markets with a large share of so-called 'outsiders' lacking security and the opportunity to make the transition to more permanent employment, paralleled by strict regulation of open-ended contracts" (European Expert Group on Flexicurity 2007, p. 19). As mentioned, such countries include Spain and Portugal, but it seems that this pathway is also becoming more relevant to the Netherlands (Muffels, Wilthagen, and Dekker 2011).

Challenge: to reduce asymmetries between non-standard and standard employment by integrating non-standard contracts fully into labour law, collective agreements, social security, and LLL and to consider making standard employment contracts more attractive to firms.

Challenges for the integration of temporary agency work include the following:

- The integration of temporary agency work into labour law
- The integration of temporary agency work into collective agreements
- The build-up of social security rights for TWA workers
- To encourage firms to allow TWA workers into the "core"

With respect to these challenges, the first three can clearly not be dealt with at the level of the triangular relationship between worker, agency, and firm. However, TWAs can lobby for regulation and/or integration into collective agreements. At the same time, both the temp agency sector and employer's representatives would support this lobby at the sectoral and national levels if they were convinced that it would not lead to lower levels of flexibility. The fourth challenge is one for firms, which can be encouraged to allow TWA workers into the "core" (e.g., by means of subsidies). In addition, agencies that are successful in converting many temporary agency workers to permanent employees could be rewarded, for example, by a reduction in taxes or social security premiums by the national government.

When trying to meet these challenges, TWAs can focus on offering workers more employment security by combining offers of temporary employment and training, thereby improving the employability of TWA workers. Furthermore, TWAs can take up the broader role of employer[8] and provide workers with more job security. In a tight labour market, this would be an interesting strategy in the "war for talent," especially when lobbying efforts at the sectoral and national levels mentioned previously are integrated into this strategy.

FLEXICURITY PATHWAY 2: SECURING TRANSITIONS FROM JOB TO JOB

The second pathway emphasizes safe and successful job-to-job transitions. Built-in contractual guarantees and human resources management policies should ensure timely progress into new jobs either within a company or outside if the necessity arises. Furthermore, it may be feasible to introduce individualized transition guarantees to redundant workers, to be borne jointly by employers, social partners, and public employment services, in order to prevent unemployment. A strong system of LLL and vocational training may form the basis for productive labour market transitions both within and outside companies. Such a system should allow for quick access to effective training funds and facilities at the branch level. Within this pathway, strengthening *internal flexicurity* (the balance between job security and functional flexibility) is also relevant, especially to enhance the employability and skills of workers. Typical countries in which flexicurity pathway 2 is relevant are Austria and the Netherlands.

CHALLENGES FOR PATHWAY 2

Pathway 2 is relevant for countries that have "labour markets characterized by relatively limited dynamism with a large share of workers with high job security, but lacking sufficient opportunities to find new employment in the event of redundancy" (European Expert Group on Flexicurity 2007, p. 20). A typical example of such a country would be the Netherlands, where employees who lose their job, older workers in particular, have major difficulties finding new gainful employment.

Challenge: to enhance companies' and workers' adaptability by developing and strengthening transition security.

Challenges for TWAs include the following:

- Widen the scope for use of TWA work by firms
- Set up agreements with firms to take on a certain number/percentage of former TWA workers

As in pathway 1, these challenges—especially the first—imply that lobbying on behalf of TWAs is necessary. Such lobbying would involve striving for a "normalization" of temporary agency work and to give TWAs a more formal role in employment security systems aimed at stimulating job-to-job transitions at the sectoral, regional, or national levels. The integration of Dutch TWAs into so-called Mobility Centres set up by the public employment agency UWV in response to the recent financial crisis is an example of such a formal role.

Irrespective of policy and their integration into the broader institutional context, the role of TWAs in meeting these challenges would be to ensure specific arrangements for specific target groups (e.g., unemployed older workers), offering them employment security to compensate for their loss of job security. These arrangements would have to involve some potential for re-entering the regular labour force, in accordance with the theoretical notions of the rent model (Polavieja 2003). As in pathway 1, these arrangements can benefit from lobbying efforts mentioned previously. This can be operationalized in the subcontracting of "employment security" arrangements by the public employment office to TWAs, leading to improvements in both the quality and quantity of the labour supply at the aggregate level. Furthermore, TWAs could set up more strategic cooperative agreements with firms (see Goudswaard and De Leede, Chapter 4 in this volume) to take on more former TWA workers, possibly coupled with lobbying for support in the form of financial stimuli from the government.

FLEXICURITY PATHWAY 3: ACCESS TO LEARNING AND GOOD TRANSITIONS FOR ALL

This pathway recommends strengthening investment in skills and research and development on the basis of existing levels of labour market dynamism. The employment and security opportunities and options of specific groups in the labour market can thereby be enhanced and productivity growth boosted. A broad-ranging approach is needed to keep the labour market accessible to the low skilled and other groups, such as minorities, older workers, women, and early school leavers, at risk of becoming long-term unemployed or excluded in other ways. Flexicurity will benefit from the possibility of concluding binding agreements at branch or regional levels that combine provisions on how to address the flexibility needs of both employers and workers by investment in training. Where the institutional structures for such agreements are not yet in place, support from social partners and government is needed. As mentioned above, a prime example of a country that might use this pathway is Great Britain. As a typical Anglo-Saxon country, there is a need to enhance functional flexibility through training efforts that complement external numerical flexibility.

CHALLENGES FOR PATHWAY 3

Pathway 3 is relevant for countries that have "labour markets that are sufficiently dynamic but [are] faced with opportunity and skills gaps, which may curb productivity growth." (European Expert Group on Flexicurity 2007, p. 20). This pathway is relevant for Anglo-Saxon–style labour markets, such as that in Great Britain, which have dynamism in abundance, but the short-term focus associated with that dynamism leads to underinvestment in training.

Challenge: to address opportunity and skills gaps within the workforce by broadening and deepening investments in skills.

The challenge for temporary agency work is as follows:

• Facilitate training efforts, especially for TWA workers

In the triangular employment relationship, each of the three parties involved has an incentive to wait until either one of the other two parties provides funding for training. Because three parties are involved, this is a more serious problem than in a traditional employment relationship with only two parties. There is scope for policy to "break this deadlock" by setting up funds for training or opening up existing funds by giving workers more rights to draw from these funds. The particular challenge for TWAs would then consist of establishing this right for their workers or setting up specific training funds for them.

In addition to the policy challenge mentioned previously, TWAs can strive to set up joint or other training funds especially geared towards the specific needs of TWA workers. At the same time, this would include negotiating possibilities for training periods with the firms that employ TWA workers. This would be relatively easy when the training is specific to the current assignment but more cumbersome when the training is aimed at those leaving the current sector/firm.

FLEXICURITY PATHWAY 4: COMPREHENSIVE SOCIAL SECURITY SUPPORTING TRANSITIONS TO REGULAR WORK

This pathway starts from the urgent need to increase the employment and job opportunities of people who are currently on social security benefits or working in the informal sector. ALMPs and social security should offer sufficient opportunities and incentives—in terms of increased conditionality of benefits—to return to work and to facilitate this transition, meaning that long-term welfare dependence can be prevented. Informal work can be made regular by offering flexi-secure contracts, lower payroll taxes, and a skills perspective for these sectors. By formalizing informal economic activities, increased financial resources can be raised to build up a more comprehensive social security system. Stronger institutional capacity needs to be developed by stimulating various social partners to negotiate the key elements of working conditions and by better cooperation between the labour market and benefit institutions. Social dialogue can be further developed at the sector and regional levels, and both bipartite and tripartite dialogue can be strengthened.

CHALLENGES FOR PATHWAY 4

Pathway 4 is relevant for countries that have "labour markets offering insufficient opportunities to groups that are outside the formal labour market due to benefit dependence or involvement in informal work" (European Expert Group on Flexicurity 2007, p. 21). These countries are typically found among the new entrants to the EU from Eastern Europe. However, this pathway is also relevant to southern European countries (e.g., Greece, Italy, and Spain) with substantial "shadow economies" of between 20 and 30 per cent of the labour market (Schneider 2010).

Challenge: to enhance employment opportunities for benefit recipients, prevent long-term welfare dependence, formalize informal work, and build up more institutional capacity for change.

Challenges with respect to temporary agency work and for TWAs include the following:

- Use TWAs as labour market intermediaries, including cooperation with public employment service systems
- Subsidize TWAs to focus on specific target groups in the labour market[9]

As in pathway 1, this challenge is primarily aimed at integrating TWAs into the broader context of labour market institutions. TWA jobs can serve as entry-level jobs for people currently on benefits and/or active in the informal sector. To prevent issues of labour market segmentation as described in pathway 1, it is important to keep in mind that these jobs must provide real opportunities for more stable inclusion in the formal labour market. For specific target groups such as the long-term unemployed and disabled people, this can involve subsidies and/or the use of benefits when providing employment.

TWAs can play an active role themselves in offering employers specific recruitment and selection services for entry-level jobs and at the same time provide formal employment opportunities to workers currently not included in the formal labour market. In so doing, TWAs can benefit from the "formalization" of labour markets currently characterized by high levels of informal employment.

CONCLUSIONS AND DISCUSSION

The flexicurity policy framework is especially relevant to all types of atypical and non-standard forms of work, including temporary agency work. These non-standard employment relations are the primary basis for the flexibility aspect of the flexicurity nexus because they are examples of numerical external flexibility (Wilthagen and Tros 2004). At the same time, it is clear that these flexible work arrangements are typically associated with lower levels of job security. In the EU, the flexicurity framework is also used as a basis for re-regulating security. Based on an open method of coordination, it can be said to be supported by law, that is, by EU directives on fixed-term and part-time work (which were based on European social partner agreements) and, very recently and after a very lengthy process, agency work. The main purpose of the Agency Worker Directive is to guarantee the appropriate protection of temporary agency workers through the application of the principle of equal treatment and to address unnecessary restrictions and prohibitions on the use of agency work.

The development of flexicurity can follow different routes. Not only can the mapping out of flexicurity pathways contribute to the better use and adequate protection of agency work, but agency work can, in its turn, also facilitate the development of distinct flexicurity pathways. The latter is the key topic of this chapter. We explored, predominantly in an analytical and theoretical way, how and under which conditions temporary agency work can play a role in the mapping out of flexicurity pathways as distinguished by the European Commission.

We have analyzed the challenges posed by the pathways to flexicurity for the actors involved in triangular employment relationships, in particular temporary agency work. The general conclusion is that the role of these actors in achieving flexicurity at the level of the firm is highly dependent on progress at the level of social partnerships, collective agreements, and national policies.

Having said that, TWAs should play an active role in influencing sectoral agreements and national policies along the lines described in the previous paragraphs. Furthermore, in most countries, there is still room for TWAs to play a greater role in providing employment security and training to their workers. In addition, the hiring firm and workers themselves must play their part in the triangular employment relationship to achieve higher levels of employment security for the temporary agency workers involved. In relation to training opportunities, the triangular employment relationship bears a higher risk of underinvestment because it is inherently more difficult to align the interests of the three (rather than two) parties involved and the scope for evading financial and other responsibilities with respect to training efforts is greater. It seems natural to look to national governments when these "coordination" problems arise, but TWAs themselves can also take strategic action to break the deadlock. By doing so, they can both strengthen their position alongside the formal institutions of the labour market and their competitive edge in the war for talent.

Furthermore, it is important that hiring firms and TWAs are more aware of the fact that the higher the "conversion" probability, the higher the "incentive effect" for temporary agency workers. By providing a real possibility of employment security and a labour relationship with a longer time horizon, the quality and productivity of the triangular employment relationship can be enhanced.

We thus conclude that depending on the nature of the labour market in which the TWA operates and thus depending on the relevant flexicurity pathways, temporary work agencies have ample opportunity to contribute to the better functioning of labour markets, thereby simultaneously enhancing both employment security and labour market flexibility. This chapter has made suggestions for these contributions along the lines of the four EU flexicurity pathways.

NOTES

1. "Job security" can be defined as the security of continuous employment with the same employer, whereas "employment security" is the security of employment that can be derived from the labour market at large.
2. "Towards common principles of flexicurity—Council conclusions" document 16201/07, SOC 523, Economic and Finance Ministers Council, 503, 6 December 2007.
3. 2007/2209 (Own-Initiative Report Procedure).
4. "Key Challenges Facing European Labour Markets. A Joint Analysis of the European Social Partners," available at www.etuc.org/a/4119.
5. Commission of the European Communities (2007) (359).
6. Commission of the European Communities (2006) 708 final.
7. Commission of the European Communities (2010) 193/3.
8. For example, in the Netherlands, the TWA is the formal employer, but this only fully materializes after a substantial period of time (3.5 years).
9. For an example of a positive contribution of the TWA industry in Italy, see Regalia (Chapter 10), in this volume.

REFERENCES

Amuedo-Dorantes, Catalina, Miguel A. Malo, and Fernando Munoz-Bullon. 2008. "The Role of Temporary Help Agency Employment on Temp-to-Perm Transitions." *Journal of Labor Research* 29 (2): 138–161.
Autor, David H. 2001. "Why Do Temporary Help Firms Provide Free General Skills Training?" *Quarterly Journal of Economics* 116 (4): 1409–1448.

Autor, David H., Frank Levy, and Richard J. Murnane. 1999. *Skills Training in the Temporary Help Sector: Employer Motivations and Worker Impacts.* Report to the U.S. Department of Labor Employment and Training Administration. Cambridge: Massachusetts Institute of Technology.

Barker, Kathleen, and Kathleen Christensen. 1998. *Contingent Work: American Employment Relations in Transition.* Ithaca, NY: Cornell University Press.

Boeri, Tito, Pierre Cahuc, Sanja Crnkovic, Csilla Kollonay-Lehoczky, and Ton Wilthagen. 2007. *Flexicurity Pathways: Turning Hurdles into Stepping Stones.* Report by the European Expert Group on Flexicurity.

Booth, Alison, L., Marco Francesconi, and Jeff Frank. 2002. "Temporary Jobs: Stepping Stones or Dead Ends?" *Economic Journal* 112 (480): F189–F213.

De Graaf-Zijl, Marloes. 2006. "Economic and Social Consequences of Temporary Employment." PhD diss., University of Amsterdam.

Dekker, Ronald. 2007. "Non-Standard Employment and Mobility in the Dutch, German and British Labour Market." PhD diss., Tilburg University.

Dekker, Ronald. 2012. Een zekere mate van zekerheid. *Economisch-Statistische Berichten*, 97(4647S), 6–9. (in Dutch)

Delsen, Lei. 1991. "Atypical Employment Relations and Government Policy in Europe." *Labour* 5 (3): 123.

European Commission. 2007. *Council Conclusions towards Common Principles of Flexicurity.* COM: 359 final. Brussels: European Commission.

European Expert Group on Flexicurity. 2007. *"Flexicurity Pathways. Turning Hurdles into Stepping Stones"*, report by the European Expert Group on Flexicurity. Brussels, European Commission.

Forrier, Anneleen, and Luc Sels. 2003. "Temporary Employment and Employability: Training Opportunities and Efforts of Temporary and Permanent Employees in Belgium." *Work Employment and Society* 17 (4): 641–666.

Freeman, Richard B. 1998. "War of the Models: Which Labour Market Institutions for the 21st Century?" *Labour Economics* 5 (1): 1–24.

Giesecke, Johannes. 2009. "Socio-Economic Risks of Atypical Employment Relationships: Evidence from the German Labour Market." *European Sociological Review* 25 (6): 629–646.

Kalleberg, Arne L. 2000. "Nonstandard Employment Relations: Part-Time, Temporary and Contract Work." *Annual Review of Sociology* 26: 341–365.

Keller, Berndt, and Hartmut Seifert. 2000. "Flexicurity—Das Konzept für mehr soziale Sicherheit flexibler Beschäftigung." *WSI Mitteilungen* 53 (5): 291–300.

Koene, Bas, Jaap Paauwe, and John Groenewegen. 2004. "Understanding the Development of Temporary Agency Work in Europe." *Human Resource Management Journal* 14 (3): 53–73.

Marsden, David W. 1999. *A Theory of Employment Systems: Micro-Foundations of Social Diversity.* Oxford: Oxford University Press.

Muffels, Ruud, Ton Wilthagen, and Ronald Dekker. 2011. "Flexibiliteit en werkzekerheid, diversiteit en dynamiek op de Nederlandse arbeidsmarkt." In *Wat is de zekerheid in Flex en Zeker?* edited by Els Sol and Charles Nysten, 25–49. Amsterdam: University of Amsterdam.

Picchio, Matteo. 2008. "Temporary Contracts and Transitions to Stable Jobs in Italy." *Labour* 22 (1): 147–174.

Picchio, Matteo, and Jan C. van Ours. 2010. "Market Imperfections and Firm-Sponsored Training." *Labour Economics* 18 (5): 712–722.

Polavieja, Javier G. 2003. "Temporary Contracts and Labour Market Segmentation in Spain: An Employment-Rent Approach." *European Sociological Review* 19 (5): 501–517.

Scherer, Stefani. 2004. "Stepping-Stones or Traps?" *Work, Employment & Society* 18 (2): 369–394.

Schmidt, Stephanie, and Kirsten Thommes. 2007. "Incentives to Invest in the Human Capital of Temporary Agency Workers." *Zeitschrift für Personalforschung* 21 (3): 232–251.

Schneider, Friedrich. 2010. "The Influence of Public Institutions on the Shadow Economy: An Empirical Investigation for OECD Countries." *Review of Law and Economics* 6 (3): 441–468.

Sorensen, Aage B. 1994. "Forms, Wages and Incentives." In *Handbook of Economic Sociology*, edited by Neil Smelser and Richard Swedberg, 504–528. Princeton, NJ: Princeton University Press.

Sorensen, Aage B. 2000. "Toward a Sounder Basis for Class Analysis." *American Journal of Sociology* 105 (6): 1523–1558.

Storrie, D. 2002. *Temporary Agency Work in the European Union*. Dublin: Eurofound.

Wilthagen, Ton. 1998. "Flexicurity: A New Paradigm for Labour Market Policy Reform?" Discussion Paper No. FS I 98–202, Wissenschaftszentrum Berlin für Sozialforschung, Berlin.

Wilthagen, Ton, and Frank Tros. 2004. "The Concept of 'Flexicurity': A New Approach to Regulating Employment and Labour Markets." *Transfer: European Review of Labour and Research* 10 (2): 166–186.

Wynn, Michael. 2000. "European Social Dialogue: Harmonisation or New Diversity?" In *Legal Regulation of the Employment Relation*, edited by Hugh Collins, Paul L. Davies, and Roger Rideout, 491–511. London: Kluwer Law International.

Part II

Organization of the Triangular Employment Relationship

4 Organizing Sustainable Partnerships between Employment Agencies and Hiring Companies
The Dutch Case

Anneke Goudswaard and Jan de Leede

The cooperation between employment agencies and organizations that hire temporary personnel is still limited. The relationship tends to focus on short-term transactional conditions, where the highest degree of work flexibility has to be delivered at the lowest possible price. Based on an analysis of nine best practice case studies in the Netherlands, we conclude that there is much to be gained from more sustainable strategic relationships between the hiring organization and the supplier of personnel. However, to be successful, this kind of cooperation requires the genuine commitment of all parties. In our cases, aspects such as quality of the service, degree of flexibility, and required competencies played an important role above and beyond the price component. We studied the cooperation between agency and hiring company and evaluated the benefits for the hiring company, employment agency, and workers.

Our findings show that the flexibility requirements differed. The nature and reason for the cooperation can be distilled into three types of cooperative focus: (1) efficiency and cost control, (2) short- and long-term flexibility, and (3) labour market and education. The cooperation can benefit both the hiring organization and the employees. The hiring organization achieves flexibility, cost control, process improvement, and better availability of employees. Employees benefit from education and training as well as from the opportunities for personal and intrinsic job development, placing them in a stronger position in the labour market. This, in turn, has an additional positive impact for the hiring organization that acquires a pool of more motivated and satisfied employees.

The factors that contribute to the success of this kind of cooperation include openness about company data to the partner organization, a willingness to invest together, a shared view of human resources management (HRM) that attends to both permanent and flexible personnel, and professional operation supported by a basic level of experience with organizational flexibility and labour market institutions. In our cases, these conditions provide the basis for a sustainable cooperation that has a positive outcome for both organization and (flexible) employee alike. However, the relationship remains vulnerable to changes in the level of support or sense of urgency within the organization, indicating that the perceived value of structural cooperation in this area of HRM is still not self-evident. Organizations are constantly subject to changes occurring in their environment. To stay competitive, organizations search for resources to anticipate these dynamics, such as the flexibility of personnel, processes, and organization (Volberda 1998; De Leede and Goudswaard 2008). The search for organizational flexibility is a global trend. We have observed an increased need for flexibility in almost all developed countries and in many markets, due to economic uncertainty and international competition. European companies have paid increasing attention to flexibility, although the flexibility profiles differ between countries. According to the *European Company Survey 2009* (Kerkhofs, Roman, and Ester 2010), Dutch companies show high flexibility profiles. Within this profile, Dutch establishments belong to the high operational flexibility category, which means that they make extensive use of flexibility arrangements (including work at irregular hours, part-time work, overtime, fixed-term contracts, and autonomous teamwork and temporary agency work) and that they use these flexibility instruments mainly to improve operating performance (Kerkhofs, Roman, and Ester 2010). Given this flexibility profile, it is valuable to investigate how agency work fits in the profile and how employment agencies cooperate with their client companies.

The Dutch context is an interesting one. The Netherlands, with a penetration level of 2.5 per cent, is Europe's second-largest temporary employee market after the United Kingdom in terms of size (Eurociett 2007). Furthermore, it is a relatively mature and liberalized market with a long history of actively regulating and developing employment flexibility (e.g., Goudswaard 2003; Van Driel and Koene 2011). The *European Working Conditions Survey* data reveal that temporary employees tend to be part of lower-income groups and receive only limited training (Pedersen, Hansen, and Mahler 2007; Storrie 2002; Eurociett/UNI-Europa 2008). In the Netherlands, we have observed a gradual increase in the average educational level of temporary employees (Donker van Heel, Van Nuland, and Van der Ende 2007). Empirical data show that Dutch companies rely heavily on personnel flexibility in terms of both internal (flexible attitude, flexible working schedules, and multifunctional flexibility) and external flexibility (all kinds of temporary and agency contracts), and the use of external flexibility is gradually increasing (Goudswaard et al. 2007).

Since the regulation of temporary work through labour law in 1999—Law on Flexibility and Security—the debate about temporary work has been less about the desirability of agency work and more about enhancing the possibilities for training and development for flexible workers and about the role of temporary work agencies in dealing with specific labour market challenges relating to unemployment, qualitative and quantitative shortages, and protection and support of vulnerable groups in the labour market.

At the same time, we see an increased emphasis on short-term opportunistic hiring, where the highest degree of work flexibility has to be delivered at the lowest possible price. Developmental cooperation between employment agencies and hiring companies cannot be taken for granted in a market where employment agencies have to discuss fees with their customers time and again, and where a new tender can undo a relationship that has been hitherto established.

The question is whether longer-term cooperation between hiring companies and employment agencies can deal with this dilemma of high service and low price and, if so, when it is sustainable. It is in this context that we present our cases of what might be considered relatively sophisticated, strategically oriented relationships between hiring companies and suppliers of flexible labour. Our hypothesis is that within these partnerships, some innovative power might be possible based on a mature, sustainable relationship. One of the preconditions for this is the need to view flexible labour in a much broader perspective than the traditional approach of only ad hoc and opportunistic use of agency workers, based on short-term cost considerations. In our case studies, we ask the following question: Can relationships with a more long-term orientation improve the possibilities of employment agencies to better respond to the needs of hiring companies?

To study this question, we asked employment agencies to provide us with cases of sustainable and successful cooperation. We investigated what made these cases of cooperation successful. Here, we report on this explorative study. First, we present the theory on partnerships between employment agencies and their client companies. Then we report on the research method used. We then present the results and discuss the nature of the forms of cooperation. This provides insight into the reason for the cooperation and the sustainable character of the cooperation. Next, we discuss the possible pay-offs for the hiring company and the employees. Finally, we look at the factors that facilitate successful cooperation and make it sustainable.

SOME THEORETICAL NOTIONS ON THE PARTNERSHIPS BETWEEN AGENCIES AND COMPANIES

In the literature, five reasons are mentioned as hiring motives for flexible labour (Volberda 1998; Donker van Heel, Van Nuland, and Van der Ende 2007; Goudswaard et al. 2007): (1) quantitative and qualitative demand fluctuations in the product market; (2) absenteeism by the core workers (sickness and other leaves); (3) the wish to cover risks of economic downturns and to act as a buffer for the security of the core workers; (4) as an important recruitment channel (the employer and employee can become accustomed to each other, and the temporary work agency takes over most of the recruitment effort); and, finally, (5) to shelter core workers from severe labour conditions and instead spread these risks among many flexible workers who work only temporarily within these varying workplaces.

Despite the majority of temporary employees taken on during production peaks or for sick personnel, a greater diversity of services is occurring in the offerings of employment agencies to companies that not only want quickly deployable and qualitatively flexible personnel, but also attach value to a professional employment agency that may co-develop and co-create with its client (Goudswaard et al. 2007; Vidal and Tigges 2009). The emphasis is shifting from a purely transactional and quantitative need (supplying the right number of people for the lowest price) to a more transformational need (by supplying properly educated personnel with the required level of competence and by being proactive in terms of strategic personnel planning; Lepak, Bartol, and Erhardt 2005). This shift implies that the relationship between the hiring company and the employment agency is no longer focused on the exchange of flexible contracts but is also focused on a more significant cooperation, or even a partnership (Morris, Snell, and Lepak 2005; Lepak, Bartol, and Erhardt 2005). In a sustainable partnership, the goal is to improve the implementation of the process and to create new possibilities and services (Wucherer 2006). The common goal is to respond better to the flexibility need of the hiring organization that wants a guarantee of flexible work for the future.

The flexibility need of the hiring company differs by organization and often depends on the dynamics of the organizational environment (Kalleberg and Marsden 2005; Volberda 1996) or disruptions and restrictions in the internal process (De Leede et al. 2002). Aspects such as price, quality, flexibility, and innovation play a role in the need of an organization to respond to the sales market (Bolwijn and Kumpe 1990). In addition, the labour market is a relevant environmental factor, so organizations also have to be able to respond to shortages or necessary innovation in the labour market (De Leede and Goudswaard 2008). If we translate this into the potential added value of temporary employees, we arrive at four kinds of flexibility needs among customer organizations.

The first type of flexibility need is based on price, allowing the fastest and cheapest response to production peaks and staff shortages. The flexibility strategy is focused on low costs and has a short-term focus. In practice, this tends to be a master contract at the lowest price with one or more employment agencies. This is not a partnership or sustainable relationship.

When price is supplemented by quality, more cooperation is needed: on the one hand, the need to optimize processes, and on the other, a reduction of costs and disruptions. This is the second type of flexibility need. The cooperation between hiring company and employment agency is focused on supplying the right employees for the best price/quality ratio. The nature of the cooperation has a medium-term perspective, in contrast to the first type, but is still transactionally structured.

The third type of flexibility need derives from a mismatch between the dynamic of the market demand and an organization that is insufficiently flexible to move with the fluctuations. The hiring organization and the employment agency work more closely together to more quickly and competently anticipate changes. Because the employment agency offers new services, such as training and planning, the hiring organization can be furnished in the long-term with the requisite personnel at the right moment.

The last type of flexibility need comes from a tight labour market and the demand for certain competences. Innovation within the labour market means new relationships between employment agencies and hiring companies. The employment agency caters to the education and training of the employees of the hiring company, making the right people with the right competences available for the longer term. The character of the cooperation is no longer transactional, but focused on supplying competences and specialism.

In our study, we investigate what flexibility needs of client organizations can be met in agency–client relationships that are rated as strategic and sustainably successful.

METHOD

To study the possibilities of successful cooperation between employment agencies[1] and hiring companies (see also Goudswaard et al. 2007), we selected nine cases for our study. For each case, we investigated three main questions: (1) What are the intended objectives of sustainable cooperation between agencies and companies? (2) What are the results of this type of cooperation? (3) What are the key success factors for sustainable cooperation? For all cases, we interviewed contacts from the hiring company (director, human resources [HR] manager, operational manager, and/or purchaser) and contacts from the employment agency (account manager and/or in-house assistant). We talked with those responsible for drawing up the cooperation agreement as well as those responsible for implementing it in daily business. Where possible, we also obtained information on company performance and personnel data (absence and turnover) and posed questions about the reason for the cooperation, the nature of the cooperation, and the pay-off for the hiring company and employee, comparing the situation before and after cooperation.

Our nine cases were supplied by a total of eight temporary employment and secondment agencies. At a secondment agency, the employees have an open-ended contract with the agency and will be posted to the hiring company to perform a specific task. The cases cover various sectors, namely, the food industry, the energy sector, logistics, aviation, the government, engineering, and financial and business services (see Table 4.1). The selection was based on the assessments of the employment agencies that these cases were best practices of sustainable cooperation. Furthermore, the cases met our criteria, such as long-term relationship (more than three years), coverage of various sectors, and coverage of various aspects of the cooperation.

Table 4.1 Overview of the Nine Cases (of the Interviewed Hiring Companies)

Case	Reason for cooperation	Sector	Form of cooperation
1	Inefficient use of (flexible) personnel, need to save costs	Food industry: production personnel	Employment agency in-house, responsible for personnel planning
2	Slow and inefficient recruitment and selection process	Food industry: all personnel	Outsourcing recruitment and selection to employment agency
3	Mismatch in use of flexible personnel, high turnover	Energy: call centre staff	Employment agency in-house, joint improvement of hiring process and operational planning
4	Slow and inefficient outplacement program, surplus personnel	Financial services: all personnel	Cooperation with a very large number of partners, supported by various information and communications technology systems (internal and external labour market)
5	Expand flexibility within the whole organization, more systematic use of personnel deployment	Business services: all personnel	Employment agency in-house, joint improvement of HR processes and personnel flexibility
6	Company focus on core business (logistics) and transfer of personnel matters to partner	Logistics: production personnel	Joint venture between logistics company and employment agency, with the latter responsible for HR task and operational planning
7	Fluctuating work supply, unpredictable future	Aviation: engineering personnel	Secondment organization supplies personnel to company (flexunit)
8	Scarcity in labour market, local authority image	Government: engineering personnel	Traineeships set up by local authority (work), engineering firm (mentor) and secondment organization (employer role)
9	Scarcity of competent personnel, competency development	Engineering: engineering personnel	Secondment organization organizes specific education to ROC (Regional Education Centre) together with hiring companies

RESULTS

Here we present the results of the study. First, intended objectives for the cooperation are discussed, as agreed on by the agency and the hiring organization. Then, the reported gains (the effects) are presented. Finally, we describe key conditions for successful cooperation.

The Reason for and Nature of the Cooperation

The interviews suggest the presence of a sustainable relationship in which both parties (employment agency and hiring company) have a stake in a successful and long-term relationship. Common to the cases is a more structural approach. The cooperation with employment agencies is closer and more sustainable in those cases where the need for flexibility shifts from optimizing processes to more flexibility and availability of competent personnel. In most cases, we see a need among the hiring companies to structurally improve the personnel deployment and to build a more coherent HR policy (recruitment, selection, retention, mobility, and outflow) for both permanent and flexible employees. All organizations are conscious of the fact that greater flexibility for the hiring company is vital and that flexible employees play a key role in this.

Based on the reason for the cooperation, we distinguish three types of cooperation structure. In the first type (cases 1 to 4), the focus is on efficiency improvement, whereas in the second type (cases 5 to 7), the cooperation focus is on enhancing the flexibility of the hiring company. In the last type (cases 8 and 9), the focus is on labour market and training. We observe a strong connection between type of reason and type of flexibility need referred to earlier, whereby efficiency improvement can be seen as a combination of price and quality adjustment. Table 4.2 presents an overview of the reasons for cooperation mentioned and the nature of the cooperation for each type.

In the first type of cooperation, the hiring companies enter into close cooperation with one or more employment agencies to achieve efficiency improvements, going beyond the supply of personnel for the lowest price. This may involve outsourcing the entire recruitment and selection process, giving the employment agency responsibility for personnel planning (see the example below), or establishing new HR services (such as a marketplace, competency management, and retention planning). The employment agency will tend to be in-house at the hiring company. Results have to be achieved quickly, so the initial period will see a focus on establishing a more sustainable structure. This type of cooperation focused on efficiency improvement. At the same time, the cooperation also focused on enhancing quality through offering extra services.

Example: Inefficient use of personnel and quality issues at the production site of a company in the food industry threatens the continuity of the company. The employment agency and hiring company will come together to produce a smarter approach to the use of permanent and temporary personnel. The result is a modification of the job profiles and planning method. The employment agency is in-house and responsible for all personnel planning,

Table 4.2 Different Kinds of Reasons and the Nature of the Cooperation

	Reason/need	Nature of the cooperation
Type I Efficiency	Inefficient planning of personnel	In-house construction
	Inefficient recruitment and selection process	Structural use of temporary employees
	Mismatch between demand and supply of temporary employees	Outsourcing personnel process (recruitment, selection, and planning)
	High turnover	On-site recruiter
	Surplus personnel	New HR services (modify job profiles, competency management, training, internal and external labour marketplace, and retention plan)
	Business continuity threatened	
	Need to save costs	
Type II Flexibility	Focus on core activities (potential market growth)	Strategic cooperation (e.g., joint venture)
	Cost saving	Structural use of temporary and seconded employees
	Unpredictable work supply pattern	Outsourcing capacity management and labour market and work supply analysis
	Inadequate flexibility of permanent personnel	Outsourcing development and management of personnel pool
		Educational program for flexworkers
		Broad deployability, location flexibility
Type III Development	Tight labour market	Set up traineeships and education courses
	Undesired outflow of experienced personnel	Outsourcing education personnel
	Poor image in the labour market	Use of seconded employees
	Lack of suitable education courses	Shared role of employership, supervision, and coaching among several organizations

including training and competency management. The hiring company supplies the production planning, and the employment agency organizes the permanent and temporary personnel around it. Agreements are made on the full scope of personnel deployment (including individual development). This adjustment allows for better use of the potential qualities of the personnel.

The second type of cooperation is motivated by the need to enhance flexibility. It is not only efficient use of personnel that is important here, but beyond that, the real need to respond better to changes in the market. Organizations experiencing growth are confronted by an unpredictable work supply pattern, with inadequate flexibility among permanent personnel or fear for the future of the company if they fail to succeed in operating more flexibly. The employment agencies disencumber the hiring company by taking over operational and tactical personnel processes (both management and capacity planning) or by offering educated, flexible employees.

Example: A company that supplies both engineering and personnel for repro services is looking for ways of reducing costs and enhancing flexibility between its sites. The contract with the regular employment agency has been extended to incorporate a more strategic relationship, implying working together in a structural and project-based way to improve processes and enhance flexibility. Thus, the employment agency conducts regular work supply analyses and labour market analyses. The hiring company, in turn, must ensure better annual planning for the sites. An improved planning and information system provides for both a more efficient hiring and invoicing process and a clear overview of the flexibility need. For the flexible employees, a retention and education plan is established (development and mobility).

In the third type of cooperation, labour market and education are key in a situation where the labour market is tight, competent personnel are few, and recruitment power is lacking, resulting in undesirable outflow of experienced personnel. Cooperation might then focus on setting up traineeships (see example below) or customized education courses at the regional education institutes. The role of the employment agency is threefold: employer, supervisor, and coach between the respective organizations.

Example: A local authority is experiencing an undesirable outflow of experienced personnel attracted to the profit sector. There was clear need for the influx of new, young civil engineers, so the local authority established cooperation with two parties: a secondment agency to select trainees and supervise their personal development and an engineering firm that supplied a mentor, coached by the secondment agency. The trainees work within the local authority.

Reported Gains

Based on our case analyses, we tentatively conclude that sustainable forms of cooperation can indeed be beneficial for the hiring company. Because the employment agency is highly familiar with the processes of the hiring company and has information at its disposal early on, it can respond better and faster to the needs of the hiring company, whose benefits include cost saving, better vacancy filling, and more utilization of employment potential. Differences are apparent in the types of cooperation arrangements in terms of both the nature of the gains and their timing (see Table 4.3).

In the first type of cooperation, the focus is on short-term results, although longer-term gains also appear to be attainable. In the short term, the companies report faster lead times in the hiring process, a higher ratio of placements, and a reduction to the number of hired hours. In the medium term, management will see more commitment and motivation from flexible personnel, and therefore less undesired outflow and absence. In the longer term, broader deployment and placement of personnel can be expected, with wider multifunctionality within the organization and with a better labour market position.

Example: For the company in the food industry, the effect of smarter planning is a decrease in the number of hired hours by more than 10 per cent and a cost reduction of 15 per cent. The employment agency staff experiences enlargement of their task and more training and education.

In the second type of cooperation, the focus is on longer-term flexibility, although short-term results are also gained. The organization is better placed to move flexibly with market changes, maintaining and assuring quality and the desired expertise. Even more gains can be expected in the longer term, namely, market expansion, better and more flexible use of personnel, and less (undesired) personnel turnover. In addition, the company gains better insight into its own flexibility need (insight into the market demand and translation to required capacity).

Example: The repro services company gains in terms of cost saving in the hiring process. The vacancies are better and more quickly filled. The work on and between the sites is better planned, and there is more adequate management information. For the flexible personnel, this implies a new way of working, as well as more personal attention, career supervision, and education. Absence and turnover among the flexible workers is lower, and their employment term is longer.

For the third type of cooperation, the benefits relate to a better response to the challenges of the labour market. Companies see a higher inflow of new employees and a lower turnover of employees in the short term, whereas in the longer term, companies experience retention of competence and quality (depending on the duration of the cooperation). Personal training and coaching will be organized for employees, which will enhance employee motivation and satisfaction.

Example: The advantage of the new way of working for the local authority is that new people are drawn in. Support from the engineering firm gives the local authority immediate gains in knowledge and new insights, while the trainees gain advantage in the labour market as well as positive personal development through supervision from three parties.

Table 4.3 Gains Reported for the Hiring Company and the Employees

	Gains for the hiring organization	Gains for the employee
Type I Efficiency	**Short term:** • Cost saving • Fewer hire hours/use of external agencies • Faster throughput times • Reduction of time to hire Longer term: • Continuity and mobility • Better use of employment potential • Fewer surplus personnel • Lower turnover • Less absence	**Short term:** • Better supervision • People more suitably placed • Higher satisfaction and motivation • More involvement • Broader job scope Longer term: • Training and education • Possibility for career development
Type II Flexibility	**Short term:** • Cost reduction • Faster and better filling of vacancies • No risk of exodus • More efficient hiring process • Better personnel planning • Higher productivity • Removal of concern for hiring company Longer term: • Better insight into flex need • Higher productivity and quality of work • Faster response to the market • Retention of competence and quality • Lower turnover • Less absence	**Short term:** • Career supervision • More personal attention • Better insight into own development possibilities • Work guarantee (at various hiring companies) Longer term: • More work-intrinsic development options • Development of competence • Stronger position in labour market
Type III Development	**Short term:** • Higher inflow of new employees • Fostering inflow Longer term: • Employee commitment with specialist knowledge • Retention of competence and quality • Higher level of personnel deployability	**Short term:** • Higher satisfaction and motivation • Access to new knowledge • Work-intrinsic and personal development options Longer term: • Value upgrade in labour market

In addition to the benefits for the hiring organization, a sustainable cooperation also seems to lead to positive results for the flexible workers. A key reason for this is the joint and explicit attention given by the cooperating parties to a more future-oriented HR policy. The personnel figures reveal a lower rate of absence and turnover among flexible employees. Work-intrinsic and personal development options give the employees a stronger position in the labour market as well as more job security. Furthermore, a more personal level of coaching and career supervision as well as broader deployability were mentioned—quite extraordinary aspects as far as temporary employees are concerned.

Characteristics of Successful Cooperation and Partnership

An important issue is covered by our third research question: Which characteristics are key to successful cooperation? Irrespective of success factors that apply to the parties separately, there are certain characteristics in the nature of the cooperation that can produce success. Due to the context of this exploratory phase, we cannot weight these factors because it is not clear which factors are decisive, although we can state what they are. We do not differentiate between the different types of cases because the success factors cited are too general (see Table 4.4).

Some of the principal factors in successful cooperation include the openness in relationships with other organizations and the willingness to invest together in the cooperation. All organizations involved share the need for change and are open towards each other about this. This enables a common search for solutions and options for cooperation. Once there is mutual trust and the will to invest together in the solution, a solid foundation is created for cooperation. An essential factor is a sufficient sense of urgency at the hiring company. The sense of urgency or support may change if, for instance, reorganizations and mergers imply changes in management. Cooperation may even be ended, regardless of actual successes. Partnerships have to deal with tensions between short-term policy and the gradual development of a sustainable relationship. Therefore, a key success factor is a joint and shared vision of HR policy; for both parties, it is self-apparent that investments in both permanent and flexible personnel are critical. We even observe that the agencies take over some parts of HR processes, not only for the flexible workers but also for the permanent workers. A success factor for the longer term is tangible agreements concerning the efficiency of the hiring process and the broad sphere of HR management (including education and career supervision). A risk to the cooperation is the need for patience and long-term engagement, and also the full range over which the cooperation has to be implemented. It is not easy to bring everyone together for the common purpose and then keep them there: from purchasing to HR, and from the board to the line managers.

Table 4.4 Success Factors for Strategic Cooperation

	Success factors
Organization of the hiring company	• Need for change
	• Offer good management information, with annual planning well organized
	• Provide insight into flexibility need (short and long term) and capacity need
	• Support from the board
	• Authorization to change processes
Organization of the employment agency	• Quality of employment agency personnel
	• Continuity among intermediaries
	• Being on the spot (as in in-house construction)
	• Offer work supply and labour market analyses
	• Improved automation system
	• HR policy (retention plan, education program, and career supervision)
	• Direct contact with flexworkers
Nature of the cooperation	• Structural approach (phased and long-term focus)
	• Tangible agreements in terms of cost saving, process improvement, and HR management
	• Common vision and commitment
	• Partnership with joint responsibility
	• Willingness to invest together
	• Openness towards other organizations
	• When cooperating in network, supplementing something to all parties

CONCLUSION

In conclusion, our cases show that hiring companies have a variety of flexibility needs and respond to them in different ways. Although the requirement to structurally deliver high-quality flexibility at the lowest possible price seems difficult to attain, our cases show examples of sustainable cooperative relationships between employment agencies and hiring companies that aim to reduce costs, enhance flexibility, and improve the labour market position of the hiring organization. In addition, we have seen that cooperation offers more security and development opportunities for employees.

The cases also reveal that achieving a balance between organization and flexible employees is not confined to high potentials connected to specialist secondment agencies. Production employees or call centre staff with an agency employment contract also appear to profit from a more structural approach from hiring companies and employment agencies in respect to capacity and competence management. Our findings do show that in all cases, a sense of urgency in terms of labour market shortages, for example, was present to support the development of these relatively novel and complex strategic labour-sourcing agreements. The findings indicate the relevance of longitudinal research to assess the sustainability of the relationships and the balance between the interests of the organization, its employees, and the employment intermediaries. It also warrants further investigation of the effects of these types of cooperation for employees.

None of our cases indicates the establishment of a relationship to support innovation capabilities. This is in line with much of the literature on the traditional role of temporary work agencies, where innovation is regarded as a core activity that cannot be externalized (Atkinson 1984; Houseman 2001). Nevertheless, it is not a role that can be excluded. Studies by Matusik and Hill (1998) and Nesheim et al. (2007) have indicated that companies can also outsource core activities for this reason when they operate in highly dynamic markets. Whereas our cases focused on flexibility in low- and medium-skilled jobs, further research is needed into strategic forms of cooperation between hiring companies and employment agencies for high-skilled employees in core processes. The chapter by Nesheim, Fahle, and Tobiassen (Chapter 5) in this volume, for example, addresses the managerial dilemmas inherent in working with highly skilled specialists in core processes. Here, other factors that are related to organizational learning and work coordination seem to become important, in addition to the factors of openness, determination, shared vision, and operational excellence, which helped to make the strategic labour-sourcing relationships in our case studies sustainably successful.

NOTE

1. In this chapter, we talk of employment agencies and hirers. In practice, this concerns the provision of flexible personnel by employment or secondment agencies to organizations that hire them. This may involve temporary employees according to the employment need or temporary or seconded employees with a short-term or fixed contract with the employment or secondment organization. Where we speak of flexible employees or flexworkers, all of these groups are concerned.

REFERENCES

Atkinson, John G. 1984. *The Flexible Firm and the Shape of Jobs to Come*. Labour Market Issues, No. 5. Oxford: Ruskin College Oxford.
Bolwijn, Pieter T., and Ted Kumpe. 1990. "Manufacturing in the 1990s—productivity, Flexibility and Innovation." *Long Range Planning* 23 (4): 44–57.
De Leede, Jan, Ellen Cox-Woudstra, Anneke Goudswaard, Gu van Rhijn, José van Schie, Bert Tuinzaad, and Aris van Veldhuisen. 2002. *Flexibele inzet van personeel in productiebedrijven. Praktijkvoorbeelden, trends, effecten, instrumenten.* Hoofddorp, The Netherlands: TNO Arbeid/TNO Industrie.
De Leede, Jan, and Anneke Goudswaard. 2008. "Flexibele organisatie: Nieuwe inzichten over de afstemming tussen strategie, personeel en proces." In *Waardevol*

werk: Van arbeidskwaliteit naar sociale innovatie, edited by Steven Dhondt, and Fietje Vaas, 216–230. The Hague: Lemma.

Donker van Heel, Peter, Etienne van Nuland, and Martin van der Ende. 2007. *Instroom uitzendkrachten 2006*. Rotterdam, The Netherlands: Ecorys.

Eurociett. 2007. *More Work Opportunities for More People. Unlocking the Private Employment Agency Industry's Contribution to a Better Functioning Labour Market*. Brussels: Eurociett.

Eurociett/UNI-Europa. 2008. *Joint Declaration on the Directive on Working Conditions for Temporary Agency Workers*. Brussels: Eurociett/UNI-Europa.

Goudswaard, Anneke. 2003. "Flexibele arbeid—duurzame arbeid? De stand van zaken na twintig jaar flexibilisering." PhD diss., Katholieke Universiteit Nijmegen. Hoofddorp, The Netherlands: TNO Arbeid.

Goudswaard, Anneke, Jan de Leede, Madelon van Hooff, Tony Brugman, John Klein Hesselink, Marc de Leeuw, Gu van Rhijn, and Rob Gruyters. 2007. *De toekomst van flexibele arbeid: hoe flexibel is Nederland?* Hoofddorp, The Netherlands: TNO.

Houseman, Susan N. 2001. "Why Employers Use Flexible Staffing Arrangements: Evidence from an Establishment Survey." *Industrial and Labor Relations Review* 55: 149–170.

Kalleberg, Arne L., and Peter V. Marsden. 2005. "Externalizing Organizational Activities: Where and How U.S. Establishments Use Employment Intermediaries." *Socio-Economic Review* 3 (3): 389–416.

Kerkhofs, Marcel, Amelia Roman, and Peter Ester. 2010. *European Company Survey 2009; Flexibility Profiles of European Companies*. Dublin: European Foundation for the Improvement of Living and Working Conditions.

Lepak, David P., Kathryn M. Bartol, and Niclas L. Erhardt. 2005. "A Contingency Framework for the Delivery of HR Practices." *Human Resource Management Review* 15 (2): 139–159.

Matusik, Sharon F., and Charles W. L. Hill. 1998. "The Utilization of Contingent Work, Knowledge Creation and Competitive Advantage." *Academy of Management Review* 23 (1): 680–697.

Morris, Shad S., Scott A. Snell, and David Lepak. 2005. *An Architectural Approach to Managing Knowledge Stocks and Flows: Implications for Reinventing the HR Function*. CAHRS Working Paper 05-15, School of Industrial and Labor Relations, Center for Advanced Human Resource Studies, Cornell University, Ithaca, NY.

Nesheim, Torstein, Karen M. Olsen, and Arne L. Kalleberg. 2007. "Externalizing the Core: Firms' Use of Employment Intermediaries in the Information and Communication Technology Industries." *Human Resource Management* 46 (2): 247–264.

Pedersen, Henrik S., Claus B. Hansen, and Susan Mahler. 2007. *Temporary Agency Work in the European Union*. Dublin: European Foundation for the Improvement of Living and Working Conditions. www.eurofound.europa.eu/publications/htmlfiles/ef04104.htm.

Storrie, Donald. 2002. *Temporary Agency Work in the European Union*. Dublin: European Foundation for the Improvement of Living and Working Conditions.

Van Driel, Hugo, and Bas Koene. 2011. "The Rhetoric of Restraint: The Struggle for Legitimacy of the Dutch Temporary Work Agency Industry, 1961–1996." *Enterprise & Society* 12 (3): 562–600.

Vidal, Matt, and Leann M. Tigges. 2009. "Temporary Employment and Strategic Staffing in the Manufacturing Sector." *Industrial Relations* 48 (1): 55–72.

Volberda, Henk W. 1998. *Building the Flexible Firm. How to Remain Competitive*. Oxford: University Press.

Volberda, Henk W. 1996. "Toward the Flexible Firm: How to Remain Vital in Hypercompetitive Environments." *Organization Science* 7: 359–374.

Wucherer, Klaus 2006. "Business Partnering—a Driving Force for Innovation." *Industrial Marketing Management* 35 (1): 91–102.

5 When External Consultants Work on Internal Projects

Exploring Managerial Challenges

Torstein Nesheim, Bjørnar Fahle, and Anita E. Tobiassen

In this chapter, we analyze a focal firm's use of non-employed human resources on time-limited contracts, who cooperate and work together with standard employees. Starting with Atkinson's (1984) model of the flexible firm, there has been extensive research on various types of employment relations. The emphasis has been on atypical employment arrangements characterized by short-term contracts that constitute alternatives to long-term, open-ended employment relations. Such arrangements include people leased from other firms such as external consultants and contractors who often work on the premises of the focal firm.

We focus on a particular employment arrangement: a focal firm's use of leased, highly skilled technical consultants (engineers) that work on the premises of the firm and cooperate closely with the employees of the focal firm. This is a triangular employment relation because these consultants have an external employer, while their work is directed and controlled by the focal firm. The first research theme we address is why firms use external consultants in the form of triangular employment relations. By engaging in such contracts on a large scale in a setting where externals and employees work closely together, a number of management challenges arise. The second research theme is the identification and analysis of these challenges. Thus, the chapter demonstrates how external flexibility (use of non-standard work arrangements) is closely linked to the organization of work and internal flexibility.

The empirical setting for our research is the petroleum sector in Norway during a period of high demand for engineers and technical expertise. A vital characteristic of firms in this sector is that project units and temporary teams are used extensively alongside traditional organizational forms, such as permanent departments and functional units. In terms of project organization, the focus here is on internal (rather than inter-organizational) projects governed by a focal firm, with important contributions from external human resources (i.e., persons not employed by the firm).

We will show that—with regard to high-competence resources such as consultants and technical experts—a model where external workers are perceived as decoupled from the ordinary employees is not useful. The two categories of personnel often interact closely, and the focal organization may become dependent on the external consultant or technical expert (Barley and Kunda 2004). We identify and discuss four management challenges derived from the manner in which firms actually use external consultants in the sector.

PREVIOUS RESEARCH ON NON-STANDARD EMPLOYMENT RELATIONS

There has been extensive work on non-standard and contingent work during the past two decades. A number of themes have been covered, including the identification of types of non-standard work arrangements, the determinants of firms' use of such arrangements, and the consequences and challenges for firms and employees.

Relatively few studies have examined issues related to the management and organization of work in these arrangements (exceptions include Lautsch 2002; Barley and Kunda 2004; Bidwell 2009; see also Ashford, George, and Blatt 2007).

Studies of management and organization have mainly focused on the employees of a given, focal firm (i.e., inside the boundaries of the organization). There are some exceptions to this pattern, such as studies on inter-organizational teams and projects. However, management challenges when a focal firm combines its own employees with external consultants have been largely neglected.

Why should there be specific managerial challenges related to these "externals" when external consultants cooperate with employees of the focal firm? First, a triangular employment relation is created when personnel not employed by the firm interact with employees and are to be directed by representatives of the focal firm; the functions usually associated with the employer are split between the formal employer (often a temporary help firm) and the focal firm (Bidwell and Fernandez-Mateo 2008). Secondly, "externals" and employees tend to have different roles and functions in the organization, where employees are preferred in core functions that provide the (intended) competitive advantage of the firm (Atkinson 1984; Lepak and Snell 1999). Further, one would expect the "externals" to have a different relation to the firm compared to employees because "externals" do not tend to have a long-term attachment to, nor expectations of a career inside, the customer firm. Employees will tend to have greater loyalty and be more committed to the firm than an external consultant. "External" workers will tend to act to promote their career across firms and have different sources of identification. External consultants are usually only partly integrated into the organizational culture of the client firm (McLean Parks, Kidder, and Gallagher 1998; Kalleberg 2000; Connelly and Gallagher 2004; Ashford, George, and Blatt 2007; Bidwell 2009).

In their review article, Ashford, George, and Blatt (2007) address the challenges of managing non-standard workers in terms of commitment and control. They identify four research streams that emphasize different "tools" of management: (1) job design and fit, (2) social exchange and psychological contracts, (3) relationships, and (4) identity. We take a different approach in this chapter and structure the analysis on the basis of four managerial challenges when external employees work together with the employees of the firm: (1) external consultants possess unique competencies, (2) share of external consultants, (3) integration versus separation of external consultants, and (4) social comparisons.

EMPIRICAL CONTEXT, METHODS, AND DATA

The empirical context of the paper is the Norwegian petroleum sector. This is a core economic sector in Norway and includes companies that control the operation of the plant and equipment to pump oil and gas from well heads; sub-contractors producing rigs, production facilities, and equipment; sub-contractors providing operational, maintenance, modifications, drilling and well services, and so forth; and a number of specialized consultancy and technical firms.

The practice of leasing employees from a third party has been an institutionalized part of this economic sector in Norway for more than two decades. The main rationale has been that it allows for numerical flexibility and a buffer for ordinary employees in a world of fluctuating demand. Before 2000, this work arrangement was regulated through dispensations from the law that prohibited employee leasing. After 2000, more liberal regulations were introduced, which still restrict the situations in which the leasing of employees may take place. Due to the regulatory schemes, the practice has been explicitly framed as leasing of employees (providing "heads") and clearly differentiated from ordinary employment on the one hand and consultancy services where the provider is responsible for the product on the other hand. It is a triangular employment relationship because the consultants in question work for a customer firm, while they are employed by a third party, most often a specialized unit of a large temporary help agency (such as Manpower and Adecco) or a technical consultancy firm. The external consultants are mostly engineers and technical specialists; thus, our focus is on a highly qualified category of human resources. At the time of the study (2006–2009), due to high oil prices and large demand, there tended to be an under-supply of external consultants with the relevant competence.

The paper is primarily based on content analyses of 23 semi-structured, qualitative interviews with managers at different levels in nine firms, located in Western Norway. We also draw on information gained from a total of 40 interviews with representatives of third parties/leasing firms, external consultants (with two exceptions employed by an intermediary), and ordinary employees. The interviews cover firms in different phases of the value chain in the petroleum sector, including operator firms, firms in maintenance and modifications and drilling and well services, and producers of specialized equipment. The interviews were conducted over a three-year period, starting in the winter of 2006.

The purpose of the chapter is to identify and explore a number of themes related to the management of external consultants, not to make statistical generalizations. Based on the information from the interviews, we are able to describe and exemplify some vital patterns and mechanisms related to the management of external consultants. Our main contribution is to shed light on the four management challenges described previously, based on the qualitative data on the actors' descriptions and perceptions of various aspects of these challenges. These were identified from the analysis of the interview data.

WHY EXTERNAL CONSULTANTS ARE USED

All firms in our sample combine standard open-ended employment relations with a specific form of non-standard employment relation: the use of leased, external consultants. In a triangular employment relation, the employer functions are shared between two firms. A third party—often a temporary help agency—acts as the formal employer and is responsible for contracts and wages. The employee is leased out to the customer firm, which is responsible for job assignment and the organization of work. Thus, the external consultant is part of the customer's work organization.

The preference for this triangular employment form—rather than direct two-party contracts with external consultants—is an institutionalized practice among the firms in the petroleum sector. The main managerial motivations for the practice in our interviews were the following:

- The contract has low termination costs and may be easily terminated. Such an arrangement enables numerical flexibility.
- The focal firm does not act as the formal employer (the third party does). The focal firm therefore has an arm's length relationship and no contractual relation with the consultant, and thus no responsibility for further employment.
- The third party provides quality control in selection of consultants.
- Administrative simplification occurs through a reduction in the number of contract partners.

Although the preference of using a third party was clearly stated among firms, there were some exceptions in actual practice. Consultants with specialized expertise and experience were in high demand. In some instances, the third party was not able to provide a competent person; in other cases, the person identified preferred a two-party consultancy contract. However, only a small fraction of consultants obtained such two-party contracts.

The Core-Periphery Question

Conventional wisdom assumes that organizations should internalize their core value-creation activities, and that non-standard work arrangements such as external consultants should not be used in the core areas of the organization (Nesheim, Olsen, and Kalleberg 2007). Use of external contracts should occur in non-core functions and in situations where numerical flexibility is vital. However, Matusik and Hill (1998) argue that external staffing arrangements are likely to be useful in the core value-creation areas of firms that compete in dynamic environments where there is rapid technological change, short product cycles, and "creative destruction." Two studies in the information and communications technology sector have found support for this perspective (Nesheim 2003; Nesheim, Olsen, and Kalleberg 2007).

In our interviews, we differentiated between the intentions of focal firms to use consultants on the one hand and actual practices on the other. A typical response was that their own employees should staff management positions related to a certain task or a certain project. Other key resources should be also internal. Examples include people with long and broad experience, those with knowledge of a particular oilfield or production site, specialists in a particular area of knowledge, as well as those possessing knowledge of the particular knowledge architecture/production system of the firm in question. External consultants should primarily supplement these employees, through the provision of more standardized knowledge and support functions.

The respondents also reported the following specific situations in which employees were preferred:

- When there are high learning costs; when it takes a certain time to obtain the necessary knowledge and the tasks are complex
- Situations where one is dependent on a single person or few persons
- Positions that give access to strategic information
- Positions that are seen as part of an internal career ladder

Thus, in general, the strategic assessment of and intentions behind the use of external consultants fit easily with a core-periphery model of the firm, and a clear hierarchy of tasks and authority exist between the two categories. However, for some of the firms, the core-periphery model was difficult to implement fully. There was a gap between intentions and actual practices. External consultants held key positions in project management or were the most knowledgeable persons in a specific field of expertise. This pattern is partly explained by the high demand of knowledge and preferences for working as an external consultant (and not ordinary employee) among the group in question. In addition, managing capacity is not easy in the sector because of the fact that the production processes are complex and varied, and technological development and demand of competencies are not always predictable.

For other firms, the intentions resembled a loose, less restrictive core-periphery model, in order to fit the practice of increasing use of external consultants. This will be illustrated by two firms/units specializing in maintenance and modifications. External consultants were not to be used in ordinary positions in line management, but elsewhere there were no differences between the two categories. The share of consultants in these units ranged from 30 to 40 per cent of all personnel. Consultants were involved in every function—procurement, cost calculation, planning, and engineering—where they had similar tasks as employees. Consultants were also used in positions that required firm-specific knowledge. External consultants in one firm were involved as unit project managers, the level above project managers in the project hierarchy.

MANAGING EXTERNAL CONSULTANTS: FOUR ISSUES

We observed an increase over time in the number external consultants and thus the ratio of "externals" to employees in the period 2006–2009. Firms found it increasingly difficult to base their staffing decisions on a core-periphery model, with a clear differentiation in tasks and functions between its own employed engineers and external consultants. Externals and internals worked closely together in projects and teams, and externals often had long experience, specialized knowledge, and vital positions in projects. Based on the observations from interviews, managerial challenges were categorized in four groups. Table 5.1 gives an overview of these challenges, their causes, and particular issues to be analyzed in the chapter.

External Consultants Possess Unique Competencies

External consultants often have key roles in the firm's organization. Especially in a situation where demand exceeds the supply of the human resources, power and dependence relations are changed in favour of the consultant. An example is a person who worked in a position as team leader in a unit involved in the development of oil reservoirs. This role gives the external consultant access to firm-specific knowledge. The consultant had been involved in several interesting tasks, including scientific studies, innovation projects with sub-contractors, and marketing related to international projects. Firms often chose external consultants for important positions, mainly due to the lack of available internal competencies. After obtaining such a position, the incumbent had the opportunity to gain further experience and knowledge, thus strengthening his/her power vis-à-vis the firm.

Table 5.1   Managing External Consultants: Overview

Management challenge	Drivers	Particular management issues
External consultants possess unique competencies (1)	Mismatch between demand and supply Preferences for working as an external consultant Unpredictability	Dependency on external consultants Vulnerability and loss of competence Hamper development of internal employees Exchange of information Opportunistic actions
Proportion of external consultants (2)	Mismatch for working as an external consultant Preferences for working as an external consultant Unpredictability	Less use of the voice option among external consultants External consultants have to be managed in a different manner Options for reducing the proportion of consultants
Integration versus separation of consultants (3)	Teamwork and operational interdependencies Different employment status	Developing trust and identification with the team Common localization of employees and consultants Limits to integration Information leakage
Social comparisons (4)	Differences in rewards Visibility of rewards Organizational justice considerations	Reward comparisons motive for leaving Taking (too) good care of consultants Job assignment dilemma Reward comparison latent issue

Vulnerability and Loss of Competence

There are many examples where consultants hold key positions in project management or possess firm-specific or production-unit-specific knowledge. The production systems are complex and often have unique characteristics. Obtaining the necessary knowledge is costly and requires training and experience. In order to provide maintenance and modification services, for example, installation-specific knowledge is often needed. If the production-specific knowledge is rare and is possessed by external consultants rather than employees, the firm is vulnerable to the exit of consultants. Presently, many opportunities have been available for these consultants, and the loss of external consultants in key positions is frequent. In today's labour market, and especially with regard to "key consultants," it is they who benefit from the low termination costs of contracts, enabling them to seek more profitable assignments elsewhere.

Development of Employees and Exchange of Information

Whereas the firm is dependent on many external consultants to get the job done, those consultants also occupy vital positions and development opportunities for employees. In this manner, when external consultants have vital positions, they often block development of knowledge and reduce career opportunities for the insiders. Further, respondents perceive that consultants share less information and knowledge than employees. The knowledge possessed by the consultants is to a large extent their basis for future work and negotiations with the customer firm. Typically, external consultants will tend to protect their knowledge in order to strengthen their competitive position.

Although our respondents tended to have strong opinions on sharing of information and knowledge between consultants and employees, there were few procedures in place among the firms in order to stimulate such sharing. Managing information and knowledge sharing with regard to consultants is related to the lack of procedures on information sharing and transfer of experience in general. Priority is given to the day-to-day tasks and to finishing projects on time. The pressure to execute the operative tasks is large, and there are few slack resources available. Transfer of experience consumes time and resources and tends to have low priority.

Opportunistic Actions

In firms where one is dependent on the special knowledge of external consultants, the potential for opportunistic actions—self-interest seeking with guile (Williamson 1985)—on part of the consultants increases. Whereas respondents agreed that knowledge sharing and bargaining power were vital issues, the respondents perceived the actions of the consultants differently.

Some respondents reported that consultants acted strategically, even opportunistically, for their own benefit. They were first and foremost concerned with their own output in the short run as well as their own career prospects. Consultants often tended to "feather their own nest" and try to increase the domain for their services and knowledge. When they possessed key knowledge for the firm, they were reluctant to pass this on. If they obtained a managerial position in a team or a department, they tended to use it as a resource to strengthen their own agenda.

Not all respondents shared this perception. Some found that the consultants were not different compared to employees; they were influenced by the norms of teamwork and the necessities of information sharing in order to do a proper job. Many of the consultants in key roles had long-term relations with the customer firm and were perceived as a vital part of the firm culture and had developed high-trust relations with their colleagues.

The Proportion of External Consultants in Projects

In the period of the study, external consultants' share of total personnel on many projects was 25 per cent or higher. Although all firms wanted to use consultants in projects, the numbers were higher than one would prefer. First, and related to the previous discussion on dependency on consultants' special knowledge, the challenges of vulnerability, information sharing, and opportunistic actions increase with the number of consultants in critical positions. Seen from the point of view of the firm, it is easier to handle one external consultant in a critical position compared to five such consultants.

Voice

Second, in our findings, the ratio of consultants influenced the psychosocial work environment in an organizational unit or project. External consultants are perceived to be more careful in using the "voice" option in order to raise problems and make complaints on work issues. Typically, there is pressure on delivery and focus on the operative tasks at hand. Consultants tend to focus on doing their job properly, without any "fuss" and without "creating problems."

Due to a combination of power perceptions and short-time perspective, consultants are sometimes reluctant to voice their concern on work-related issues. Feedback is vital for improving work processes, for coordination, and for maintaining social relations in a work setting. The higher the ratio of consultants and the more vital their roles, the greater the impact of these mechanisms.

Managerial Capabilities

Some of the respondents noted that the ratio of consultants had implications for managerial capabilities. This is due to factors such as locus of identity, sense of responsibility, and motivation. One respondent noted that consultants require strong leaders because they have their focus on earning money. Another said that they tended to take a more hands-on approach and monitor projects closer when consultants were involved.

On the other hand, several respondents said that few managers were conscious of these challenges. There may be a "consultancy paradox" here. One would expect a higher ratio of "externals" to draw attention to issues related to the management of this category of engineers. However, what is observed is that the increased use of consultants has strengthened the norm of using consultants, and this practice is taken for granted in the firms in the sector. Among some of those managers that accepted this practice as matter of fact, we found a low emphasis on the challenges of managing external consultants. As a consequence, in some firms consultancy use tends not to be an issue as such, and potential problems and issues do not receive much attention.

An alternative to more active management of consultants was to reduce their numbers. We observed two measures taken to reduce the proportion of consultants.

- One alternative is to train new employees, who after a period of training work "virtually." One firm had set up offices in Gothenburg (Sweden), enabling the firm to tap into the labour market in Sweden and to avoid using consultants for those positions.

- Many of the consultants were offered employment contracts after the initial consultancy assignment ended. The leasing contract had an element of "try and hire" and was a vital mechanism for recruiting new employees. Through this measure, the proportion of employees on projects should increase.

Integration versus Separation of Consultants

Although firms (to some extent) strive to implement a hierarchy of competences, tasks, and authority between employees and consultants, this policy does not imply the decoupling of consultants from employees in the actual organization of work. Respondents said that people should cooperate, work in teams, and exchange information. In order for a team to function, one has to create cooperative relations and develop trust. This might be challenging when time horizons, commitment, and loyalty differ among the two categories of workers. There is a dilemma with regard to the integration and separation of consultants. All of our respondents stated that integration is vital. A typical statement was the following:

> "It is vital to make them feel part of the team, support them in the beginning. They should be assigned sensible tasks, and feel a sense of belonging. Consultants are part of an integrated work group, where there is a high degree of dependence between those who participate in the project" (manager, firm A).

One of the firms has even started to use a human resources management tool usually exclusively associated with employees (appraisal interviews) for consultants as well. The reasoning is to show that the firm cares for the consultants and that they are part of the team.

Barley and Kunda (2004) found that firms often had a number of formal policies to set consultants apart from employees, including badges and lower quality of workspace. We found no such policies to create outsiders in our study. Rather, the pattern is that information exchange and cooperation were stimulated through common localization of consultants and employees.

Limits to Integration

Based on the information from respondents, there are limits to the level of integration of consultants. To understand such limits, one has to look at the time perspective. At the project and team level, integration is emphasized, as described previously. However, firms differ with regard to the consultants' integration into the firm in a more long-term perspective. A typical response is that consultants are not involved in strategic processes, meetings at the department level, and measures taken to ensure career development. One firm that involved consultants in the management of projects and other key areas in projects stated clearly that it didn't intend to use "externals" as line managers at the department level, in management teams, and in strategic planning at this level.

Information Leakage

There is the potential for leakage of information and critical knowledge to other firms when "externals" move on to other customers. In a few of the firms, limited access to information and databases for consultants prevailed in order to handle this challenge. However, the typical response was that the benefits of information access and task integration outweighed the potential costs of information leakage. Given the consultants' involvement in key functions and tasks, they are perceived to need (with some exceptions) similar information as employees. As a consequence, there is bound to be some information leakage that may benefit competing firms in the future.

Although leakage of information can hardly be stopped, the respondents cite two mechanisms that are perceived to reduce direct transfer of sensitive information to competitors. First, consultants sign confidentiality agreements when they start an assignment. Second, there are reputation effects. The consultant's market value is dependent on having a reputation as a trustworthy person. If his/her actions are perceived as dishonest or deceitful, the consequences for him/her will be very negative. A condition for such reputational effects is that the engineers and technical specialists are part of rather closely knit networks.

Social Comparisons and Organizational Justice

In groups where people work closely together, there tends to be a comparison of attitudes, actions, and contributions. When consultants and employees cooperate in projects and teams, one would expect that such social comparisons are stimulated, and that one evaluates oneself compared to others. Considerations of equity and justice—the wish to be treated fairly with regard to the allocation of responsibility, work tasks, and financial outcomes—are usually vital in such processes (Connelly and Gallagher 2004).

The respondents said that such comparisons were a "part of the game" in the sector. Typically, such evaluations were framed as "pros and cons" of working as an employee or a consultant. Consultants as rule earn more than employees who are in similar positions and have similar responsibilities and similar work tasks. This gap in earnings is not exactly popular among employees and is usually compensated for by the higher job security and better pension and insurance rights among employees. Furthermore, although consultants have more freedom in terms of assignments outside a customer firm, employees should benefit from career opportunities, courses, training, and interesting work tasks in the firm.

Comparisons of outcomes are vital in explaining why employees leave to work as consultants. Many respondents cite retaining employees as a big challenge where differences in remuneration are a vital factor. However, with the exception of exit decisions among employees, it seems that differences in financial remuneration between consultants and employees are not considered problematic by our respondents. One explanation may be that the differences are perceived to be fair among employees, and compensated for by other long-term benefits that employees obtain. Another explanation may be that although justice considerations are a latent issue, they are not triggered due to do to the high level of general satisfaction in these jobs.

We observed several dilemmas with regard to organizational justice considerations. Many respondents stated that they tended to treat the two categories equally. This policy of "taking good care of consultants" is not beyond discussion among the employees of the firm. Some of them raise the question about whether the firm takes too good care of them:

> "We have had some reactions on this policy in lately; why are they treated so well? Such perceptions are more usual among younger employees, who have not yet experienced recessions and downsizing. Others have internalized that our own employees have more job security, and herein is the most vital difference between employees and consultants" (manager, firm B).

What the respondent is implying is that in the long run employees have a fair deal; it is inevitable that there will be lower demand, fewer projects, and downsizing in a few years' time. All the same, given the labour market characteristics at the time of the study, we would argue that there are lots of opportunities outside the organization and that consultants are more prone than employees to exploit these. In order to keep the consultants and maintain the staffing needed, there is clearly a pressure to cater to consultants. What is accepted as a fair deal for the two categories in question seems to be influenced by external labour market pressures.

Job Assignment

Justice considerations get attention when people are assigned to positions and when decision responsibilities are allocated to employees or consultants. Some respondents stated that it was fair that employees should be assigned to critical positions as a reward for loyalty and staying with the firm when earnings were higher in the external labour market. In other words, consultants could not expect to earn both the going rate and be assigned to the most prestigious positions in a project or a department. The managerial dilemma was whether one should choose the best person for a certain job or use an employee even if there were more competent external consultants available. This dilemma was acknowledged by several of the managers we interviewed.

In sum, organizational justice considerations have both manifest and latent aspects. When consultants are extensively used and they possess scarce and specialized knowledge, managers more often confront "justice-laden" dilemmas when staffing positions and assigning people to various tasks. These choices have vital consequences for development opportunities and trigger justice considerations among employees and consultants. Social comparisons of financial rewards seem to have a more latent character but may be activated in times of change, for example, if demand is reduced or there are qualitative shifts in demand and competencies needed.

CONCLUDING DISCUSSION

In this chapter, we have identified and analyzed a number of managerial issues that arise when employees and non-employees cooperate on projects. These issues have to be understood in the particular context of work. Firms in the petroleum sector in Norway have institutionalized the practice of using external consultants employed by a third party as a supplement to ordinary employees. However, in the period studied, they tended to use more consultants than they preferred because of the high demand and lack of qualified personnel in the market.

We have approached these issues by taking a managerial perspective on non-standard work. This line of enquiry includes contributions from (among others) Lautsch (2002), Barley and Kunda (2004), Bidwell (2009), and Ashford, George, and Blatt (2007). Although we recognize and are inspired by these contributions, we have followed a different line of inquiry. Based on qualitative interviews with actors involved in triangular employment arrangements in the Norwegian oil industry, we have identified and analyzed particular management challenges. These have been grouped in four categories: (1) consultants possess unique competencies, (2) the proportion of external consultants, (3) integration versus separation, and (4) social comparisons.

The first challenge, that consultants possess specialized knowledge or scarce managerial competence, is an unintended effect of the lack of available human resources in the labour market, preferences (among some) for consultancy work, and unpredictability in demand. Although teamwork and cooperation between employees and consultants is an issue when consultants are used, the use of externals having key knowledge and key positions changes the equation in favour of consultants. We have described consequences related to dependencies on consultants, vulnerability and loss of competence, development of employees, and exchange of information, as well opportunistic actions by consultants.

The relatively high proportion of consultants is an unintended effect of the labour market in the particular field. This is a quantitative rather than a qualitative aspect of the use of consultants and refers to numerical shortage, rather than unique competencies or skills. The respondents were concerned about the low propensity for consultants to use the voice option, and many stated that a large proportion of consultants required more hands-on leadership.

The challenges on integration/separation are related to teamwork and interdependencies between employees and consultants. Respondents emphasized the importance of trust, cooperative relations, and common localization. At the same time, there are limits to integration, and information leakage may be an issue. Social comparisons and justice considerations were also found to be important. Comparisons of rewards were a motive for employees leaving the firm. We also identified dilemmas regarding job assignment and how "well" the consultants should be treated.

The particular challenges analyzed in this chapter are grouped in categories that are analytically distinct. However, there are interdependencies between the categories in the sense that the degree of importance of one challenge has an impact on other issues. For example, questions of integration and access to/leakage of information (3) take on a higher importance when there is a high proportion of consultants (2) and some of those consultants possess unique competencies (1). Social comparisons (4) probably become more pressing and challenge psychological contracts and justice perceptions when external consultants make the most of their strong market situation (1).

A number of characteristics of the empirical setting should be noted in evaluating the generalizability of our results. We have studied non-standard employees in the high end of the market: engineers with a professional education working as external consultants. The study took place at the time of high demand for the competence in question. Thus, the context may be seen as an "extreme" case in terms of non-standard employment in general. Nevertheless, our findings should provide the basis for conceptual development and hypotheses that can be tested more systematically on larger samples of consultants and employees. Further research should take care to study questions in different settings and with different institutional practices, types of competence, and labour market situation.

REFERENCES

Ashford, Susan J., Elizabeth George, and Ruth Blatt. 2007. "Old Assumptions, New Work: The Opportunities and Challenges of Research on Nonstandard Employment." *Academy of Management Annals* 1: 65–117.
Atkinson, John. 1984. *Flexibility, Uncertainty and Manpower Management.* Institute of Manpower Studies. Report No. 89. Brighton, UK: Sussex University.
Barley, Stephen R., and Gideon Kunda. 2004. *Gurus, Hired Guns and Warm Bodies: Itinerant Experts in a Knowledge Economy.* Princeton, NJ: Princeton University Press.
Bidwell, Matthew. 2009. "Do Peripheral Workers Do Peripheral Work? Comparing the Use of Highly Skilled Contractors and Regular Employees." *Industrial and Labor Relations Review* 62 (2): 200–225.
Bidwell, Matthew, and Isabel Fernandez-Mateo. 2008. "Three's a Crowd. Understanding Triadic Employment Relationships." In *Employment Relationships.*

New Models of White-Collar Work, edited by Peter Cappelli, 142–178. Cambridge: Cambridge University Press.

Connelly, Catherine E., and Daniel G. Gallagher. 2004. "Emergent Trends in Contingent Work Research." *Journal of Management* 30: 959–983.

Kalleberg, Arne L. 2000. "Nonstandard Employment Relations. Part-Time, Temporary and Contract Work." *Annual Review of Sociology* 26: 341–365.

Lautsch, Brenda A. 2002. "Uncovering and Explaining Variance in the Features and Outcomes of Contingent Work." *Industrial and Labor Relations Review* 56 (1): 23–43.

Lepak, David P., and Scott A. Snell. 1999. "The Human Resource Architecture: Toward a Theory of Human Capital Allocation and Development." *Academy of Management Review* 24: 31–48.

Matusik, Sharon F., and Charles W. L. Hill. 1998. "The Utilization of Contingent Work, Knowledge Creation, and Competitive Advantage." *Academy of Management Review* 23 (4): 680–697.

McLean Parks, Judi, Deborah L. Kidder, and Daniel G. Gallagher. 1998. "Fitting Square Pegs into Round Holes: Mapping the Domain of Contingent Work Arrangements onto the Psychological Contract." *Journal of Organizational Behavior* 19 (7): 697–730.

Nesheim, Torstein. 2003. "External Work Arrangements in the Core of the Firm." *European Management Journal* 21 (4): 528–537.

Nesheim, Torstein, Karen M. Olsen, and Arne L. Kalleberg. 2007. "Externalization of the Core: Firms' Use of Employment Intermediaries in the Information and Communication Technology Industries." *Human Resource Management* 46 (2): 247–264.

Williamson, Oliver E. 1985. *The Economic Institutions of Capitalism: Firms, Markets, Relational Contracting*. New York: Free Press.

6 Towards Sustainable Employment Schemes at the Inter-Organizational Level

Virginie Xhauflair and François Pichault

In order to deal with the increased demands for flexibility and adaptability linked to globalization, companies constantly test new forms of work organization and employment (Marchington et al. 2004; Cooke et al. 2004). During the past two decades, temporary work has emerged as one of the preferred managerial means of fostering flexibility. It has led to important changes in the employment relationship rooted in the Fordist compromise: By creating a triangular relationship (employer, worker, and user), temporary work creates a major challenge for employment regulation because it disassociates economic from social responsibilities (Sobczak 2003; Havard, Sobczak, and Rorive 2009) and thus reinforces the risk of job insecurity for workers.

Despite its unquestionable popularity, temporary work seems unable to respond to the diverse needs of employers and workers: Managers and workers continuously design innovative new practices in an attempt to reconcile opposing demands for flexibility and job security. In Belgium and neighbouring countries, many of these new practices rely on work pooling or posting principles. Yet, in many European countries, the lending or sharing of workers remains forbidden, except by temporary work agencies. As a consequence, the rise of new inter-organizational employment schemes often occurs in a regulatory vacuum.

In Belgium, employment law makes provision for two exceptions to the ban on workers' posting: temporary work and employer pools (i.e., workforce pooling between partner companies). However, the Belgian legal framework for employer pools is more restrictive than the French model: Employment contracts must be full time and open ended, and the workers concerned must be long-term job seekers. Therefore, the few existing employer pools sometimes break the law in order to ensure their efficient operation and provide the best possible answer to the needs of both member companies and pooled workers: They hire workers with very short periods of unemployment (as little as one day), offer part-time contracts to those who wish it, or use the same joint agreement for all shared workers despite differences in the tasks they perform.

Because of legal limitations, many inter-organizational practices develop in clandestine fashion, growing at the margin of, or in the gaps in, the existing legal framework. In Belgium, this is the case for *umbrella company services*, which allow professionals to act as freelancers whilst benefiting from the status and associated rights of salaried employees. Although the practice is forbidden in Belgium, it is on the way to being legally accepted in France. We also observe practices such as *skill pooling* and *co-sourcing*, which, by exploiting existing loopholes in the law, enable one company to make its workers available to another, either part time or for the duration of a particular project.

In many cases, these new practices seem to satisfy the various stakeholders concerned. However, the lack of regulatory framework creates a risk that, especially in the case of asymmetrical power relationships, these employment schemes become unbalanced and untenable in the longer term because they reinforce the precarious position of certain actors. Until now, little research has focused on the micro, inter-organizational, and emergent aspects of social regulation (Regalia 2006). It is therefore important to determine the conditions for sustainable social regulation and inter-organizational employment partnerships. Our research may also help to fill a gap in the research about *flexicurity*, which is presented in Europe as *a new paradigm for labour market policy reform* (Wilthagen 1998; Wilthagen and Rogowski 2002; Wilthagen and Tros 2004) but which remains both normative and ideological (Auer 2010). Its micro-level aspects in particular remain under-investigated (Pichault and Xhauflair 2007). Understanding the conditions that support the construction of durable inter-organizational employment practices may help to reveal the processes needed to develop sustainable flexicurity solutions, such as skill pooling or co-sourcing.

Based on action research in various contexts, we developed an analytical grid containing eight dimensions characterizing the collective process that leads to the development (and maintenance) of sustainable inter-organizational employment schemes. In this chapter, we present the model and explain it through a case study of an emerging inter-organizational employment practice—namely, multi-employership—that was designed to resolve the labour-sourcing needs of an international airfreight company. We attempt to answer the following question: What kind of new employment schemes are developed at the inter-organizational level and under which conditions can they be considered to be balanced and sustainable?

METHODOLOGICAL CONCERNS

In order to uncover the characteristics of processes leading to the implementation of sustainable inter-organizational employment schemes, we adopted an inductive action-research methodology, based on stimulating and providing follow-up for emerging practices, in collaboration with labour market stakeholders. A purely deductive approach appeared premature, considering how little research there is about sustainable inter-organizational employment schemes (Regalia 2006). The inventiveness of actors confronted with a lack of institutional answers to their flexibility and security needs, however, provides fertile ground for insights into the dimensions of attractive and durable inter-organizational employment practices. However, we rapidly discovered that all actors had different perspectives on the process, depending on their particular experience and expectations. The challenge of the study was thus to come up with an overarching model.

We had the opportunity to access such practices through a European research project aimed at identifying, designing, and implementing innovative employment practices—such as flexpool in the logistics sector, EEIG[1] for social enterprises, employer pools among small and medium-sized enterprises (SMEs), and so forth—that allow local actors to deal with new flexibility and job security needs. Our action-research methodology both allowed and obliged us to go beyond a simple case study to stimulate and support the targeted practices. The empirical basis of our study is thus a number of action research projects that aimed to develop innovative inter-organizational employment schemes in the Liège area of Belgium.

These projects were initiated, accompanied, and evaluated in a participative manner. Within the framework of the European research project, we involved multiple stakeholders at the micro-level of the labour market: human resources (HR) managers in various companies, representatives of the Belgian temporary work federation, shop stewards and union workers from diverse companies and sectors, representatives of private- and public-sector organizations responsible for vocational training and/or the (re)integration of job seekers, representatives of local authorities in charge of regional redevelopment, Chamber of Commerce representatives, and so forth. Drawing on the experience and information given by these local labour market stakeholders, we conceptualized the micro-level process required to develop sustainable schemes. This participative action-research process strengthens the social legitimacy of our model, by anchoring it in the daily practices of actors.

We use Trilogi, one of our case studies in the logistics sector, as an illustrative example throughout this chapter. We first conducted a questionnaire survey at Trilogi[2] to clarify the needs of workers, then carried out 15 qualitative interviews with multi-employed workers. Subsequently, we shared and discussed the information gathered with the stakeholders concerned, in order to co-develop new sustainable employment solutions. Based on the entire set of field experiences, we identified a set of dimensions that characterize the experimental processes supporting the development of inter-organizational employment arrangements.

After briefly describing the Trilogi case and the way we worked with the company in the section "The Case of Multi-Employership at Trilogi," we introduce our analytical grid in the section "An Analytical Grid for the

Effective Development and Maintenance of Inter-Organizational Employment Schemes" and apply it to the case. In the section "Shifting the Conditions towards More Sustainable Employment Solutions," we show how its descriptive dimensions can be used to discuss the sustainability of emerging inter-organizational practices. Finally, in the section "The Pivotal Role of the Third Party," we highlight the pivotal role of third-party actors in introducing such a transformation process.[3]

THE CASE OF MULTI-EMPLOYERSHIP AT TRILOGI

The main employment issue in Trilogi at the start of our study was the income insecurity faced by its warehouse workers as a result their atypical working conditions. Trilogi is the European hub of a transnational airfreight express company and is based at a Belgian regional airport. Its activity is heavily constrained by the special characteristics of the logistics profession. This organization's core activity, at the heart of an international network operating on "just-in-time" principles, consists of receiving thousands of parcels from numerous European countries and ensuring that they are sorted overnight for delivery to their final recipients the next morning. At the centre of a process involving multiple entities, the company is subject to very strict time objectives, the meeting of which is of prime importance from a financial point of view. Each minute late costs thousands of Euros because any delay in delivering parcels means paying compensation to the clients.

Working conditions are particularly difficult in such a context: The work is carried out almost exclusively at night, within a framework of atypical contracts where part-time employment is the rule. The majority of staff members (1,100 out of the 1,500) work 4 hours per night, or 20 hours a week. Moreover, the nature of the warehouse tasks and the work of sorting parcels—a humdrum and tedious activity—favour the hiring of a poorly qualified, multicultural workforce that proves very complex to manage.

Still, the work can be planned, and peaks of activity are mainly seasonal and therefore predictable. In consequence, Trilogi offers most of its employees open-ended contracts. The workers value the predictability of their night shifts and the fact that this leaves them long periods of free time during the day. Yet they all express a need for greater income security. Whilst the salary paid for these 20 hours a week is considered reasonable, it is not enough to live on, and certainly not enough to support a whole family. As a result, many devote their free time during the day to other paid activity, sometimes as an employee or a self-employed worker, sometimes in the informal economy.

The results of our survey confirmed the need to undertake complementary work: 81 per cent of respondents considered that an extra job was necessary, and 22 per cent of respondents admitted to having an extra job. They also pleaded for support: 76 per cent of respondents considered that Trilogi should help people who were looking for an additional job, and 67 per cent would want to receive this assistance.

In Western European countries, the dominant model continues to be a full-time job with one employer, and many workers still consider that employers have a duty to offer full-time employment contracts. Multi-employership is viewed as a second choice and is difficult to manage in administrative terms. Our qualitative interviews showed, however, that needs and expectations differ according to individual living conditions, such as changes in the family situation, but also according to the "primacy" of the job at Trilogi: Is this job considered as supplementary to another activity, or is it viewed as the main activity? In the latter case, workers wished to keep their jobs for as long as possible and even to increase the number of hours they worked. All our interviewees believed that the various mechanisms to increase job security that Trilogi could provide had to remain available to them. Some workers thought that Trilogi had a moral obligation to offer additional work, whereas others considered that "security" needs belonged in the private domain and that the employer should not interfere.

Through our qualitative interviews, we discovered that approximately 30 workers combined part-time work at Trilogi with part-time employment at PiecElec, a company whose activity peak takes place between 5 p.m. and 9 p.m., just before Trilogi's activity peak. PiecElec is part of a global group that distributes electronic, electrical, and computer components. The arrangement at the time was organized completely informally, on the sole initiative of workers wanting to earn an income equivalent to a full-time job. This arrangement also allowed them to organize their working day in such a way as to keep a large portion of time available for rest and private activities, which constituted an important aspect of security from their point of view. Nonetheless, the informal nature of this arrangement generated harmful effects and risks for employers and workers alike, including fatigue, difficulty in handling health and safety incidents, difficulty in working extra hours at PiecElec and/or in attending training sessions before the shift at Trilogi, administrative complexity linked to the combination of two work contracts, and so forth. Both parties wondered how to transform this casual practice into a more sustainable and desirable arrangement.

AN ANALYTICAL GRID FOR THE EFFECTIVE DEVELOPMENT AND MAINTENANCE OF INTER-ORGANIZATIONAL EMPLOYMENT SCHEMES

Our involvement as action researchers changed the conditions of this informal practice, first by clarifying the respective needs, expectations, and individual situations of various actors, and second through the collective exploration of a scenario that would allow some formalization of the hitherto informal multi-employership practice: the creation of an employer pool by Trilogi and PiecElec (and possibly other partners) to hire the workers and share them between its members.

Between 2006 and 2008, we conducted a participative analysis of the whole process from its informal stage to its transformation through our action research. In addition to the study in Trilogi, we investigated similar situations and processes in three other projects. The description and evaluation of these innovation processes were carried out collectively during European project partnership meetings, which brought together the stakeholders of the projects themselves and other relevant actors. The action-research dynamic permitted the identification of approximately 30 dimensions characterizing the development of sustainable inter-organizational employment practices. The diversity of actors involved in the various projects generated a multitude of analytical categories, given the specific issues and interests related to each group to which they belonged (see Table 6.1).

In meeting after meeting, through multiple iterations between progress in the projects and our own theorization about the process, we revised and refined our inventory of dimensions. Approximately two-thirds of the original categories were eventually deleted either because the group considered them irrelevant—for instance, the degree of permanence of the practice, the type of collective guarantee provided by the practice, or its potential for extension—or because the categories were reformulated and integrated into other dimensions because of redundancy: For example, the "double voluntary action" category, defined as the "degree of respect for the principle of voluntary commitment to the practice for all parties concerned," was abandoned and integrated into the "deliberate/emergent" dimension. The description of the dimensions reflects the debate and negotiation among partner members of the projects. If we take, for example, the category "Formalized/informal," it was necessary to find a formulation that took into account the fear of bureaucracy expressed by employers as well as the need expressed by workers' representatives for an explicit, documented agreement.

Table 6.1 Specific Concerns of Partners

Type of partner	Concern
Workers	Informal, individual, optional, and flexible nature of the scheme
Workers unions	Area, modes of application, and systems of control of the scheme
Managers	Respect for the variation in respective needs for flexibility and security, and the voluntary involvement of various stakeholders
Public authorities	Formal nature of the agreements and integration of the latter into existing labour law
Local authorities	Intervention of third parties to ensure the coordination and management of the whole inter-organizational employment scheme

It is important to note that our descriptive grid essentially refers to procedural (Rawls 1971) and processual features of the scheme. As an analytical tool, it does not aim to characterize the content of the arrangement, but rather the conditions under which it can emerge and be sustained. The contingency of employment regulation practices makes it difficult to identify substantive features with universal relevance because they vary due to contextual evolution, respective needs, and power relationships among actors. Indeed, most of the dimensions we abandoned were related to the substance of arrangements: status, working conditions, cost effectiveness of the practice, well-being at work, and so forth. Table 6.2 presents an overview of our final set of descriptive dimensions.

These dimensions represent polarized categories to describe the various compromises characterizing each inter-organizational employment solution. If we apply these dimensions to the multi-employership practice at Trilogi, we can observe that this solution was purely *emergent*, based on a spontaneous initiative by workers. This arrangement was also *unilateral*, as multi-employed workers activated it autonomously. It appeared to be not very *reflexive*, in the sense that each stakeholder acted in accordance with its

Table 6.2 Analytical Dimensions for the Evaluation of Sustainable Development of Inter-Organizational Employment Schemes

Dimensions	Descriptions
Deliberate/ emergent	Voluntary negotiation, in reference to clearly expressed needs and accepted by the parties, versus gradual or recurring adjustments, in reference to needs that appear progressively
Multilateral/ unilateral	Involvement of the various stakeholders at each step of the process leading to the agreement versus involvement limited to some actors only
Reflexive/ not reflexive	Ability to make stakeholders depart from their usual roles in order to go beyond the defence of their initial interests versus upholding of pre-existing identity divides between stakeholders
Generic/ specific	Scheme applied uniformly to all members of one of the negotiating groups versus compromise responding to specific problems expressed by an individual or restricted group
Evolving/ static	Possibility of adapting and enriching the scheme versus rigidity of the negotiated scheme
Formalized/ informal	Scheme based on an official agreement between the stakeholders (explicit, documented, and accessible) versus informal agreement
Normed/ not normed	Existence (versus non-existence) of control modes allowing measurement of the gap between an objective and its implementation, and of a system of sanctions linked to non-compliance with norms
Consistent/ inconsistent	Coherent (versus dispensatory) linking of the scheme to other levels of regulation

traditional role and sphere, without considering other possibilities. In spite of the high number of workers who expressed the need to improve their income by holding two jobs simultaneously, such arrangements remained very *specific* because they were tailor-made by individuals who were more proactive and probably had more resources (social capital, professional qualifications, etc.) at their disposal than their colleagues. Moreover, we noted that multi-employership was here not subject to any kind of *formalization*: The employers were hardly aware of it. The consequence of this informal character was that no *norms* had been defined. Finally, we observed that the current arrangements, whilst shaky, were still *consistent* with the existing legal framework, apart obviously from cases of moonlighting.

SHIFTING THE CONDITIONS TOWARDS MORE SUSTAINABLE EMPLOYMENT SOLUTIONS

After this descriptive process, the second methodological step was to identify the most desirable position on the spectrum for each polarized category. Each dimension was discussed with each project's stakeholders and the European project partnership in order to find agreement on the characteristics of a sustainable inter-organizational employment solution in similar cases. Some dimensions needed little debate between parties. The *multilateral* nature of the process, the *evolving* nature of the employment scheme, and its *normativeness* were unanimously considered to be desirable goals in the interests of sustainability.

As far as the formalized/informal dimension was concerned, there was far more discussion about which position was the more desirable. Formalization was demanded by unions but was feared by managers concerned about too much bureaucracy and diminished room for manoeuvre. Eventually, the partners found agreement by introducing temporal dynamics into various dimensions: *Formalization* was thus considered as an objective, but one that could be developed progressively, with adjustments if needed.

Both workers and employers were indeed seeking flexible, customized, and voluntary arrangements. However, unions thought there was a risk of increased individualization, which might be beneficial for some (groups of) workers but detrimental to the community as a whole. They argued in favour of *generic* schemes while emphasizing the prior importance of a formalized framework agreement. Both parties agreed on the principle of making the new employment scheme accessible but optional for all workers to suit individual preferences.

This paradox between informality and openness to innovation, on the one hand, and the need expressed by many partners to design a new employment scheme consistent with the existing regulatory framework, on the other hand, also produced a lively debate. The conclusion, similar to that reached for the formalization dimension, was that the final target should be a *consistent* scheme emerging from lobbying efforts to transform existing employment regulation.

The researchers meanwhile appealed for *reflexivity* among the various stakeholders, explaining that distancing oneself from one's usual roles and ideas was a precondition for any kind of innovation. The acceptance of this dimension was the outcome of a long-running debate about the necessary involvement (or not) of third-party actors and the nature of the support they could provide to emerging partnerships. It was eventually agreed that the inclusion of third parties added value by ensuring a reflexive process among all stakeholders.

Some partners argued that emergent new employment schemes that allowed gradual adjustments should be retained, but after long debate, it was agreed that the voluntary engagement of each stakeholder could pave the way for other desirable dimensions. This meant as a consequence that *deliberate* schemes should be preferred to emerging ones.

Through this second methodological step, we converted descriptive dimensions into action variables that could enhance the sustainability of interorganizational employment solutions. Such dimensions reflect the way in which the various stakeholders considered "what could work" in developing sustainable solutions. This conversion process from descriptive into "prescriptive" variables relies on concrete experience, multiple debates, interactions, and iterations, rather than on ideological premises. It does not result from speculative normativity anchored in an ideal vision of labour regulation, but from a pragmatic process based on the observation of hard realities and orientated towards action (Dorf and Sabel 1998).

As shown in Figure 6.1, this set of "action" variables provides labour market actors with useful guidelines as they try to reconcile different needs for flexibility and security and seek to balance the interests concerned. The positions on the dimensions considered as allowing sustainability are circled with a dotted line. However, these polarized dimensions should not be understood as rigid dichotomies where a single position—left or right—for each category is favoured, but rather as pointers indicating a process from the right-side categories to the left-side categories, the latter being considered as dimensions for sustainability. Moreover, practices that do not satisfy the whole set of dimensions for sustainability should not be ruled out. Figure 6.1 indicates the initial state of multi-employership practice at Trilogi and shows which dimensions have scope for further effort to enhance its sustainability.

Even if the multi-employership solutions found by workers are by nature *evolving* because they change continuously according to needs and opportunities for supplementary work, the various stakeholders expressed a wish to move towards a more *deliberate* and *formalized* situation. The multi-employed workers as well as their employers noted that the initial situation generated numerous negative effects, notably in terms of health and safety at work and psychosocial risks. They also highlighted the fact that the

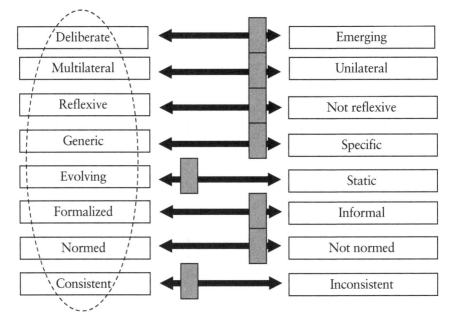

Figure 6.1   Characterization of the Emerging Multi-Employership Solution at Trilogi

frequent scheduling problems they encounter could threaten organizational flexibility.

In practice, we can observe some relationships, whether sequential or circular, between the dimensions. The intervention of a third-party actor—the research team—helped HR managers and union representatives to become aware of these issues and to become progressively involved. This gradually increased the *multilateralism* of the process and constituted a first step towards a more *deliberate*—because it aimed to clarify respective needs and expectations—and *reflexive* dynamic, allowing actors to glimpse possible new interactions within the emerging partnership.

These attitudinal changes also paved the way for greater *formalization* of the solution and the setting up of new *norms*. Until this point, this had been inconceivable because neither employers nor workers unions had felt fully involved. Previously, employers felt the need to exchange information and create informal rules in order to make coordinating different shifts easier, but now they admitted that such informality was probably suboptimal.

In the process, employees also agreed that durable compromises had to be more *generic*, in order to avoid reinforcing dualities: Multi-employership should become a full right available to any worker, rather than based on the initiative of those who are shrewder and more resourceful than their colleagues.

This scenario of formal pooling of workers between Trilogi and PiecElec must also take into account the need for *consistency* with existing regulations. In Belgium, the "employer pool" formula implies legal constraints in terms of a target (providing full-time and open-ended jobs to long-term job seekers) that does not correspond to the profile of multi-employed workers seeking greater financial security. It was thus a matter of obtaining the agreement of relevant authorities. But such agreement reinforced the need for an official commitment by employers and the formalization of their interactions.

THE PIVOTAL ROLE OF THE THIRD PARTY

This multi-employership case study shows how the descriptive categories can attain the status of conditions for a sustainable inter-organizational employment scheme. Our assumption is that moving the majority of pointers towards the left-hand side of Figure 6.1 will enhance the desirability and efficiency of the new employment solution.

As the theoreticians of institutional entrepreneurship have demonstrated (Fligstein 1997; Maguire, Hardy, and Lawrence 2004), a changing field may favour the political initiatives of organized actors. In such a context, frequent, short-term opportunistic strategies may reinforce asymmetrical power relations. There is a very high risk of achieving solutions beneficial to some parties only, to the detriment of the others. For these reasons, it is by no means sure that emergent practices will develop into balanced and sustainable solutions.

The debates among partners in the European project revealed that intervention by third-party actors may be crucial. In the Trilogi case, we—as researchers—tried to play this role in collaboration with the Chamber of Commerce, a prominent member of a local employers union, and others. It can be said that our reflexive actions helped to stimulate new dynamics and coax actors out of their normal routines.

The third-party actions we carried out were of two types. One was of a cognitive nature: Our actions consisted of supporting reframing processes (Schön and Rein 1994) and theorizing emergent practices (Maguire, Hardy, and Lawrence 2004), which helped to "de-enroll" and then "re-enroll" the actors in a renewed pattern of interactions that lay beyond their conventional power relationships. The idea was to build a decision-making process that was not based on the perpetuation of existing practices.

The second type was pragmatic, following the "democratic experimentalism" developed by Dorf and Sabel (1998). The main objective was to support the involvement of actors in experimental work in order to effect an inferential movement that gradually transforms perceptions and concepts and thereby permits incremental change to occur. The role of the third party thus consists of structuring intermediate stages, guiding the actors to test out alternatives, and reducing the uncertainty of the relational system through a gradual institutionalization of the new practices. However, we must admit that this role is precarious and requires permanent renegotiation (for further details, see Xhauflair and Pichault 2012).

CONCLUSION

Employment schemes are increasingly organized at the inter-organizational level, in order to deal with the need for flexibility and job security emanating from both employers and employees. However, a legal black hole remains at this level, together with a growing risk of asymmetrical power relationships. The challenge is thus to transform these emerging arrangements into sustainable and desirable forms of social regulation. The action research we carried out allowed us to develop an analytical grid to describe the process of such inter-organizational initiatives using a specific set of dimensions that reflect the attitudes of the various stakeholders involved in developing and evaluating the employment solutions. This model was then used to evaluate the sustainability of the initiatives and to design a collective strategy to gradually transform the current schemes into more sustainable solutions. The reflexive dynamic required during the entire action-research process also revealed the pivotal role of third-party actors in establishing the cognitive and pragmatic conditions that allow the various stakeholders to gradually modify their routines. Given the exploratory character of our research, further empirical research is needed on the role of third-party actors in the emergence of sustainable inter-organizational employment schemes.

NOTES

1. European Economic Interest Grouping.
2. The questionnaire was distributed to 1,172 of the company's workers, of every status and at every level of the organization, and achieved a response rate of 67 per cent (i.e., 785 respondents).
3. The two latter sections were designed within the framework of interdisciplinary research supported by the Belgian Science Policy Office (IAP Demogov, Belgian Scientific Policy, Phase IV, 2007–2011).

REFERENCES

Auer, Peter. 2010. "What's in a Name? The Rise (and Fall?) of Flexicurity." *International Journal of Industrial Relations* 52 (3): 371–386.
Cooke, Fang Lee, Jill Earnshaw, Mick Marchington, and Jill Rubery. 2004. "For Better and for Worse: Transfer of Undertakings and the Reshaping of Employment Relations." *International Journal of Human Resource Management* 15 (2): 276–294.

Dorf, Michaël, and Charles Sabel. 1998. "A Constitution of Democratic Experimentalism." *Columbia Law Review* 98 (2): 267–473.

Fligstein, Neil. 1997. "Social Skill and Institutional Theory." *American Behavioral Scientist* 40: 397–405.

Havard, Christelle, André Sobczak, and Brigitte Rorive. 2009. "Client, Employer and Employee: Mapping a Complex Triangulation." *European Journal of Industrial Relations* 15 (3): 257–276.

Maguire, Steve, Cynthia Hardy, and Tom B. Lawrence. 2004. "Institutional Entrepreneurship in Emerging Fields: HIV/AIDS Treatment Advocacy in Canada." *Academy of Management Journal* 47 (5): 657–679.

Marchington, Mick, Damian Grimshaw, Jill Rubery, and Hugh Willmot, eds. 2004. *Fragmenting Work: Blurring Organisational Boundaries and Disordering Hierarchies.* Oxford: Oxford University Press.

Pichault, François, and Virginie Xhauflair. 2007. "Rethinking Flexicurity at the Level of Work Situations." In *Flexicurity and Beyond*, edited by Per K. Madsen and Henning Jorgensen, 481–501. Copenhagen: DJOF.

Rawls, John. 1971. *A Theory of Justice.* Cambridge, MA: Harvard University Press.

Regalia, Ida, ed. 2006. *Regulating New Forms of Employment. Local Experiments and Social Innovation in Europe.* London: Routledge.

Schön, Donald A., and Martin Rein. 1994. *Frame Reflection: Toward the Resolution of Intractable Policy Controversies.* New York: Basic Books.

Sobczak, André. 2003. "Quelle régulation des relations de travail dans l'entreprise-réseau?" *Revue interdisciplinaire d'études juridiques* 51: 1–37.

Wilthagen, Ton. 1998. "Flexicurity: A New Paradigm for Labour Market Policy Reform?" Discussion Paper No. FS I 98-202, Wissenschaftszentrum Berlin für Sozialforschung, Berlin.

Wilthagen, Ton, and Ralf Rogowski. 2002. "Legal Regulation of Transitional Labour Markets." In *The Dynamics of Full Employment: Social Integration through Transitional Labour Markets*, edited by Gunther Schmid and Bernard Gazier, 233–273. Cheltenham, Northampton, UK: Edward Elgar.

Wilthagen, Ton, and Frank Tros. 2004. "The Concept of 'Flexicurity': A New Approach to Regulating Employment and Labour Markets." *Transfer* 10 (2): 166–187.

Xhauflair, Virginie, and François Pichault. 2012. "Du Tiers à la Tercéisation. Modalités d'une fonction essentielle pour l'émergence d'une regulation à l'échelon inter-organisationnel." *Négociations*, 2/2012 (18): 43–59.

Part III

Managing the Temporary Workforce

7 The Potential "Spillover" of Temporary Agency Work

Catherine E. Connelly, Daniel G. Gallagher, and Christa L. Wilkin

Worker behaviours do not take place in isolation; they are affected by what happens both within and outside the workplace. An illustration of this basic premise can be found in the extensive body of research that has been directed towards the study of "work–family" balance. Most basically, research on work–family balance is predicated on the underlying assumption that the demands and experiences that workers encounter in the workplace are likely to have an impact on their family relationships (Cousins and Tang 2004; Lewis and Cooper 1995). In a related vein, "family–work" balance suggests that family-related experiences influence an individual's workplace-related attitudes and behaviours (Karatepe, Kilic, and Isiksel 2008; Kinnunen and Mauno 1998). It has also been observed, in the "work–leisure" literature, that negative experiences, such as work-related stress or perceptions of unfair treatment, affect how workers spend their leisure time (e.g., Wilensky 1960). Inherent in these streams of research is the application of "spillover theory," which suggests that "positive or negative feelings in one life area may reach out and carry over into other facets of life" (Wiener, Vardi, and Muczyk 1981, 51). The notion of spillover has important implications for many types of work because it helps to account for the extent to which treatment or experiences in one context contribute to attitudes and behaviours in another environment.

We argue that spillover theory is especially relevant to the experiences of workers employed under temporary employment contracts because these individuals deal with multiple contexts either simultaneously or sequentially. For workers employed under temporary employment contracts, the potential relevance of spillover theory is even more apparent in the case of temporary agency workers. As frequently noted, the structure of most temporary employment arrangements can be characterized as intermediated or "triangular" in nature (Biggs and Swailes 2006). Under the structural relationship found in most temporary agency work (TAW) arrangements, workers have a contractual assignment and reporting relationship with the "agency," as well as a responsibility to fulfil work obligations to "client" firms (Galais and Moser 2009; Gallagher and McLean Parks 2001). As a result, temporary agency workers operate in an environment of multiple work-based organizations (i.e., agencies and clients). In such an arrangement, it is hypothesized that, in addition to the well-explored spillover between work and non-work relationships, there is a potential for spillover in multiple work arrangements. In other words, the nuanced aspects of TAW enable different kinds of spillover within the domain of their employment arrangements that are not as applicable to permanent work. This chapter will specifically focus on categories of spillover within the employment domain.

Temporary agency workers encounter potential spillover in the context of simultaneous associations with both temporary agencies and client firms. For example, an agency's treatment of a temporary worker can in turn affect that worker's relationship with a client firm. Conversely, there is the question as to what, if any, spillover for permanent employees might occur as the result of introducing temporary agency workers into client firms. Pushing the application of spillover even a step further, given the nature of TAW, one could anticipate that attitudinal and behavioural "spillover" might occur as temporary workers are assigned from one client firm to another. Attitudes such as commitment, trust, and loyalty, as well as citizenship or counterproductive behaviours, will therefore span organizational boundaries and affect other facets within the employment domain.

As implied in the previous discussion, we have divided possible "spillover" into three general categories: (1) temporary agency workers' responses that span the boundaries between temporary agencies and client firms (agency–client spillover), (2) the impact that temporary agency workers have on permanent employees (temporary worker–permanent employee spillover), and (3) the way in which temporary agency workers' experiences with current client firms affect their future experiences (client spillover). We discuss each type of spillover in the following sections of the chapter and provide a commentary concerning specific gaps in the extant literature, as well as avenues for future research. We will also seek to offer some practical implications for the management and organization of temporary agency workers.

AGENCY–CLIENT SPILLOVER

Temporary workers interact with multiple organizations. As a result, their behaviours, emotions, attitudes, and perceptions will not be limited to just one organization; workers' responses will flow across organizational boundaries. We define agency–client spillover as (1) that which occurs when temporary agency worker's attitudes and behaviours relating to their clients affect their attitudes and behaviours relating to the temporary agency and (2) when temporary agency worker's attitudes and behaviours relating to their agencies affect their attitudes and behaviours relating to the client organization.

Agency–client spillover is especially important to consider because it implies that temporary agencies and client firms will influence how workers respond to other organizations to which they are affiliated. One reason for this spillover is that because temporary agency workers interact more frequently with client firms, they are likely to respond to client firms as a means of reciprocating attitudes and behaviours towards temporary agencies. Another plausible explanation is that the psychological contracts of temporary agency workers are more complex than permanent employees because they hold more than one psychological contract with the multiple organizations that they are affiliated with (Guest 1998). Workers simultaneously fulfil their obligations to multiple organizations, namely, client firms and temporary agencies, through the same behaviour (Gallagher and McLean Parks 2001). Although these contracts are separate, there may be spillover between them, especially when one is breached. In this section, we draw on empirical research to discuss how temporary agency workers' attitudes and behaviours result in spillover between agencies and clients; we also discuss the positive and negative implications for organizations.

Organizational commitment is a particularly interesting attitude because temporary agency workers are, by definition, affiliated with multiple organizations, so the question of the source of workers' commitment is inherently interesting (Gallagher and Sverke 2005). Although one might expect that temporary agency workers should be only committed to or identify with their employer of record (the agency), there is substantial evidence that this is not the case. As Galais and Moser (2009, 591) observe, temporary workers "often feel like they belong to and 'work for' the client organization." There is further evidence to suggest that these workers often have simultaneously high levels of commitment to their agencies and their clients (e.g., Coyle-Shapiro and Morrow 2006; Hesselink and Van Vuuren 1999). As such, temporary agency workers' commitment to one organization (e.g., temporary agencies) is likely to magnify commitment to other organizations (e.g., client firms). Indeed, research findings suggest that commitment to the client firm is positively related to commitment to the temporary agency (Camerman, Cropanzano, and Vandenberghe 2007). This spillover is especially likely when values, norms, and expectations are congruent between organizations (McLean Parks, Kidder, and Gallagher 1998).

Despite research findings to the contrary, managers often expect temporary agency workers who are highly committed to their temporary agencies to be less committed to their client firms (Liden et al. 2003). This expectation may be due to a zero-sum mentality among managers that suggests that any gains in commitment for one organization result in losses for another organization. Further research is required to further explore implications of these assumptions.

For the same reasons that "organizational" commitment of temporary agency workers is inherently interesting, perceived "organizational" support (POS) of these workers is also worthy of further examination. Managers who support their workers by demonstrating concern for their well-being and valuing their contributions will spur reciprocal behaviours from workers in forms of higher commitment and better performance (Eisenberger et al. 1986). The effects of this support, however, may result in spillover between the agency and the client. Specifically, POS from one source (e.g., the agency) will affect workers' responses towards other sources (e.g., the client). Indeed, some empirical findings suggest that workers who perceive support from their client firms are more committed to their client firms and agencies (Connelly, Gallagher, and Gilley 2007). This finding is important because it suggests that both temporary agencies and client firms play a part in demonstrating that they care about temporary agency workers' well-being and value their contributions.

Despite the importance of POS from client firms, it is often difficult for temporary agency workers to obtain support from managers and colleagues (Isaksson and Bellagh 2002). Because agencies have a contractual obligation with workers, managers in client firms often believe that their only role is to assign job duties and not to support or encourage workers. Obtaining support is especially problematic with highly transitory workers, who often work for client firms for a short period of time. Some managers avoid investing in their temporary workforces and instead create strictly transactional agreements (Rousseau 1995).

As noted above, temporary agency workers' attitudes towards their temporary agencies and client firms span organizational boundaries, and as such, their behaviours also flow both within and between organizations. Temporary agency workers engage in organizational citizenship behaviours (OCBs) as a way to reciprocate favourable treatment from organizations, by engaging in discretionary behaviours that are "not directly or explicitly recognized by the formal reward system" but are important because they help organizations function more effectively (Organ 1988, 4). Indeed, research findings suggest that temporary agency workers may demonstrate their loyalty and commitment to their agencies through lower absenteeism, better job performance, and more OCBs towards client firms (e.g., Moorman and Harland 2002; Van Breugel, Van Olffen, and Olie 2005). It is interesting to note that not all studies have shown significant relationships between workers' job attitudes towards temporary agencies and their client-directed OCBs (e.g., Liden et al. 2003). These inconsistent findings may be partly explained by De Gilder (2003), who suggests that the level of OCBs directed towards client firms may also be affected by temporary agency workers' commitment to their co-workers.

Although there is some research to support the spillover of positive behaviours between temporary agencies and client firms, little research has examined spillover of negative behaviours. From time to time, temporary workers engage in counterproductive workplace behaviours (CWBs), or "voluntary behavior that violates significant organizational norms and in so doing threatens the well-being of an organization, its members, or both" (Robinson and Bennett 1995, 556). Some temporary workers say unfavourable things about their agencies or yell at their agents (Connelly, Gallagher, and Webster 2011). In the client context, they call in sick when not ill (Rogers 2000), work slower to extend billable hours (Henson 1996), or sabotage work processes (Rogers 2000).

Because temporary agency workers are affiliated with multiple organizations, spillover between contexts is able to occur. For example, it is not uncommon for temporary agencies to be dishonest about whether assignments will lead to full-time positions (Feldman, Doerpinghaus, and Turnley 1994). These misrepresentations are likely to result in negative reactions by temporary workers (e.g., resentment and lower commitment) towards client firms, even though the client was not necessarily involved in the initial misleading promises. Because both client firms and temporary agencies play an important role in shaping workers' psychological contracts, we see why both temporary agencies and clients should endeavour to make realistic promises to temporary agency workers.

Although both organizations are at risk of being harmed, there are some examples of CWBs that actually benefit client firms even though they are motivated by a desire to harm the agency. For example, if temporary agency workers are unsatisfied with their assignments, they can secretly agree to work "off the record" for client firms (Connelly, Gallagher, and Webster 2011). These actions are intended to harm the interests of the temporary agencies because the agency would thereby forfeit the income generated by the temporary worker as well as "kill fee" or contract termination penalty that would normally be paid by the client organization.

TEMPORARY WORKER–PERMANENT EMPLOYEE SPILLOVER

Another type of spillover that is applicable to temporary agency workers stems from the integration of temporary workers into a workforce composed primarily of permanent employees. We define temporary worker–permanent employee spillover as spillover that occurs when the presence of temporary agency workers affects the attitudes and behaviours of permanent employees. The hiring of temporary agency workers often has negative outcomes for permanent employees, even though blended workforces have the potential to benefit client firms through reduced employment costs and increased flexibility (Chattopadhyay and George 2001). Studies suggest that employing temporary workers negatively affects the attitudes and behaviours of permanent employees (e.g., Broschak and Davis-Blake 2006; Chattopadhyay and George 2001; Davis-Blake, Broschak, and George 2003). This negative spillover is reported to stem from conflict between workers as a result of internal competition, lower status for permanent employees, or an extra burden for permanent employees to train and supervise temporary workers (Broschak and Davis-Blake 2006).

The treatment of temporary agency workers may also affect permanent employees' perceptions of organizational fairness. For example, excluding temporary agency workers from task-related or social gatherings, such as team meetings and social events (Mitlacher 2008), is likely to lead permanent employees to perceive that temporary agency workers are treated unfairly (Feldman, Doerpinghaus, and Turnley 1994; Ashford, George, and Blatt 2007). Permanent employees frequently question this unfair treatment, but feel reluctant to bring such concerns to management (Geary 1992; Pearce 1993). As a result, perceptions of unfair treatment can negatively affect the ways in which permanent employees feel and behave towards their organizations, in terms of lower commitment and fewer OCBs. Because few empirical studies have explored the link between fair treatment and potential outcomes (Connelly and Gallagher 2004), future research is required to empirically determine how treating temporary agency workers affects permanent employees.

Spillover as a result of blending workforces negatively affects a broad range of permanent employees' attitudes, including their loyalty towards their organization, morale, organization-based self-esteem, and organizational attraction (Chattopadhyay and George 2001; Davis-Blake, Broschak, and George 2003; Morishima and Feuille 2000). Permanent employees also report lower trust towards their co-workers and organizations when they work with contingent workers such as temporary workers (Chattopadhyay and George 2001; Morishima and Feuille 2000). Permanent employees' trust is an important concern to organizations because higher trust is associated with more desirable individual behaviours, such as improved job performance and higher organizational commitment, as well as important organizational outcomes, such as increased profits and lower employee turnover (Dirks and Skarlicki 2004). Thus, when permanent employees work alongside temporary agency workers, permanent employees are typically less trusting, loyal, and attracted to their organizations and, consequently, less committed and more likely to resign.

The presence of temporary agency workers also has the potential to affect the interactions between permanent employees and supervisors. Conflicts can arise between temporary workers and permanent employees if the latter are unwilling to provide assistance or engage in other interpersonally aggressive behaviours towards their temporary colleagues. Because blending workforces may result in conflicts and tensions among workers, supervisors may thus be required to intervene to resolve worker differences (Geary 1992; Smith 1994). The impact of temporary employment on other individuals, such as supervisors, has rarely been studied in the temporary agency worker literature, and as a result, an opportunity exists for future research to explore this potential type of spillover in greater depth.

Although the findings of these studies have important theoretical and practical implications, there have been calls to more specifically address how temporary workers affect the attitudes and behaviours of permanent employees (Gallagher 2002, 2005). One approach would be to make clearer distinctions as to which type of contingent worker is under observation (e.g., direct hires or temporary agency workers) because spillover may depend on the form of contingent worker arrangement, as well as other aspects of the environment in which the work takes place (Aronsson, Gustafsson, and Dallner 2002; Davis-Blake, Broschak, and George 2003).

Based on the accumulated empirical literature, the reach of positive or negative attitudes or behaviours is therefore not limited to within-individual effects, as suggested by the current definition of spillover theory, which proposes that workers' positive or negative feelings affect other facets of their lives. A broader definition of spillover theory, which includes the influence of individuals' responses on other individuals and organizations, would imply that it is necessary to widen the parameters when considering the impact of TAW. Thus, we suggest that spillover theory should also be reframed with consideration of the potential impact that TAW has on more permanent workers.

CLIENT SPILLOVER

Our discussion thus far has focused on the interplay between temporary workers' affiliations with permanent employees, agencies, and client firms and has focused on the possible direct and indirect effects of one entity on another. It is possible, however, that this phenomenon also occurs between current and subsequent client firms. We define client spillover as that which occurs when temporary agency workers' attitudes and behaviours, in relation to one client, affect attitudes and behaviours towards subsequent clients. This possibility has not yet received substantial attention from empirical researchers, but it may lead to important practical and theoretical implications. For example, as we discuss subsequently, the use of contingent workers has the potential to result in the spillover of information between client firms.

Although temporary agency workers are not generally supposed to influence work practices of client firms (Furusten and Garsten 2005), contingent workers are exposed to different practices in client firms and use their skills in different settings. As such, they bring with them innovative practices and a depth of knowledge that can result in the transfer of valuable knowledge to client firms (Nesheim 2003). In a related vein, contingent workers who leave client firms may take private information with them; some competitors use contingent workers to imitate and adopt strategically important knowledge rather than develop it independently (Matusik and Hill 1998).

We similarly expect a potential spillover of temporary agency workers' attitudes and behaviours between client firms. For example, workers' responses elicited during one assignment are expected to affect their responses in subsequent assignments to the extent that workers' feelings about their current jobs are influenced by their prior experiences. These contrast effects would occur when workers compare their current jobs to their previous assignments with different clients. Such a phenomenon would be broadly analogous to what has been demonstrated in prior research; individuals tend to compare the treatment they receive from previous and subsequent supervisors (Van den Boss et al. 2005). When comparing their assignments, we expect that temporary workers will take into account contextual factors. Workers will be more likely to compare assignments that are similar in duration and job requirements.

Temporary agency workers who are treated favourably by client firms respond to this treatment by expressing higher commitment to their client organizations (Liden et al. 2003). These positive responses then influence workers' responses towards subsequent clients in such a way that workers who are treated fairly by previous clients will expect to be treated fairly by future clients. Based on this expectation, workers are more likely to feel and behave positively towards subsequent client firms, even before receiving fair treatment. Engaging in these positive behaviours would not be considered to be "altruistic," in the sense that temporary agency workers are not performing these behaviours for entirely unselfish reasons; however, these behaviours can still be classified as OCBs because they are not explicitly recognized by formal reward systems and they benefit the client. When temporary agency workers behave positively to subsequent client firms, they are likely to invoke similar reciprocal behaviours from client firms. This spillover will have especially important implications for client firms, because treating workers fairly should lead to a more committed workforce that engages in a greater number of OCBs.

Spillover between client firms, however, would be less positive when temporary agency workers experience and anticipate unfair treatment. Because they experience unfair treatment from co-workers and supervisors, temporary agency workers are "keenly attuned to how they are treated by others" (Ashford, George, and Blatt 2007, 82). For example, temporary agency workers are often marginalized because of their exclusion from work and social functions (Mitlacher 2008). This unfair treatment is expected to negatively affect their attitudes (e.g., lower commitment and trust) and behaviours (e.g., CWBs) towards future client firms. In essence, temporary agency workers reasonably base their responses to their current or future client firm on the social exchanges that they experienced with their previous client firms. These past negative responses could then invoke similar unfavourable responses (e.g., shorter contracts, less desirable contracts, contract termination) from subsequent client firms. Thus, as already noted with positive responses, the social exchange process between client firms and temporary agency workers originates with workers' negative responses towards client firms.

Because negative experiences have a far greater effect on individuals than positive experiences (Baumeister et al. 2001), as a result, we would expect a much stronger spillover of negative than positive responses. This stronger spillover is supported by affective events theory, which proposes that "negative events produce stronger physiological responses and stronger subjective feelings of affect" (Weiss and Cropanzano 1996, 320). Affective event theory suggests that work events trigger individuals' positive or negative emotional reactions, which influence their short-term and long-term attitudes and behaviours (Weiss and Cropanzano 1996). Work events, in the form of unfair treatment, therefore trigger negative responses from temporary agency workers and affect their expectations of unfair treatment from subsequent client firms. Temporary agency workers who respond negatively in later assignments pose detrimental consequences for client firms. In particular, they are at risk of having workers that exhibit lower levels of commitment and trust, and that engage in actions that are damaging for client firms and their members. Because negative spillover between assignments is stronger than positive spillover, organizations need to pay particular attention to the fair treatment of temporary agency workers.

The temporal element in the spillover between subsequent client assignments becomes especially salient. Spillover between current and subsequent client firms occur over time and flow from one domain (e.g., temporary agencies) to another (e.g., client firms). Individuals' responses to current client firms therefore influence their future responses towards subsequent client firms. Because this spillover occurs over time, longitudinal research is required to examine how workers' responses span multiple client firms. A summary of the different types of spillover is shown in Table 7.1.

PRACTICAL IMPLICATIONS

This chapter has shown that the employment of temporary agency workers has the potential to create positive and negative spillover, which results in direct and indirect consequences for the effective management and organization of the organizations that hire or employ them. Both client firms and temporary agencies, therefore, have legal and ethical obligations to manage temporary workers carefully. Temporary agencies have contractual requirements towards their workers, as well as an obligation to provide reasonable levels of support and fair treatment. Most client firms, in contrast, have fewer legal obligations, but we argue that they still have a responsibility to treat their agency workers carefully. Client firms are instrumental in shaping workers' psychological contracts and the conditions in which they work, so one would hope that managers would help to establish fair working conditions and mitigate potential staffing problems (e.g., turnover of temporary workers) that also affect permanent employees (Koene and Van Riemsdijk 2005). Creating fair working conditions also makes good business sense because positive attitudinal and behavioural spillover can be expected.

Table 7.1 Summary of Spillover Types

	Agency–client spillover	Temporary agency worker/permanent employee spillover	Client spillover
Definition	Temporary agency workers' attitudes and behaviours relating to client affect attitudes and behaviours relating to the temporary agency. Temporary agency workers' attitudes and behaviours relating to agency affect attitudes and behaviours relating to the client organization.	The presence of temporary agency workers affects the attitudes and behaviours of permanent employees.	Temporary agency workers' attitudes and behaviours in relation to one client affect attitudes and behaviours towards subsequent clients.
Entities involved	Temporary agencies, temporary agency workers, client organizations	Temporary agency workers, permanent employees	Temporary agency workers, client organizations
Examples of relevant attitudes and behaviours	• Organizational commitment • Perceived organizational support • Organizational citizenship behaviours (OCBs) • Counterproductive workplace behaviours (CWBs)	• Loyalty • Morale • Organization-based self-esteem • Organizational attraction • Trust • OCBs • CWBs	• Knowledge sharing • Organizational commitment • Trust • OCBs • CWBs

Managers at the client firm are able to improve work conditions through equitable treatment practices and policies (Isaksson and Bellagh 2002; Torka and Schyns 2007). Although there are some reasons why temporary agency workers must sometimes be treated differently than their permanent counterparts, organizational policies should clarify any necessary differentiation in order for this treatment to be fair. For example, excluding temporary agency workers from social gatherings is likely not defensible, but a compelling rationale could exist for excluding them from meetings where confidential personnel matters are discussed.

Because breached psychological contracts in one context may cause negative consequences in another context, it is also important for temporary agencies to make realistic promises to temporary agency workers. In particular, they need to be transparent in how assignment decisions are made (Galais and Moser 2009). Temporary agencies that mislead workers about the likelihood of permanent assignments are likely to breach workers' expectations, which can lead to negative attitudes (e.g., resentment) and behaviours (e.g., CWBs) towards the client. This outcome is particularly important for temporary agencies because they often operate in highly competitive environments; if their workers express negative attitudes and behaviours, client firms are more likely to employ their competitors.

FUTURE RESEARCH

Integrating temporary workers into an organization's workforce is potentially detrimental to relationships between managers and permanent employees (Davis-Blake, Broschak, and George 2003), so it is important that organizations carefully weigh potential benefits gained from using temporary agency workers against potential costs. Using temporary workers is one means for client firms to increase their flexibility, reduce their costs, and increase their knowledge (Matusik and Hill 1998), but employing temporary agency workers may cause negative spillover for permanent employees and require managerial resources to resolve conflicts and tensions among workers. Thus, temporary agency workers should be integrated into work groups with caution (Broschak and Davis-Blake 2006). Future research can empirically compare various possible approaches, such as an "integration" approach, whereby temporary workers and their permanent counterparts have similar responsibilities, or a "segregation" approach, where temporary workers' assignments are notably different, in terms of tasks, work organization, and compensation.

Longitudinal research is also suggested, in order to ascertain how contingent workers' attitudes change over time. It is possible that initial experiences, when the worker is introduced and socialized into the temporary agency and the client organization will affect how the worker interprets the way that he or she is treated. For example, a temporary worker who has a positive first interview with the agency and subsequent bad experiences with client assignments may be less likely to retaliate against the agency, in comparison to a temporary worker who has a neutral first impression. However, it is also possible that the protective effects of the initially positive interactions will wear off over time, or that negative behaviours or CWBs will escalate. These effects should be investigated empirically.

Although we have framed our discussion in the Canadian context, we encourage more research in a variety of international settings. In Canada, about 4 in 10 workers are employed in non-standard work arrangements, and close to 2 per cent of the workforce is employed through temporary agency arrangements (Galarneau 2005; Kapsalis and Tourigny 2004). Most Canadian temporary agency workers are employed on a full-time basis (83.9 per cent), almost half are young workers between 25 and 34 (43.5 per cent), and slightly more than half are male (52.5 per cent; Galarneau 2005). Large-scale international studies are necessary to examine whether worker and client attitudes towards temporary work are more positive in countries where TAW is more or less common.

Certain characteristics of the Canadian labour and sociopolitical environment may make this context particularly appealing to temporary workers. Unlike in the United States, Canadian workers have universal access to taxpayer-funded health care. As such, workers may be more inclined to take temporary jobs without benefits and be less likely to seek permanent employment solely in order to secure health care for themselves or for family members. Canada also has a larger proportion of low-paid work than European countries, especially in service industries (LaRochelle-Côté and Dionne 2009). This point is important because much of the employment growth has been in the service industry (Lin 2008). Again, future research is necessary to determine how national differences affect temporary workers' reasons for pursuing this type of employment.

CONCLUSION

The employment and treatment of temporary agency workers creates positive and negative spillover for organizations and their members. When client firms support temporary agency workers and treat them fairly, workers reciprocate by exhibiting higher levels of commitment to client firms and temporary agencies and engaging in more OCBs. Nevertheless, this spillover may also have negative organizational implications, in that employing temporary agency workers has the potential to negatively affect permanent employees' trust towards their peers and organizations. Both positive and negative spillover, however, have far-reaching implications for temporary agencies and client firms, especially when workers engage several agencies and hold multiple assignments (Gallagher and McLean Parks 2001). In order to be responsive to the growing numbers of temporary agency workers, we suggest that it may be useful to expand the traditional definition of spillover theory beyond a narrow focus on within-person effects. The expansion of "spillover" to include the impact of workers' attitudes and behaviours on co-workers, temporary agencies, and client firms provides a more nuanced understanding of these workers' experiences.

REFERENCES

Aronsson, Gunnar, Klas Gustafsson, and Margareta Dallner. 2002. "Work Environment and Health in Different Types of Temporary Jobs." *European Journal of Work and Organizational Psychology* 11 (2): 151–175.

Ashford, Susan J., Elizabeth George, and Ruth Blatt. 2007. "Chapter 2: Old Assumptions, New Work." *Academy of Management Annals* 1 (1): 65–117.

Baumeister, Roy F., Ellen Bratslavsky, Catrin Finkenauer, and Kathleen D. Vohs. 2001. "Bad Is Stronger than Good." *Review of General Psychology* 5 (4): 323–370.

Biggs, David, and Stephen Swailes. 2006. "Relations, Commitment and Satisfaction in Agency Workers and Permanent Workers." *Employee Relations* 28 (2): 130–143.

Broschak, Joseph P., and Alison Davis-Blake. 2006. "Mixing Standard Work and Nonstandard Deals: The Consequences of Heterogeneity in Employment Arrangements." *Academy of Management Journal* 49 (2): 371–393.

Camerman, Julie, Russell Cropanzano, and Christian Vandenberghe. 2007. "The Benefits of Justice for Temporary Workers." *Group & Organization Management* 32 (2): 176–207.

Chattopadhyay, Prithviraj, and Elizabeth George. 2001. "Examining the Effects of Work Externalization through the Lens of Social Identity Theory." *Journal of Applied Psychology* 86 (4): 781–788.

Connelly, Catherine E., and Daniel G. Gallagher. 2004. "Emerging Trends in Contingent Work Research." *Journal of Management* 30 (6): 959–983.

Connelly, Catherine E., Daniel G. Gallagher, and K. Matthew Gilley. 2007. "Organizational and Client Commitment among Contracted Employees: A Replication and Extension with Temporary Workers." *Journal of Vocational Behavior* 70 (2): 326–335.

Connelly, Catherine E., Daniel G. Gallagher, and Jane Webster. 2011. "Predicting Temporary Agency Workers' Behaviors: Justice, Volition, and Spillover." *Career Development International* 16 (2): 178–194.

Cousins, Christine R., and Ning Tang. 2004. "Working Time and Work and Family Conflict in the Netherlands, Sweden and the UK." *Work, Employment & Society* 18 (3): 531–549.

Coyle-Shapiro, Jacqueline A.-M., and Paula C. Morrow. 2006. "Organizational and Client Commitment among Contracted Employees." *Journal of Vocational Behavior* 68 (3): 416–431.

Davis-Blake, Alison, Joseph P. Broschak, and Elizabeth George. 2003. "Happy Together? How Using Nonstandard Workers Affects Exit, Voice, and Loyalty among Standard Employees." *Academy of Management Journal* 46 (4): 475–485.

De Gilder, Dick. 2003. "Commitment, Trust and Work Behaviour: The Case of Contingent Workers." *Personnel Review* 32 (5): 588–604.

Dirks, Kurt T., and Daniel P. Skarlicki. 2004. "Trust in Leaders: Existing Research and Emerging Issues." In *Trust and Distrust in Organizations: Dilemmas and Approaches*, edited by Roderick M. Kramer and Karen S. Cook, 7: 21–40. The Russell Sage Foundation Series on Trust. New York: Russell Sage Foundation.

Eisenberger, Robert, Robin Huntington, Steven Hutchinson, and Debora Sowa. 1986. "Perceived Organizational Support." *Journal of Applied Psychology* 71 (3): 500–507.

Feldman, Daniel C., Helen I. Doerpinghaus, and William H. Turnley. 1994. "Managing Temporary Workers: A Permanent HRM Challenge." *Organizational Dynamics* 23 (2): 49–63.

Furusten, Staffan, and Christina Garsten. 2005. "'New' Professionalism: Conditions for Expertise in Management Consulting and Temporary Administrative Staffing." In *Dealing with Confidence: The Construction of Need and Trust in Management Advisory Services*, edited by Staffan Furusten and Andreas Werr, 19–38. Denmark: Copenhagen Business School Press.

Galais, Nathalie, and Klaus Moser. 2009. "Organizational Commitment and the Well-Being of Temporary Agency Workers: A Longitudinal Study." *Human Relations* 62 (4): 589–620.

Galarneau, Diane. 2005. "Earnings of Temporary versus Permanent Employees." *Perspectives on Labour and Income* (Statistics Canada catalogue no. 75-001-XIE) 6 (1): 5–18.

Gallagher, Daniel G. 2002. "Contingent Work Contracts: Practice and Theory." In *The New World of Work: Challenges and Opportunities*, edited by Cary L. Cooper and Ronald J. Burke, 115–136. Oxford: Blackwell.

Gallagher, Daniel G. 2005. "Part-Time and Contingent Employment." In *Handbook of Work Stress*, edited by Julian Barling, E. Kevin Kelloway, Michael R. Frone, 517–541. Thousand Oaks, CA: Sage.

Gallagher, Daniel G., and J. McLean Parks. 2001. "I Pledge Thee My Troth . . . Contingently: Commitment and the Contingent Work Relationship." *Human Resource Management Review* 11 (3): 181–208.

Gallagher, Daniel G., and Magnus Sverke. 2005. "Contingent Employment Contracts: Are Existing Employment Theories Still Relevant?" *Economic and Industrial Democracy* 26 (2): 181–203.

Geary, John Francis. 1992. "Employment Flexibility and Human Resource Management: The Case of Three American Electronics Plants." *Work, Employment & Society* 6 (2): 251–270.

Guest, David E. 1998. "Is the Psychological Contract Worth Taking Seriously?" *Journal of Organizational Behavior* 19 (7): 649–664.

Henson, Kevin Daniel. 1996. *Just a Temp*. Philadelphia, PA: Temple University Press.

Hesselink, D. J. Klein, and Tinka van Vuuren. 1999. "Job Flexibility and Job Insecurity: The Dutch Case." *European Journal of Work and Organizational Psychology* 8 (2): 273–293.

Isaksson, Kerstin S., and Katalin Bellagh. 2002. "Health Problems and Quitting among Female 'Temps.'" *European Journal of Work and Organizational Psychology* 11 (1): 27–45.

Kapsalis, Constantine, and Pierre Tourigny. 2004. "Duration of Non-Standard Employment." *Perspectives on Labour and Income* 17 (1): 5–13.

Karatepe, Osman M., Hasan Kilic, and Bengi Isiksel. 2008. "An Examination of the Selected Antecedents and Outcomes of Work-Family Conflict and Family-Work Conflict in Frontline Service Jobs." *Services Marketing Quarterly* 29 (4): 1–24.

Kinnunen, Ulla, and Saija Mauno. 1998. "Antecedents and Outcomes of Work-Family Conflict among Employed Women and Men in Finland." *Human Relations* 51 (2): 157–177.

Koene, Bas, and Maarten van Riemsdijk. 2005. "Managing Temporary Workers: Work Identity, Diversity and Operational HR Choices." *Human Resource Management Journal* 15 (1): 76–92.

LaRochelle-Côté, Sébastien, and Claude Dionne. 2009. "International Differences in Low-Paid Work." *Perspectives on Labour and Income* 10 (6): 5–13.

Lewis, Suzan, and Cary L. Cooper. 1995. "Balancing the Work/Home Interface: A European Perspective." *Human Resource Management Review* 5 (4): 289–305.

Liden, Robert C., Sandy J. Wayne, Maria L. Kraimer, and Raymond T. Sparrowe. 2003. "The Dual Commitments of Contingent Workers: An Examination of Contingents' Commitment to the Agency and the Organization." *Journal of Organizational Behavior* 24 (5): 609–625.

Lin, Jane. 2008. "Trends in Employment and Wages, 2002 to 2007 (Catalogue 75–001-X)." *Perspectives on Labour and Income* 9 (9): 5–15.

Matusik, Sharon F., and Charles W. L. Hill. 1998. "The Utilization of Contingent Work, Knowledge Creation, and Competitive Advantage." *Academy of Management Review* 23 (4): 680–697.

McLean Parks, Judi, Deborah L. Kidder, and Daniel G. Gallagher. 1998. "Fitting Square Pegs into Round Holes: Mapping the Domain of Contingent Work Arrangements onto the Psychological Contract." *Journal of Organizational Behavior* 19 (7): 697–730.

Mitlacher, Lars W. 2008. "Job Quality and Temporary Agency Work: Challenges for Human Resource Management in Triangular Employment Relations in Germany." *The International Journal of Human Resource Management* 19 (3): 446–460.

Moorman, Robert H., and Lynn K. Harland. 2002. "Temporary Employees as Good Citizens: Factors Influencing Their OCB Performance." *Journal of Business and Psychology* 17 (2): 171–187.

Morishima, Motohiro, and Peter Feuille. 2000. "Effects of the Use of Contingent Workers on Regular Status Workers: A Japan-US Comparison." In *12th World Congress of the International Industrial Relations Association*, 316. Tokyo: IIRA.

Nesheim, Torstein. 2003. "Using External Work Arrangements in Core Value-Creation Areas." *European Management Journal* 21 (4): 528–537.

Organ, Dennis W. 1988. *Organizational Citizenship Behavior: The Good Soldier Syndrome*. Lexington, MA: Lexington Books/D. C. Heath.

Pearce, Jone L. 1993. "Toward an Organizational Behavior of Contract Laborers: Their Psychological Involvement and Effects on Employee Co-Workers." *Academy of Management Journal* 36 (5): 1082–1096.

Robinson, Sandra L., and Rebecca J. Bennett. 1995. "A Typology of Deviant Workplace Behaviors: A Multidimensional Scaling Study." *Academy of Management Journal* 38 (2): 555–572.

Rogers, Jackie Krasas. 2000. *Temps: The Many Faces of the Changing Workplace*. Ithaca, NY: Cornell University.

Rousseau, Denise M. 1995. *Psychological Contracts in Organizations: Understanding Written and Unwritten Agreements*. Thousand Oaks, CA: Sage.

Smith, Vicki. 1994. "Institutionalizing Flexibility in a Service Firm: Multiple Contingencies and Hidden Hierarchies." *Work and Occupations* 21 (3): 284–307.

Torka, Nicole, and Birgit Schyns. 2007. "On the Transferability of 'Traditional' Satisfaction Theory to Non-Traditional Employment Relationships: Temp Agency Work Satisfaction." *Employee Relations* 29 (5): 440–457.

Van Breugel, Gerla, Woody van Olffen, and René Olie. 2005. "Temporary Liaisons: The Commitment of 'Temps' Towards Their Agencies." *Journal of Management Studies* 42 (3): 539–566.

Van den Bos, Kees, John W. Burrows, Elizabeth Umphress, Robert Folger, James J. Lavelle, Jennifer Eaglestone, and Julie Gee. 2005. "Prior Experiences as Temporal Frames of Reference in Social Justice: The Influence of Previous Fairness Experiences on Reactions to New and Old Supervisors." *Social Justice Research* 18 (2): 99–120.

Weiss, Howard M., and Russell Cropanzano. 1996. "Affective Events Theory: A Theoretical Discussion of the Structure, Causes and Consequences of Affective Experiences at Work." In *Research in Organizational Behavior*, edited by Barry M. Staw, Larry L. Cummings, 1–74. Greenwich, CT: JAI Press.

Wiener, Yoash, Yoav Vardi, and Jan Muczyk. 1981. "Antecedents of Employees' Mental Health–the Role of Career and Work Satisfaction." *Journal of Vocational Behavior* 19 (1): 50–60.

Wilensky, Harold L. 1960. "Work, Careers and Social Integration." *International Social Science Journal* 12: 543–560.

8   Social Identity and Temporary Work

Dick de Gilder

For a long time, organization scientists have had a rather negative attitude towards temporary work. Based on a somewhat normative approach, many organization sociologists and organizational psychologists have argued that the opportunity for employers to install a flexible workforce, to hire employees on a temporary basis, mainly seems to benefit employers (e.g., Rogers 1995). It allows employers to hire—and fire—employees based on the needs of the employer, and it reduces labour costs and administrative duties (Pfeffer and Baron 1988). It can also lead to a competitive advantage over organizations that don't adopt temporary work in their human resources strategy (Lepak and Snell 1999). The needs of temporary employees are different from those of the employers, as they usually prefer a permanent position (e.g., Von Hippel et al. 1997). Several authors stated that temporary work leads to the alienation of temporary workers and to the creation of a low-status workforce in society that is dissociated from the regular labour market (Kalleberg, Reskin, and Hudson 2000; McLean Parks and Kidder 1994; Rogers 1995). Temporary employees also experience more stress, leading to poor well-being (e.g., Zeytinoglu et al. 2004). In fact, these authors suggest that negative consequences of temporary work are inherent to this form of employment. There is even some evidence that permanent workers' relationships with their colleagues (Broschak and Davis-Blake 2006), as well as their attitudes towards their organization, are affected negatively by employing temporary workers (e.g., Pearce 1993).

However, based on a social exchange, or psychological contract perspective, many authors argue that the disadvantages of temporary work are not limited to the employees alone. They argue that the relationship between the employer and the temporary worker is fundamentally different from the relationship between the employer and the permanent employees, and that this difference involves costs to the employer (e.g., McLean Parks and Kidder 1994). Temporary employees are supposed to have a *transactional* contract with the employer; they do what they have to do—provide labour for money—but nothing more. They would be inclined to withhold additional effort because they act in a calculative way: Only if it will yield them additional pay are they willing to exert themselves. They would compare themselves with permanent employees, who have all kinds of benefits that temporary employees do not have, and thus find it legitimate to expend less effort than permanent employees do. In contrast, permanent employees supposedly have a *relational* contract with the employer, a relationship that is based on much more than labour alone, such as long-term relationships with co-workers and their supervisor, investments in training by the organization and participation in pension plans. In this perspective, employees having a relational contract are more likely to be committed to the organization, perform well, and engage in organizational citizenship behaviour (OCB; e.g., Beard and Edwards 1995). OCB is discretionary, not part of the formal job description of the employee. Extensive research has shown that OCB, such as helping a colleague, volunteering for extra chores, and showing enthusiasm, contributes to organizational effectiveness (see Podsakoff and MacKenzie 1997).

However, although the social exchange perspective has dominated the discussion about the consequences of temporary work, it has received limited support. Besides a number of studies that demonstrate a relationship between contract type and behaviour, other studies do not report such differences between temporary and permanent employees (see De Cuyper et al. 2008, for an overview). In fact, there are some studies in which the opposite results are found. For instance, McDonald and Makin (2000) found no differences between temporary and permanent employees in the perceptions of psychological contract and actually report higher affective commitment and higher job satisfaction for temporary employees. One of my own studies (De Gilder 2003) showed that temporary workers were more positive about distributive justice than permanent workers but were nevertheless less committed to the organization and showed less OCB. Distributive justice can be regarded as an aspect of the psychological contract, given its definition: "the perceived fairness of the outcomes or allocations that an individual receives" (Folger and Cropanzano 1998, xxi). Given that the temporary employees in my study received less pay compared to permanent employees for similar work, it would be expected from a social exchange or psychological contract perspective that the perceived distributive justice would be lower for the temporary employees.

It is very difficult to exactly establish empirically what causes the variation in results across the reported studies. Typically, when there is much variation across studies, social scientists start searching for contingency variables, which help to explain under which circumstances phenomena occur (see De Cuyper et al. 2008; McLean Parks, Kidder, and Gallagher 1998). For instance, the study samples may differ, the status of temporary work may differ across countries, and the job characteristics may be different across studies. However, the efforts to compare work attitudes of temporary and permanent employees may be problematic because there are natural, inherent differences between these groups on a number of—potential— contingency variables.

In general, temporary employees, in comparison to permanent employees, are relatively young, have relatively low-level jobs with a low level of responsibilities, have lower tenure levels, and have lower experience levels. Furthermore, temporary employees may be heterogeneous in other respects: Some may work for temporary work agencies (TWAs), whereas others may be self-employed or seasonal workers. Variation across studies for each of these contingency variables may account for the heterogeneity in the results. However, it seems very unlikely that variation in any of these contingency variables can explain why a number of studies report findings that are opposite to the predictions that are derived from social exchange theory and the psychological contract perspective. Although it seems safe to conclude that differences in well-being and job-related attitudes are not necessarily tied to type of labour contract, there is still little understanding of the processes underlying the emergence of different attitudes and behaviours of temporary and permanent employees (see Ashford, George, and Blatt 2007).

The search for contingency variables has led to efforts to develop models and to perform studies in which a large number of contingency variables are measured in order to control for variations in the contingency variables. In a way, researchers have been trying to increase the power of measurement. However, the increasing power—and quality—of measurement cannot disguise the poor quality of the theories that are used to explain the behaviour of temporary employees. In fact, so far there is no convincing alternative for the—in this domain—insufficient social exchange approach. In line with De Cuyper et al. (2008), I argue that research should pay more attention to the motivations and expectations of temporary employees. I furthermore argue that social identity theory (SIT; e.g., Tajfel and Turner 1986) offers a theoretical basis to study these motivations and expectations, and that it can help to explain the inconsistent findings reported in the literature.

SOCIAL IDENTITY THEORY

SIT is a group dynamic theory that attempts to explain intra- and intergroup processes. The basic assumption in SIT is that individuals strive for a positive social identity. Positive identities can be derived from group membership, which lead to feelings of self-esteem. For this to occur, individuals have to be a member of a valued group, the in-group, that has qualities or characteristics that distinguishes the group from other groups, the outgroups. Individuals are likely to identify with the in-group, to contribute to the goals of this group, and to favour the other members of the in-group. For a comprehensive overview on SIT, see Haslam (2004).

The elegance of SIT is that it refers to relatively few socio-structural characteristics, identifiable and measurable aspects of the social situation, to explain why differences in identification with the in-group emerge and to what degree the level of identification with the in-group affects social interaction. An important focus of the theory—and subsequent empirical research—is on the consequences of identity threat: What happens if you are not a member of a valued group? When a group is not evaluated positively by other groups (i.e., when a group has low social status), group members are motivated to do something about the situation, to engage in action. However, there are distinct strategies that individuals may engage in, depending on the possibilities the situation has to offer.

If possible, individuals who are members of a low-status group try to leave their current group and get access to a higher-status group. This individual mobility strategy is not always possible, for instance, when you cannot leave the in-group. A simple example is that when you are a member of a disadvantaged ethnic minority, a group with a low-status position in society, it is not possible to change your ethnicity. It is also possible that the higher-status group does not allow you to become a member. In the terminology of SIT, in these situations the group boundaries are not permeable. Permeability of group boundaries is a precondition for individual mobility (e.g., Ellemers et al. 1988). Going back to the ethnic minority example, when the individual path to high-status groups is closed, groups may attempt to improve the social status of the group as a whole. This is a social change— or social competition—approach, which is also employed by the feminist movement, as well as by unions (e.g., by promulgating strikes against the— more powerful—employer to enforce better collective labour agreements).

There are marked differences in levels of identification with the in-group for individuals who believe that permeability is possible, as compared to those who don't. Individuals in low-status groups who believe they may become members of a higher-status group tend to dissociate themselves from their current low-status group members and actually display a high level of identification with the high-status group. This process is referred to as anticipatory socialization. Individuals in low-status groups who believe that the chances of moving to a high-status group are slim—or even non-existent— identify relatively stronger with their current low-status in-group. Just suggesting that permeability is a serious option can therefore have an immediate effect on the level of identification with the in-group.

SIT IN ORGANIZATIONS

Although SIT is developed to explain intra- and inter-group processes in general, it has been successfully applied to the more specific setting of organizations (for an overview, see Ellemers, De Gilder, and Haslam 2004). At first sight, SIT may seem to be inapplicable to temporary employees because as they are generally not really considered as core members of the organization, and it is far from evident they will identify with some indistinct group of temporary employees because they know they will be colleagues for only a short time. However, many psychological experiments have shown that even in seemingly meaningless groups, identification with the in-group can emerge, as well as in-group favouritism. The abstract concepts of status and permeability are also meaningful in organizational settings and for temporary employees as well.

It can be argued that temporary employees have a lower-status position in organizations, for a number of reasons. Employers generally don't invest in training of temporary employees, their pay level is usually lower, they can't profit from employee benefits, and they are the first to be dismissed at economic downturns, irrespective of their performance (e.g., Feldman, Doerpinghaus, and Turnley 1994). They have a high level of uncertainty, and if their attitude is critical or if they are part of a collective action, they can easily be punished with contract termination or by withholding contract extension. In line with SIT, there is already some evidence that temporary employees consider the permanent employees a high-status group and will prefer getting a permanent position too, thus joining the high-status group (Veenstra, Haslam, and Reynolds 2004; Von Hippel 2006).

As stated previously, the desire to become a member of a higher-status group is an insufficient precondition for actual actions to occur. A certain degree of permeability of group boundaries is necessary to incite individuals into action to improve their individual status. The pervasiveness of permeability in organizations has been demonstrated in research on the effects of mergers of organizations (e.g., Terry, Carey, and Callan 2001). A merger is rarely between equal-status organizations. One of the two parties usually has the lower status, and important positions in the new organization are usually taken by individuals from the higher-status organization. However, in mergers where individuals from the lower-status group believed permeability was possible, they showed high levels of identification and positive behaviour. Permeability in organization for temporary employees implies that they can get access to a more desired position, a permanent position, or, at least, a long-term contract. Opportunities to augment the status position of the group as a whole, social change, are difficult to realize (see Jordan 2003). First of all, individuals generally prefer individual mobility to efforts to attain social change (Haslam 2004). Furthermore, especially in situations where the contract duration is short, temporary employees may simply not have enough time to organize a collective action, or they may not be interested in engaging in collective action because its potential positive outcomes might not benefit the current group of temporary employees. Temporary employees usually are not represented by unions either because union membership among temporary employees is generally low (see Goslinga and Sverke 2003). Perhaps the likelihood of collective action increases when groups of temporary employees are sent out at the same time, but as yet there is no literature to support this.

Unfortunately, the application of SIT concepts in organizational settings is more complicated than in more controlled settings because individuals can be a member of several groups at the same time. Although most people find work groups important, they can also be a member of valued groups outside work situations and can derive self-esteem from these groups. Permeability is not only relevant for the organization in which individuals are working but also involves job opportunities on the labour market. When individuals have the experience—or the belief—that they can always get another job, even though it may not be in their current organization, they might not feel the need to attempt to get a permanent position in the organization for the time being. This analysis suggests that besides the feasibility of getting a permanent position, the desire to get a permanent position should be taken into account as well. In the literature, this distinction is described as voluntary versus involuntary temporary employees (e.g., Connelly and Gallagher 2004; see also Ashford, George, and Blatt 2007).

Another crucial issue is that permeability is not as fixed as suggested previously. There can be discrepancies between the objective permeability in a given situation and the perception of the situation by individuals. For instance, organizations may communicate that individual promotion is— or isn't—possible, but the individual response to the situation—and to the information—varies across individuals. Some individuals may think they have a chance despite information suggesting the opposite, and some people may be pessimistic even if there are frequent examples of temporary employees having made the transition. This attitude may even become a self-fulfilling prophecy, as these pessimistic people may be unlikely to be picked out of the group of temporary employees as candidates for a permanent position.

In line with SIT, temporary employees who believe the group boundaries are permeable (i.e., who think there is a chance to get a permanent position within the user organization) are expected to identify more strongly with the organization (which is hinted at by Chambel and Castanheira [2006])—and will display positive behaviour, such as high effort and high OCB—than temporary employees who are fatalistic about their opportunities. In the end, therefore, I argue that the effects of permeability of group boundaries can only be understood by looking at the *perceived* permeability.

A TYPOLOGY OF TEMPORARY EMPLOYEES

Basically, my proposition is that many of the results from field research on job attitudes and behaviour by temporary employees can be understood by studying (perceived) permeability and volition. Do individual temporary employees believe they have a chance to get a permanent position or not, and do they really want a permanent position within this organization or not? It is important to look at the two dimensions at the same time, in interaction. Neither one can explain sufficiently why there are so many differences in results across studies.

Adapting a model by McShane and Von Glinow (2003, 546), it is possible to propose a typology of temporary employees[1] along the two dimensions that describes four prototypes of temporary employees in different situations (see Figure 8.1):

1. Temporary employees in transition: those who strive for a permanent position and believe they can get it
2. Wannabes: those who want a permanent position but don't believe it is feasible
3. Transients: those who don't believe they can get a permanent position but who are indifferent about it
4. Free agents: those who believe they could get a permanent position but would reject it

It is conceivable that each of these prototypical temporary employees may be present in an organization. As I would predict that the combined effects of permeability and volition on individuals' attitudes and behaviour are different for each of these prototypes, results in a situation where there are several different prototypes present are likely to be inconclusive. On the other hand, reality about labour opportunities, in the sense that there is an objective permeability, is likely to steer the perceived permeability. That is, it seems likely that in any given organization there is a dominant situation that suggests which opportunities individuals have.

Of course, differences in objective—and perceived—permeability are associated with social capital as well. It is clear that better-educated temporary employees, as well as temporary employees who are trained in a field where there is a personnel shortage, have a better position on the labour market. In short, free agents and temporary employees in transition probably differ from transients and wannabes in the sense that they are likely

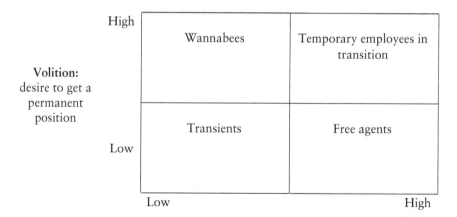

Figure 8.1 A Typology of Temporary Employees

to have more social capital. The essence may be, however, that although these groups of temporary employees are incomparable with regard to background variables and social capital, this does not mean that social capital is the explanatory variable. There are also highly educated people with many abilities who are wannabes nevertheless, who are likely to behave in line with the prototype of wannabes, not with their education level. I therefore argue that to understand the attitudes and behaviour of temporary employees it is enough to look at permeability and volition.

Although there are as yet no studies that were designed to test the validity of the typology, the results of several studies seems to lend some preliminary support. For instance, a closer look at the results from the McDonald and Makin (2000) study described previously suggests that the temporary employees in this study are temporary employees in transition: They seem to strive for a permanent position and believe they can get it. The fact that their job satisfaction and commitment to the organization is higher than for permanent employees may point to the anticipatory socialization effect described previously: They already identify with the organization, in the anticipation of becoming a member of the organization. Similar findings are reported by Von Hippel (2006), who interpreted their results using a social identity perspective. In their study, they asked the respondents—permanent and temporary employees—to distribute performance bonuses across the two groups. In the particular situation, there was no clear reason why any of the two groups would deserve a bonus. Although from an economic perspective it would make sense to favour the group you are a member of as you are likely to profit from the bonus, it turned out that not only the permanent employees but also the temporary employees allocated higher bonuses to the permanent employees, a rare phenomenon called out-group favouritism. As Von Hippel (2006) also demonstrated that the participating temporary employees generally had a preference for permanent work, the results could again point to anticipatory socialization, an explanation that is actually put forward by the authors.

Temporary employees do not regularly favour permanent employees. One study showed that some resentment of temporary employees versus permanent employees may emerge (Kossek et al. 1997). These temporary employees displayed in-group favouritism, in the sense that they indicated that temporary employees are better employees, who work harder for less pay. Because in the studied organizations temporary employees had few chances to get a permanent contract, these temporary employees could be described as wannabes: those who want a permanent position but don't believe it is feasible. In one of my own studies, I compared permanent and temporary employees who performed similar tasks in a hotel with regard to job attitudes and performance (De Gilder 2003). The temporary employees were students, who did not have the objective of staying indefinitely in the organization. It is not clear whether they could have had a permanent position within the organization, and I therefore cannot be sure whether these temporary employees should be classified as free agents or as transients. In any case, the results were not very positive for the hotel because the temporary employees scored lower on team and organizational commitment, made fewer attempts to help the organization improve their services, neglected their work more, performed less well, and were more often looking for a job outside of the organization. One study seems to compare free agents with temporary employees in transition (Marler, Woodard Barringer, and Milkovich 2002). They found that temporary employees who preferred a permanent contract with their (temporary) employer displayed higher OCB and performed better in comparison with the temporary employees who preferred a temporary contract, perhaps in the hope to attain such a permanent position. The temporary employees who might be considered free agents were relatively highly educated, had relatively high-status jobs, and were more often part of a dual-earner relationship. These temporary employees were performing relatively worse and showed less OCB.

The findings from the two latter studies involving free agents and/or transients have some intriguing implications. Free agents and probably also transients can be regarded as voluntary temporary employees. In the literature on temporary work, voluntary temping is associated with higher job satisfaction (e.g., Ellingson, Gruys, and Sackett 1998) and fewer somatic complaints (Isaksson and Bellaagh 2002). Voluntariness, therefore, is likely to be beneficial for the individual temporary employee, whereas the results from the studies by De Gilder (2003) and Marler, Woodard Barringer, and Milkovich (2002) suggest that voluntariness might lead to negative outcomes for the employers who take them into their service.

MANAGEMENT IMPLICATIONS

Based on general aspects of SIT and the typology introduced previously, some management implications can be formulated. Organizations can attempt to create permeability, to accept a relatively low motivation by temporary employees, or to increase the status of the temporary employee in the organization.

Based on the typology, it can be suggested that it makes sense for organizations to strategically create realistic opportunities for temporary employees to get a permanent position within the organization. A large majority of employees prefer permanent jobs (e.g., Von Hippel et al. 1997), and the combination of preference and feasibility is likely to enhance positive job attitudes and positive behaviour towards the organization. In this respect, it makes sense to communicate these opportunities, for instance, to make known how many employees were recruited from temporary employees in the past six months. It is important to realize that in social situations people are mainly guided by the *perceived* permeability, not necessarily the actual permeability.

Of course, there is a clear ethical issue at stake here: Employers may take advantage of employees by suggesting there are opportunities to get a permanent position while in reality there are not any. Such a strategy is likely to backfire, as temporary employees may soon realize they are duped. As is known from social justice literature, unjust treatment might lead to harmful behaviour towards the organization (for an overview, see Folger and Cropanzano 1998). Moreover, as stated before, if permanent employees perceive their employer as exploiting temporary employees, their attitudes towards the organization may be negatively affected as well (e.g., Pearce 1993).

There are many reasons why it is not always possible to create opportunities to let temporary employees make the transition to a permanent position in the organization. For instance, the economic situation may be unfavourable, the need for some specialist is just temporary, the amount of work may vary strongly, or the work may be season dependent. Based on the typology and SIT, employers may have to accept to a certain degree that temporary employees will be less motivated than permanent employees. A flexible workforce comes at a cost, but for many organizations, it will still be strategically sensible to have a partly flexible workforce. And sometimes temporary employees don't need to be extremely motivated to be valuable to the organization. For instance, some temporary employees may have special skills and may provide new knowledge that may be transferred to permanent colleagues.

Nevertheless, hiring temporary employees may have more far-reaching effects than on the attitudes and behaviour of temporary employees alone. Permanent employees are affected not only by the way employers treat temporary employees, as described previously (Pearce 1993), but also by an increase in the number of temporary employees, which may be seen by permanent employees as a threat to their position (Smith 1997; Broschak and Davis-Blake 2006) and may lead to increasing tensions and worse relationships among co-workers (Geary 1992; Chattopadhyay and George 2001; for an overview, see Davis-Blake and Broschak 2009).

For the sake of argument, I have used the concept of permeability in a very strict sense, as the actual transfer from one group to another, a change in job status. In SIT, however, permeability is not strictly tied to leaving one group and entering another. Permeability has a psychological meaning too, as it refers to group membership, becoming part of a—preferably—high-status group. Individuals can be team members and members of the larger organization at the same time and identify with both groups, just as temporary employees can be team members and temporary employees at the same time. I therefore speculate that there may be other ways for employers or for supervisors of units where the temporary employees are placed to create a certain level of—psychological—permeability in the organization. Treating people with respect generally makes people feel included in their current group and suggests that they are members of a high-status groups (Sleebos, Ellemers, and De Gilder 2006a, 2006b), which typically leads to high levels of identification. A temporary employee, who is properly welcomed, introduced, and bid farewell; who has an interesting work experience; and who has the possibility to make new friends, may have a sense of inclusion, of being a member of the organization, even if this membership has a short lifespan. In other words, such treatment and opportunities may contribute to an increase of the individual's social capital. It has been suggested previously (e.g., Feldman, Doerpinghaus, and Turnley 1994) that temporary employees should receive some training in the organization as well. Such an approach could also contribute to feelings of being included in the organization and actually contribute to the temporary employees' status and self-esteem, another increase in their social capital, as it may increase their skills that can be used elsewhere. In fact, such increased social capital may lead to a type of perceived permeability that so far has not been addressed in SIT: an individual's confidence that he or she is likely to get an interesting job elsewhere. Such confidence may buffer the individual psychologically against the prospect of having to leave the current organization.

It is not just the client organization that may have a task in treating temporary employees as valuable human resources. TWAs may also play a role in this respect, and in some cases, they are under pressure to do so or are even subjected to government laws that enforce such strategies. Dutch lawmakers have actually added another type of permeability that is specifically relevant for agency workers: Depending on the number of months—or years—an agency worker employee works for the TWA, he or she has more rights to claim from the TWA. After working one year for the TWA, the TWA is held to pay the agency worker even if there is no temporary job available, and after working three years for the TWA or 18 months for the same client organization, the TWA even has to offer a permanent position to the agency worker. Such laws are a clear incentive for the TWA to either help its agency workers to get a permanent contract elsewhere before it has to offer them a permanent position or to undertake efforts to keep finding temporary jobs for its agency workers with permanent contracts. In fact, when agency workers perceive that they are supported by the TWA, this may have positive consequences for the TWA as well because it may lead to high levels of commitment to both the client organization and the TWA (e.g., Liden et al. 2003). However, such laws might also have detrimental effects for agency workers, for instance, TWAs dismissing large numbers of their agency workers before they have been employed for a year. As yet, the laws' consequences cannot be established.

All in all, I repeat my proposition that differences in well-being, job-related attitudes, and behaviour towards the organization are not necessarily tied to the type of labour contract. It seems worthwhile to establish the validity of these speculations by studying the relative contribution of actions taken by employers or TWAs to increase the motivation of temporary employees.

NOTE

1. The line of argument pertains to all types of temporary employees, including temporary agency workers, self-employed individuals, and seasonal workers.

REFERENCES

Ashford, Susan J., Elizabeth George, and Ruth Blatt. 2007. "Old Assumptions, New Work." *Academy of Management Annals* 1: 65–117.
Beard, Kathy M., and Jeffrey R. Edwards. 1995. "Employees at Risk: Contingent Work and the Psychological Experience of Contingent Workers." In *Trends in Organizational Behavior*, vol. 2, edited by Cary L. Cooper and Denise M. Rousseau, 109–126. New York: Wiley.
Broschak, Joseph P., and Alison Davis-Blake. 2006. "Mixing Standard Work and Nonstandard Deals: The Consequences of Heterogeneity in Employment Relationships." *Academy of Management Journal* 49: 371–393.
Chambel, Maria J., and Filipa Castanheira. 2006. "Different Temporary Work Status, Different Behaviors in Organization." *Journal of Business and Psychology* 20: 351–367.
Chattopadhyay, Prithviraj, and Elizabeth George. 2001. "Examining the Effects of Work Externalization through the Lens of Social Identity Theory." *Journal of Applied Psychology* 86: 781–788.
Connelly, Catherine E., and Daniel G. Gallagher. 2004. "Emerging Trends in Contingent Work Research." *Journal of Management* 30: 959–983.
Davis-Blake, Alison, and Joseph P. Broschak. 2009. "Outsourcing and the Changing Nature of Work." *Annual Review of Sociology* 35: 321–340.
De Cuyper, Nele, Jeroen de Jong, Hans de Witte, Kerstin Isaksson, Thomas Rigotti, and René Schalk. 2008. "Literature Review of Theory and Research on the Psychological Impact of Temporary Employment: Towards a Conceptual Model." *International Journal of Management Reviews* 10: 25–51.
De Gilder, Dick. 2003. "Commitment, Trust and Work Behavior. The Case of Contingent Workers." *Personnel Review* 32: 588–604.
Ellemers, Naomi, Dick de Gilder, and S. Alexander Haslam. 2004. "Motivating Individuals and Groups at Work: A Social Identity Perspective on Leadership and Group Performance." *Academy of Management Review* 29: 459–476.
Ellemers, Naomi, Ad van Knippenberg, Nanne de Vries, and Henk Wilke. 1988. "Social Identification and Permeability of Group Boundaries." *European Journal of Social Psychology* 18: 494–513.
Ellingson, Jill E., Melissa L. Gruys, and Paul R. Sackett. 1998. "Factors Related to the Satisfaction and Performance of Temporary Employees." *Journal of Applied Psychology* 83: 913–921.
Feldman, Daniel C., Helen I. Doerpinghaus, and William H. Turnley. 1994. "Managing Temporary Workers: A Permanent HRM Challenge." *Organizational Dynamics* 23: 49–63.
Folger, Robert, and Russel Cropanzano. 1998. *Organizational Justice and Human Resource Management*. Thousand Oaks, CA: Sage.
Geary, John F. 1992. "Employment Flexibility and Human Resource Management: The Case of Three American Electronics Plants." *Work Employment & Society* 6: 251–270.
Goslinga, Sjoerd, and Magnus Sverke. 2003. "Atypical Work and Trade Union Membership: Union Attitudes and Union Turnover among Traditional vs Atypically Employed Union Members." *Economic and Industrial Democracy* 24: 290–312.

Haslam, S. Alexander. 2004. *Psychology in Organizations: The Social Identity Approach.* 2nd ed. London: Sage.

Isaksson, Kerstin, and Katalin Bellaagh. 2002. "Health Problems and Quitting among Female 'Temps.'" *European Journal of Work and Organizational Psychology* 11: 27–45.

Jordan, John W. 2003. "Sabotage or Performed Compliance: Rhetorics of Resistance in Temp Worker Discourse." *Quarterly Journal of Speech* 89: 19–40.

Kalleberg, Arne L., Barbara F. Reskin, and Ken Hudson. 2000. "Bad Jobs in America: Standard and Nonstandard Employment Relations and Job Quality in the United States." *American Sociological Review* 65: 256–278.

Kossek, Ellen E., Melissa Huber-Yoder, Domini R. Castellino, and Jacqueline V. Lerner. 1997. "The Working Poor: Locked Out of Careers and the Organizational Mainstream?" *Academy of Management Executive* 11: 75–91.

Lepak, David P., and Scott A. Snell. 1999. "The Human Resource Architecture: Toward a Theory of Human Capital Allocation and Development." *Academy of Management Review* 24: 31–48.

Liden, Robert C., Sandy J. Wayne, Maria L. Kraimer, and Raymond T. Sparrowe. 2003. "The Dual Commitments of Contingent Workers: An Examination of Contingents' Commitment to the Agency and the Organization." *Journal of Organizational Behavior* 24: 609–625.

Marler, Janet H., Melissa Woodard Barringer, and George T. Milkovich. 2002. "Boundaryless and Traditional Contingent Employees: Worlds Apart." *Journal of Organizational Behavior* 23: 425–453.

McDonald, David J., and Peter J. Makin. 2000. "The Psychological Contract, Organizational Commitment and Job Satisfaction of Temporary Staff." *Leadership and Organizational Development Journal* 21: 84–91.

McLean Parks, Judi, and Deborah L. Kidder. 1994. "'Till Death Us Do Part . . .': Changing Work Relationships in the 1990s." In *Trends in Organizational Behavior*, vol. 1, edited by Cary L. Cooper, and Denise M. Rousseau, 111–133. Chichester, UK: Wiley.

McLean Parks, Judi, Deborah L. Kidder, and Daniel G. Gallagher. 1998. "Fitting Square Pegs into Round Holes: Mapping the Domain of Contingent Work Arrangements onto the Psychological Contract." *Journal of Organizational Behavior* 19: 697–730.

McShane, Steven L., and Mary Ann von Glinow. 2003. *Organizational Behavior: Emerging Realities for the Workplace Revolution.* 2nd ed. New York: McGraw-Hill.

Pearce, Jone L. 1993. "Toward an Organizational Behavior of Contract Laborers: Their Psychological Involvement and Effects on Employee Co-Workers." *Academy of Management Journal* 36: 1082–1096.

Pfeffer, Jeffrey, and James N. Baron. 1988. "Taking the Workers Back Out: Recent Trends in the Structuring of Employment." In *Research in Organizational Behavior*, vol. 10, edited by Barry M. Staw and Larry L. Cummings, 257–303. Greenwich, CT: JAI Press.

Podsakoff, Philip M., and MacKenzie, Scott B. 1997. "Impact of Organizational Citizenship Behaviour on Organizational Performance: A Review and Suggestions for Future Research." *Human Performance* 10: 133–151.

Rogers, Jackie K. 1995. "Just a Temp: Experience and Structure of Alienation in Temporary Clerical Employment." *Work and Occupations* 22: 137–166.

Sleebos, Ed, Naomi Ellemers, and Dick de Gilder. 2006a. "Efforts by Respected and Disrespected Group Members." *Personality and Social Psychology Bulletin* 32: 244–255.

Sleebos, Ed, Naomi Ellemers, and Dick de Gilder. 2006b. "The Paradox of the Disrespected: Disrespected Group Members' Engagement in Group-Serving Effort." *Journal of Experimental Social Psychology* 42: 413–427.

Smith, Vicki. 1997. "New Forms of Work Organization." *Annual Review of Sociology* 23: 315–339.

Tajfel, Henri, and John C. Turner. 1986. "The Social Identity Theory of Intergroup Behavior. In *Psychology of Intergroup Relations*, edited by Stephen Worchel and William G. Austin, 7–24. Chicago: Nelson-Hall.

Terry, Deborah J., Craig J. Carey, and Victor J. Callan. 2001. "Employee Adjustment to an Organizational Merger: An Intergroup Perspective." *Personality and Social Psychology Bulletin* 27: 267–280.

Veenstra, Kristine, S. Alexander Haslam, and Katherine J. Reynolds. 2004. "The Psychology of Casualization: Evidence for the Mediating Roles of Security, Status and Social Identification." *British Journal of Social Psychology* 43: 499–514.

Von Hippel, Courtney D. 2006. "When People Would Rather Switch Than Fight: Out-Group Favoritism among Temporary Employees." *Group Processes & Intergroup Relations* 9: 533–546.

Von Hippel, Courtney D., Stephen L. Mangum, David B. Greenberger, Robert L. Heneman, and Jeffrey D. Skoglind. 1997. "Temporary Employment: Can Organizations and Employees Both Win?" *Academy of Management Executive* 11: 93–104.

Zeytinoglu, Isik U., Waheeda Lillevik, Bianca M. Seaton, and Josefina Moruz. 2004. "Part-Time and Casual Work in Retail Trade. Stress and Other Factors Affecting the Workplace." *Industrial Relations* 59: 516–544.

9 Double Employment Relationship in Temporary Agency Work

Psychological Contract with the Client and the Agency

Maria José Chambel

The number of temporary agency workers in Portugal almost doubled between 1998 and 2008, and the penetration rates increased from 0.6 per cent to 0.9 per cent (Ciett 2010[1]). These workers were legally employed by the temporary agency and utilized by the client organization. In these cases, the agency is the employer, and the temp must be given a written "labour contract" with detailed information on pay and working conditions at the user firm. Agencies must obtain a license to set up a business and are monitored by government, trade unions, and the Portuguese Ombudsman for the Temporary Workers. The contract between temporary agency workers and the agency can have different forms—fixed term or indeterminate—but the most common is of temporary tenure in the temporary work agency. The law restricts the type and duration of assignment at the client organization. The client can use temporary work to temporarily replace a permanent worker (e.g., with a health problem or on maternity/paternity leave), to develop a temporary task or project, or to adjust staffing levels in response to changes in market demands. The duration of the contract can vary and may be renewed but may not exceed a maximum of two years. In Portugal, in principle, the law calls for equal treatment with workers at the client organization as regards working hours, protection against accidents at work, and social security benefits.

The work arrangements of these temporary agency workers involve more transitory, lower-intensity connections with the firms in which they work, relative to traditional workers, leading Forde and Slater (2006) and Van Dyne and Ang (1998) to argue that these workers have lower levels of attachment to work organizations. From the perspective of the social exchange theory, Blau (1964) argued that people establish relationships with others according to expectations of return from invested resources and from the perspective of the norm of reciprocity. Gouldner (1960) established that people feel obliged to respond positively to favourable treatment received by others. Thus, we believe that when temporary agency workers experience an unfavourable employment situation, a more restricted employment relationship ensues.

One of the dominant frameworks used to define this employment relationship is the psychological contract theory (Shore and Tetrick 1994). The psychological contract refers to an individual's belief regarding the terms and conditions of a reciprocal exchange agreement between that focal person and the organization for which he or she works (Rousseau 1995). This psychological contract affects performance, motivation, absenteeism, extra-role behaviours, commitment, satisfaction, the intention to quit, dysfunctional behaviours, and psychological well-being, among other work behaviours and attitudinal variables (Millward and Brewerton 1999; Rousseau 1995). Therefore, we may consider that temporary agency workers' well-being, attitudes, and behaviours depend not on their worker status but on their psychological contract (see Figure 9.1; Chambel and Castanheira 2006; Guest 2004; McDonald and Makin 2000; Moorman and Harland 2002).

The first aim of this chapter is to explore the extent to which the psychological contract of temporary agency workers is related to their attitudes and behaviours. More specifically, we describe studies that have shown that temporary agency workers tend to be of the view that the client organization offers them fewer inducements and has fewer obligations towards them, and, thus, they develop a psychological contract with less emphasis on socioemotional or relational components and more on economic or transactional ones. Furthermore, this psychological contract can have a devastating effect because a relational orientation has a positive influence on outcomes both for the individual workers and for the organization, whereas the opposite pattern is found for the transactional orientation.

On the other hand, temporary agency workers render services simultaneously for two organizations. They are employed by an organization with which they have a formal contract, the agency, and they work for another organization, the client. Temporary agency workers have a psychological

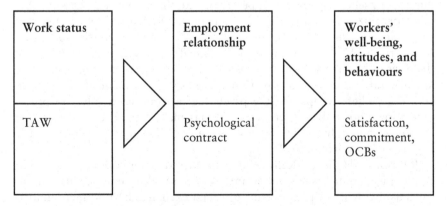

Figure 9.1 The Mediating Role of the Psychological Contract in the Relationship between Temporary Status and Workers' Outcomes

contract with both of the organizations (Claes 2005; Druker and Stanworth 2004; Liden et al. 2003). It is, therefore, an open question whether these two psychological contracts are related to each other and can influence important outcomes, such as the temporary agency workers' attitudes and behaviours (Conway and Briner 2009).

A second purpose of this chapter is to reflect on whether the psychological contract associated with the agency and the psychological contract with the client organization operate simultaneously and are related to each other. Indeed, we describe a study that shows that when temporary agency workers have extensive interaction with employees directly hired by the client organization, they consider that the agency has more obligations towards them. We also refer to another study where the perception of psychological contract fulfilment by the client is related to the perception of psychological contract fulfilment by the agency.

We consider this chapter to contribute to literature on the employment relationship as it explores the extent to which the psychological contract is applicable to temporary agency workers.

PSYCHOLOGICAL CONTRACT: MUTUAL EXPECTATIONS IN THE EMPLOYMENT RELATIONSHIP

The psychological contract is a crucial construct to explain the employee-employer relationship. It is based on the expectations of workers in terms of the kind of exchange established between them and the organization that employs them. In earlier formulations of the psychological contract, Argyris (1960) and Levinson et al. (1962) emphasized the exchange of implicit expectations where reciprocal acceptance creates the interdependence required to maintain the employer-employee relationship. It was defined by Schein as an "unwritten set of expectations operating at all times between every member of an organization and the various managers and others in that organization" (Schein 1980, 22). More recently, Druker and Stanworth (2004) and Millward and Hopkins (1998) have examined the psychological contract on the basis of beliefs and expectations regarding resource exchanges, motives, and general orientation to work. Rousseau (1995), by contrast, has considered that beliefs comprising the psychological contract involve reciprocal obligations, not only expectations. She has maintained the importance of exchange, but only of the employee's mutual obligations (Robinson and Rousseau 1994; Rousseau 1995).

Johnson and O'Leary-Kelly (2003) considered that in order to understand employment contracts it is important to conceptualize employment relationships as involving different forms of social exchange beyond mere mutual obligations. Coyle-Shapiro and Kessler (2002) analyzed the employment relationship including employer obligations and employer inducements. Guest (2004) stated that the concept of the psychological contract has been broadened to include not only mutual obligations but also fairness and trust. In this chapter, when we refer to the psychological contract, we will simultaneously analyze perceived obligations by the employee and general thoughts and feelings about work, including resource exchange and motives. These two conceptions of the psychological contract allow us to analyze different dimensions of the employment relationship. Organizational obligations are prospective and provide a way of viewing an exchange relationship as a sequence of contingent transactions that includes reciprocal promises about what will be exchanged (Dulac et al. 2008). General orientations are related to what is currently exchange and is based on the idea that the employee provides a set of resources to the organization in return for entitlements (Robinson and Brown 2004). In the first, the employee-organization relationship focuses on promises made; in the second, this relationship does not differentiate between promises and no promised expectations. When we simultaneously analyze obligations and general orientations, we acquire greater knowledge on the employment relationship exchange of temporary agency workers.

We can distinguish two *focuses* in psychological contracts. The first, the transactional psychological contract, centres essentially on economic interests and material benefits that the employee considers or expects to receive from his/her relationship with the organization. This psychological contract also includes fixed obligations or limited employment and restricted commitment/involvement. The second, the relational psychological contract, centres on socio-emotional interests like opportunities for growth, status, loyalty, and identification. This psychological contract includes obligations towards employee concerns, well-being, employment security, and providing internal and external job opportunities and more challenging goals (Anderson and Schalk 1998).

PSYCHOLOGICAL CONTRACT WITH THE CLIENT

As far as the relationship with the client is concerned, some studies have shown that when compared with workers directly hired by clients, these employees tend to develop a different psychological contract and consequently present lower levels of satisfaction, commitment, and organizational citizenship behaviour. Van Dyne and Ang (1998) developed a study in a bank and a hospital in Singapore and verified that contract status influenced the way in which employees perceived the employer's obligations in terms of job security, access to training, and opportunities for career development. For permanent employers, the content of the psychological contract included a broader set of obligations compared to temporary employees who perceived fewer and a narrower range of employer obligations.

Consequently, temporary agency workers showed less commitment to the client and fewer organizational citizenship behaviours. Coyle-Shapiro and Kessler (2002), in a study focusing on the local government in England, showed that temporary agency workers had a less favourable view of the exchange relationship—fewer organization obligations and inducements—and they were less inclined to hold positive attitudes towards the organization and less likely to engage in organizational citizenship behaviours. In the Portuguese context, we carried out a study with factory workers, in which we compared temporary agency workers with workers hired directly by the company, with permanent and fixed-term contracts (Chambel and Castanheira 2006). We found that in spite of carrying out identical tasks and sharing similar work contexts with the workers hired directly by the company, temporary workers received fewer benefits (they had a lower wage and fewer chances of prolonging their employment). In response, they restricted their employment relationship, highlighting the transactional motives, resources, and obligations and de-emphasizing the socio-emotional motives, resources, and obligations. This more restricted nature of the employment relationship tends to lead to less favourable attitudes and behaviours, which can become harmful to the client organizations for which they work.

Such findings have important analytical and theoretical implications and may well have significant consequences for the way in which temporary agency workers are managed. These findings are consistent with the predictions of the psychological contract theory whereby the temporary workers breach the traditions of relational contracting and are more likely to view their relationship with their employer in more narrow terms and receive fewer organizational inducements from that relationship. Consequently, they reciprocate this underinvestment by the client organization with less positive attitudes and are less likely to engage in organizational citizenship behaviours.

In addition, we may consider that a social comparison process could also be important to explain these differences between temporary agency workers and traditional employees. The worker establishes a comparison between him- or herself and his or her peers, and this process could be an important source of information for psychological contract evaluations (Ho and Levesque 2005) and fairness determinations (Lamertz 2002). These psychological evaluations are not limited solely to comparisons between promises made and present conditions but include comparisons throughout the duration of these workers' employment (O'Neill, Halbesleben, and Edwards 2007). When they work at the client, temporary agency workers establish a social comparison between their own situation and the one experienced by their *peers*—the workers hired directly by the client company. Temporary agency workers view the client organization as having a different employment relationship with their peers holding a permanent status: They have higher salaries, more promotion possibilities, and more employment security. When the temporary agency workers feel underestimated in terms of what they receive or would receive, they restrict their relationship.

This finding suggests that temporary agency workers need to be treated well in terms of inducements and obligations by the client and on the same level as the permanent workers, as recommended by the European Union (EU) commission that proposed a directive on temporary work, which includes equal-pay and equal-treatment principles (Commission of the European Communities 2002). Only with this action can management mitigate potential unfair perceptions from temporary agency workers and contribute towards the development of positive cognitive schemas that influence subsequent psychological contracts (Morrison and Robinson 1997).

In support of this, Koene and Van Riemsdijk (2005) verified with two case studies that client human resources management had effects on the temporary agency workers' employment relationship with the client. A narrow and transactional employment relationship defined by one of the given companies, based on calculation and on the expendability of temporary workers, resulted in a transactional psychological contract and a weak performance for workers. The other enterprise focused on special attention in selection, training, and support and in evaluation and appraisal, whereby temporary workers showed a socio-emotional psychological contract, affective attitudes, and appropriate behaviours.

Nevertheless, with temporary agency workers, the client transfers responsibility for staff to an agency, and the control of worker management may well be lost. Probably, in order to guarantee such suitable treatment offered on the part of the client, the agency would need to develop a close relationship. In order to guarantee a workforce of temps with a relational psychological contract with the client, related to appropriate attitudes and behaviours, the agency needs to make sure the clients support the temporary workers, showing concern for their well-being, paying attention to their needs, and complying with their different obligations.

SIMULTANEOUS ANALYSIS OF THE DOUBLE PSYCHOLOGICAL CONTRACT OF TEMPORARY AGENCY WORK

Agency workers differ from other employees in that they maintain a simultaneous employment relationship with two organizations: the agency, which is responsible for assigning resources to its clients and is considered to be the workers' employer; and the client, for whom the workers' perform a job and who provides direct supervision. The agency and the client organization have negotiated a shared employer relationship, creating a triangular system of employment relations (Kalleberg, Reskin, and Hudson 2000). Workers are, therefore, likely to be involved in two psychological contracts at the same time, one with the agency and one with the client, and simultaneously fulfil obligations to more than one employer through the same act or behaviour (Coyle-Shapiro, Morrow, and Kessler 2006; Gallagher and McLean Parks 2001).

Unfortunately, there is a scarcity of empirical studies that simultaneously analyze both psychological contracts of temporary agency workers with the agency and with the client. We could point out two studies that have compared these two psychological contracts. Druker and Stanworth (2004) developed a qualitative study—based on a mix of semi-structured interviews, non-participant observation, and focus group research—and analyzed the expectations of workers both by agencies and by the host. Their findings suggested that the temps had very limited expectations of the host organizations and developed a transactional psychological contract. On the contrary, they had positive expectations and experiences of the agency and developed a relational expectation of the psychological contract. Claes (2005) developed a study with 100 blue-collar employees from 12 agencies and compared temporaries' perceptions of the promises of their agencies and client organizations. She verified that temporary agency workers perceived more agency promises than client promises. Both studies demonstrated that temporary agency workers perceived a broader array of obligations by the agency over the client. This is more likely to occur because the agency performs human resources functions for temporary workers (recruitment, training, and compensation) and it is the agency that helps workers to gain competitive advantage in the labour market (screening possible new clients, gaining work experiences, and filling gaps in education and training) (Claes 2005). The agency recruits and selects the workers and provides them with salaries and human resources services, which can include the bureaucratic procedures, but also training, career development opportunities, performance assessment, and management. Thus, temporary agency workers develop perceptions concerning what they receive in their exchange relationships with their agencies. The agency tries to fulfil its *obligations* towards the employee, engendering a retention plan that intends not only to retain employees but also to engage them in a way that leads to positive, productive attitudes and behaviours for the period of employment (Lee 2001). Simultaneously, these workers also develop perceptions of the way in which they are treated by their client organizations (Liden et al. 2003). We can consider that the relationship they establish with the client organization relates positively to the relationship they establish with the agency. Their experience with the client has an impact on their relationship with the organization (McLean Parks, Kidder, and Gallagher 1998).

In the Portuguese context, we carried out a study with call centre workers and compared temporary agency workers that work on the premises of the client, along with workers directly hired by the client, with those working on specific premises only with other temporary agency workers (Chambel and Alcover 2011). We verified that when working at the client's premises, the temporaries worked alongside the client's employees and focused their attention on local comparisons. In spite of performing similar work tasks, the client's employees had more privileges and more career and training opportunities, they were taken on by a more prestigious enterprise providing them with the possibility of greater employability, and they had a better chance of continuing their work within that organization. Hence, the temporary agency workers that worked at the client developed a different psychological contract towards the agency when compared with temporary agency workers who were not in contact with workers directly hired by the client. The former considered the agency to have more obligations towards them, namely, those involving continued employment, training, and development, so that they could attain a situation more along the lines of their client colleagues (Ang, Van Dyne, and Begley 2003).The process of social comparison not only aids in explaining the psychological contract with the client but is also important in explaining the psychological contract with the agency. A social comparison was established by temporary agency workers between their own situation and the one experienced by their *peers*—the workers hired directly by the client company. These workers developed a perception with more obligations on the part of the agency to enable them to attain a situation more like that of their client colleagues.

On the other hand, we may consider that employees' perceived fulfilment of the client organization's obligations relates positively to their perceived fulfilment of the agency's obligations. This supposition can be supported by the idea that temporary agency workers might perceive that, as the actual employer, the agency has the *obligation* of assuring that they are being well managed by the client organization where they work. This means that they make sure that this client is fulfilling its own obligations. If the temporary agency worker perceives that the client organization is fulfilling its obligations, he or she will consider that the agency is doing a good job by fulfilling its obligations (by placing him or her with a "good" client). In a Portuguese study with white-collar temporary agency workers from four different agencies, we found that temporary agency workers established relationships with both their agencies and their client organizations and that these relationships were not mutually independent (Chambel and Fontinha 2009). As expected, we found that the perceived fulfilment of the client's obligations was positively related to the perceived fulfilment of the agency's obligations. The main statement that can be drawn from this evidence is the fact that the psychological contracts established between temporary agency workers and their agencies must not be approached alone because they are intrinsically related to the psychological contracts they establish with the client organizations where they work. In terms of practical implications, these findings support the idea that agencies that seek to increase their business are supposed to familiarize themselves with dual psychological contracts, finding a way to implement strategies where the client organization is seen as a partner (Coyle-Shapiro and Morrow 2006). These organizations should then be able to share effectively their responsibilities concerning human resources practices, meaning that agencies should define management strategies with each client organization based on the assessment of these webs of mutual expectations.

IMPLICATIONS FOR HUMAN RESOURCES PRACTICES

The social exchange theory has been approached as a major guideline to study employee organization relationships (Blau 1964). Relying on this framework, the psychological contract theory provides a solid basis for the assessment of the emerging contingent employment relationships. The web of mutual expectations created by contingent employment adds a particular relevance to the study of these relationships (Druker and Stanworth 2004). Although the EU commission proposed a directive on temporary work in 2002 that includes equal-pay and equal-treatment principles (Commission of the European Communities 2002) in its analysis of 15 countries, Nienhuser and Matiaske (2006) found that country-enforced principles of non-discrimination (e.g., in Portugal) had only limited influence on the compensation and working conditions of temporary workers. This means that the directive may be a necessary but insufficient step towards improving the terms and conditions of temporary workers. We consider the psychological contract analysis to represent another important step. The research shows that the development of a relational psychological contract is good for temporary workers as well as for permanent workers, and that it will contribute to effective equal treatment. For managers, the relationship with temporary workers is an investment, as with permanent workers, with return: the promotion of a relational psychological contract between workers and the organization, which promotes appropriate attitudes and behaviours.

Additional research is needed to explore workers' psychological contract with the agency, workers' psychological contract with the client organization, and the mechanisms that may connect these two relationships. Future research could focus on a better understanding of actions shared by the agency and the client organization, in order to assess how some particular practices affect the psychological contract fulfilment with both the agency and the client. We know that temporary workers are more responsive than permanent employees to higher levels of organizational support or higher amounts of inducements (Coyle-Shapiro and Kessler 2002) and that it is in the interest of organizations to ensure that temporary workers are well treated by the agency and the client organization (Guest 2004).

This research contributes to supporting the idea that social exchange theories are appropriate to explain temporary workers' attitudes and behaviours. As with permanent employees, temporary workers may develop a social employment relationship. It is in the interests of organizations to ensure that these workers are well treated because research demonstrates that the organizations will obtain a very positive response (Chambel and Castanheira 2006; Coyle-Shapiro and Kessler 2002; Guest 2004; Van Dyne and Ang 1998). Investments in temporary agency workers are good for both temporary workers and organizations, contributing to an effective employment relationship.

From a practical point of view, we consider that human resources practitioners focus on the dual psychological contracts established by temporary agency workers towards both their agencies and the client organizations where they work. Human resources practitioners from the agency and from the client should meet regularly and discuss human resources practices such as training and performance management, in order to define the best ways to manage these employees. Agency representatives should also frequently meet the employees and focus on their career paths—more specifically, on how working for that client can be a career advantage or not. This concern with employees' careers is quite important because human capital is regarded as the most relevant asset for an agency, and retention means placing the employees with *good* clients.

NOTE

1. In the 2011 Ciett report, data from Portugal are the same as those used in the 2010 report.

REFERENCES

Anderson, Neil, and René Schalk. 1998. "The Psychological Contract in Retrospect and Prospect." *Journal of Organizational Behavior* 19: 637–647.

Ang, Soon, Linn Van Dyne, and Thomas M. Begley. 2003. "The Employment Relationships of Foreign Workers versus Local Employees: A Field Study of Organizational Justice, Job Satisfaction, Performance, and OCB." *Journal of Organizational Behavior* 24 (5): 561–583.

Argyris, Chris. 1960. *Understanding Organizational Behaviour.* Homewood, IL: Dorsey Press.

Blau, Peter. 1964. *Exchange and Power in Social Life.* New York: Wiley.

Chambel, Maria José, and Carlos-María Alcover. 2011. "Psychological Contract of Call-Centers Workers: Employment Conditions, Satisfaction and Civic Virtue Behaviors." *Economic and Industrial Democracy* 32: 115–134.

Chambel, Maria José, and Filipa Castanheira. 2006. "Different Temporary Work Status, Different Behaviors in Organization." *Journal of Business and Psychology* 20: 351–367.

Chambel, Maria José, and Rita Fontinha. 2009. "Contingencies of Contingent Employment: Psychological Contract, Job Insecurity and Employability of Contracted Workers." *Revista de Psicología del Trabajo y de las Organizaciones/ Journal of Work and Organizational Psychology* 25: 207–217.

Ciett. 2010. *The Agency Work Industry around the World.* Economic Report. Brussels: Ciett.

Claes, Rita. 2005. "Organization Promises in the Triangular Psychological Contract as Perceived by Temporary Agency Workers, Agencies, and Client Organizations." *Employee Responsibilities and Rights Journal* 17: 131–142.

Commission of the European Communities. 2002. *Proposal for a Directive of the European Parliament and the Council on Working Conditions for Temporary Workers.* COM(2002) 149 final. Brussels: Commission of the European Communities.

Conway, Neil, and Rob B. Briner. 2009. "Fifty Years of Psychological Contract Research: What Do We Know and What Are the Main Challenges?" *International Review of Industrial and Organizational Psychology* 21: 71–131.

Coyle-Shapiro, Jacqueline A.-M., and Ian Kessler. 2002. "Contingent and Non-Contingent Working in Local Government: Contrasting Psychological Contracts." *Public Administration* 80: 77–101.

Coyle-Shapiro, Jacqueline A.-M., and Paula C. Morrow. 2006. "Organizational and Client Commitment among Contracted Employees." *Journal of Vocational Behavior* 68: 416–431.

Coyle-Shapiro, Jacqueline A.-M., Paula C. Morrow, and Ian Kessler. 2006. "Serving Two Organizations: Exploring the Employment Relationship of Contracted Employees." *Human Resource Management* 45 (4): 561–583.

Druker, Janet, and Celia Stanworth. 2004. "Mutual Expectations: A Study of the Three-Way Relationship between Employment Agencies, Their Client Organisations and White-Collar Agency Temps." *Industrial Relations Journal* 35: 58–75.

Dulac, Tanguy, Jacqueline A.-M. Coyle-Shapiro, David J. Henderson, and Sandy J. Wayne. 2008. "Not All Responses to Break Are the Same: The Interconnection of Social Exchange and Psychological Contract Processes in Organizations." *Academy of Management Journal* 51: 1079–1098.

Forde, Chris, and Gary Slater. 2006. "The Nature and Experience of Agency Working in Britain. What Are the Challenges for Human Resource Management?" *Personnel Review* 35 (2): 141–157.

Gallagher, Daniel G., and Judi McLean Parks. 2001. "I Pledge Thee My Troth . . . Contingently: Commitment and the Contingent Work Relationship." *Human Resource Management Review* 11 (3): 181–208.

Gouldner, Alvin W. 1960. "The Norm of Reciprocity." *American Sociological Review* 25: 161–178.

Guest, David. 2004. "Flexible Employment Contracts, the Psychological Contract and Employee Outcomes: An Analysis and Review of the Evidence." *International Journal of Management Reviews* 5/6 (1): 1–19.

Ho, Violet T., & Levesque, Laurie L. (2005). "With a little help from my friends (and substitutes): Social referents and influence in psychological contract fulfillment." *Organization Science, 16*(3): 275–290.

Johnson, Jonathan L., and Anne M. O'Leary-Kelly. 2003. "The Effects of Psychological Contract Breach and Organizational Cynicism: Not All Social Exchange Violations Are Created Equal." *Journal of Organizational Behaviour* 24: 627–647.

Kalleberg, Arne, Barbara Reskin, and Ken Hudson. 2000. "Bad Jobs in America: Standard and Nonstandard Employment Relations and Job Quality in the United States." *American Sociological Review* 65: 256–278.

Koene, Bas, and Maarten van Riemsdijk. 2005. "Managing Temporary Workers: Work Identity, Diversity and Operational HR Choices." *Human Resource Management Journal* 15: 76–92.

Lamertz, Kai. 2002. "The Social Construction of Fairness: Social Influence and Sense Making in Organizations." *Journal of Organizational Behavior* 23: 19–37.

Lee, Gregory. 2001. "Towards a Contingent Model of Key Staff Retention: The New Psychological Contract Reconsidered." *South African Journal of Business Management* 32: 1–9.

Levinson, Harry, Charlton R. Price, Kenneth J. Munden, and Harold J. Mandl. 1962. *Men, Management, and Mental Health*. Cambridge, MA: Harvard University Press.

Liden, Robert C., Sandy J. Wayne, Maria L. Kraimer, and Raymond T. Sparrowe. 2003. "The Dual Commitments of Contingent Workers: An Examination of

Contingents' Commitment to the Agency and the Organization." *Journal of Organizational Behavior* 24: 609–625.

McDonald, David J., and Peter J. Makin. 2000. "The Psychological Contract, Organizational Commitment and Job Satisfaction of Temporary Staff." *Leadership and Organization Development Journal* 21: 84–92.

McLean Parks, Judi, Deborah L. Kidder, and Daniel G. Gallagher. 1998. "Fitting Square Pegs into Round Holes: Mapping the Domain of Contingent Work Arrangements onto the Psychological Contract." *Journal of Organizational Behaviour* 19: 697–730.

Millward, Lynne J., and Peter M. Brewerton. 1999. "Contractors and Their Psychological Contract." *British Journal of Management* 10: 253–274.

Millward, Lynne J., and Lee J. Hopkins. 1998. "Psychological Contracts, Organizational and Job Commitment." *Journal of Applied Social Psychology* 28 (16): 1530–1556.

Moorman, Robert H., and Lynn K. Harland. 2002. "Temporary Employees as Good Citizens: Factors Influencing Their OCB Performance." *Journal of Business and Psychology* 17: 171–187.

Morrison, Elizabeth W., and Sandra L. Robinson. 1997. "When Employees Feel Betrayed: A Model of How Psychological Contract Violation Develops." *Academy of Management Review* 22: 226–256.

Nienhuser, Werner, and Wenzel Matiaske. 2006. "Effects of the 'Principle of Non-Discrimination' on Temporary Agency Work: Compensation and Working Conditions of Temporary Agency Workers in 15 European Countries." *Industrial Relations Journal* 37: 64–77.

O'Neill, Bonnie S., Jonathon R. B. Halbesleben, and John C. Edwards. 2007. "Integrating Employment Contracts and Comparisons: What One Can Teach Us about the Other." *Journal of Management Issues* 19 (2): 161–185.

Robinson, Sandra L., and Graham Brown. 2004. "Psychological Contract Breach and Violation in Organizations." In *The Dark Side of Organizational Behavior*, edited by Ricky W. Griffin and Anne O'Leary-Kelly, 309–337. San Francisco, CA: John Wiley and Sons.

Robinson, Sandra L., and Denise M. Rousseau. 1994. "Violating the Psychological Contract: Not the Exception but the Norm." *Journal of Organizational Behavior* 15: 245–259.

Rousseau, Denise M. 1995. *Psychological Contracts in Organizations.* Thousand Oaks, CA: Sage.

Schein, Edgar H. 1980. *Organizational Psychology.* Englewood Cliffs, NJ: Prentice-Hall.

Shore, Lynn M., and Lois E. Tetrick. 1994. "The Psychological Contract as an Exploratory Framework in the Employment Relationship." In *Trends in Organizational Behavior*, vol. 1, edited by C. L. Cooper and Denise M. Rousseau, 91–109. San Francisco, CA: John Wiley and Sons.

Van Dyne, Linn, and Soon Ang. 1998. "Organizational Citizenship Behavior of Contingent Workers in Singapore." *Academy of Management Journal* 41 (6): 692–703.

Part IV

Variety in the Development and the Organization of Temporary Agency Work

10 Agency Work in Italy
Limits and Unexpected Potentials of a Much-Debated Form of Employment

Ida Regalia

This chapter discusses the introduction, development, and consolidation of agency work in Italy, a process that began belatedly and in an extremely hostile context. The case enables reflection on the conditions in which a long-opposed institutional innovation may come about, on the character-istics that the subsequent process of institutionalization tends to assume, and on the prospects that open up—somewhat unexpectedly—for a socially sustainable regulation of flexible work.

The chapter consists of five sections. The first two sections ("The Intro-duction of Temporary Agency Work" and "Regulation by Initiative of the Social Partners") are devoted to the manner in which agency work was first introduced and regulated in Italy. The third section ("The Development of the Sector") presents data on the sector's development. The fourth sec-tion ("A Somewhat Unconventional Assessment") discusses the logic behind organizing and regulating the temporary supply of flexible labour in Italy. Finally, the fifth section ("Conclusion") closes with some general consider-ations suggested by the analysis.

THE INTRODUCTION OF TEMPORARY AGENCY WORK

For a long time in Italy, it was not legally permitted to use labour furnished by a subject other than the subject utilizing that labour. A law enacted in 1960 imposed an absolute ban on labour subcontracting, which was seen as a form of unacceptable labour exploitation.

The purpose of this prohibition was to put an end to uncontrolled labour intermediation by unscrupulous procurers who, in agriculture, in the con-struction industry, and in less developed areas of the country, eluded the established norms of working terms and conditions (Carinci 2011).

After Italy's *economic miracle* in the early 1960s, and with the increas-ing influence exerted by the trade unions, rejection of this odious practice of labour exploitation soon spread beyond the labour movement to public opinion at large. This was at the origin of both prolonged hostility against any form of labour supply by third parties and the close protection of labour provided by the law, which, in 1997 finally legalized the use of agency workers.

The Law of 1997

Already in the late 1970s, as firms' need for flexibility progressively increased, case law had begun to open breaches in the interpretation of the 1960 law (Carinci 2008, 26–28). Furthermore, there had developed other flexible forms of employment that were authorized and were socially accepted: in particular, various kinds of self-employment and fixed-term contracts. Alternatively, recourse was made to unlawful arrangements, such as bogus cooperatives or underground employment. Among the European countries, Italy had one of the highest levels of self-employment without employees (more than 25 per cent of all employment outside agriculture) and of irregular work (Carpo and Reyneri 1997).

However, the opportunity to introduce temporary agency work (TAW) only arose legally during the *social pacts* phase of the 1990s (Regini and Colombo 2011). Despite the persistence of strong resistance among the labour movement, a first commitment was made by the crucial 1993 tripartite agreement reached during the Ciampi technocratic government, in a period of severe political tension and high unemployment (Ferrera and Gualmini 2004). Operationally, TAW was finally legally introduced in 1997 by a centre-left government, which could guarantee that workers would be adequately protected, following the tripartite 1996 social pact on reform of the labour market.

The law 196/1997 defined the conditions in which TAW was permissible without abrogating the 1960 law. It established that labour could only be furnished by agencies formally authorized to do so by the Ministry of Labour, enrolled on a special register, and fulfilling specific requirements.[1] TAW could be used—solely as a temporary measure and in the instances and to the extent established by the sectoral collective agreements—in cases of temporary use of skills not normally present in the user firm and as a substitute for absent workers. Recourse to TAW was forbidden to replace workers on strike; at production units where collective dismissals, layoffs, or working time reductions had taken place in the same categories for which TAW was requested; or at production units that were noncompliant with health and safety norms or were considered dangerous production processes. Temps were to be hired on fixed-term or open-ended contracts by the agency, which assumed the functions of an employer. Their contracts had to be in written form, specifying the employment conditions, and had to stipulate equality of treatment with the user firm's workers of the same level.

Finally, in order to ensure suitable training for the job to be performed and adequate information on workplace health and safety, the law provided for the creation of a fund for the training of TAWs to be financed with obligatory deductions from their gross wages. The definition of further forms of worker protection was referred to collective bargaining.

In conclusion, the law was distinguished by its strong concern for preventing abuses in the use of labour by both agencies and user firms, as part of a more general endeavour to foster the growth of (regular) employment in which broad margins were left for bargained agreements between the industrial relations actors. TAW was substantially regarded as an occasion to match labour demand and supply. The restrictions imposed on its use prevented TAW from becoming a "functional substitute for the standard employment contract with the user firm" (Carinci 2008, 34).

The Reform of 2003

Some of these requirements were removed or attenuated by the provisions of a further law reforming the labour market, enacted in 2003 by the centre-right Berlusconi government, by which the use of TAW (renamed *leased labour*) was extended and liberalized.

As regards agencies, the law abolished the previous obligation that they must engage solely in labour supply, enabling their conversion into general employment agencies; however, it confirmed the prerequisites for the granting of ministerial authorization.

Some of the restrictions on the use of TAW were eliminated. Firms could now use TAWs simply for "reasons of a technical, productive, organizational or substitutive nature, even if referable to the ordinary activities of the user firm" (art. 20 of Legislative Decree n. 276/03, in Parlamento Italiano 2003). As previously, the law did not set quantitative or temporal limits on the use of TAW—referring their definition to collective bargaining—and the law confirmed the circumstances under which the use of TAW was prohibited. Finally, the law somewhat attenuated the protection of temporary labour. It reiterated the equal-treatment principle, but in a manner that might be less favourable to temps (Carinci 2008, 64–65).With the 2003 law, it became more convenient for firms to resort to TAW, given that they could also use it for reasons "referable to the ordinary activities of the user firm."[2] The potential market of the agencies therefore expanded.

REGULATION BY INITIATIVE OF THE SOCIAL PARTNERS

The legal introduction of TAW in 1997 immediately stimulated initiatives by unions and employers' associations to regulate its use more closely. New organizations were created to represent the two sides of industry, a new system of collective bargaining was launched, and specific bilateral bodies were instituted to furnish TAWs with dedicated forms of protection.

The Creation of New Actors

In regard to representation, the most innovative outcome was the creation by the three main trade union confederations of unions specialized in the crosswise representation of workers on non-standard contracts. Following previous experiences of self-organization, between 1997 and 1998 trade unions for atypical workers were set up, such as NIdiL (Nuove Identità di Lavoro), affiliated with the Cgil (the largest Italian trade union confederation); ALAI (Associazione Lavoratori Atipici e Interinali), recently renamed Felsa (Federazione Lavoratori Somministrati e Autonomi); and CPO (Comitati per l'Occupazione), now Uil-Temp, respectively affiliated with the other two large confederations, Cisl and Uil (Regalia 2003; Ballarino 2006).

These were unions that constituted a radical break with the past because they represented workers not on the basis of their sector, occupation, or firm, but on the nature of their employment contract. Hence, these were organizations that cut across the economic sectors on which the industry-based unions affiliated to the confederations are modelled in Italy. Operationally, they specialized in three areas: institutional action for the general representation of atypical labour; collective bargaining for temps and freelance workers; and the provision of individual services to workers with flexible contracts. Notwithstanding somewhat problematic relations with traditional sectoral unions, the new organizations attracted followings among workers and, above all, constituted the organizational premise for the development of collective bargaining in the TAW sector.

Regarding these agencies, they were initially organized into distinct associations according to their size or geographical location, as is typical of business associations in Italy. However, attempts were soon made to create a common front, which came about with the founding of Assolavoro in 2006, affiliated with Confindustria (the largest Italian employers' confederation). From the outset, the goals pursued included promoting the development of TAW, enhancing its image among public opinion, establishing a code of behaviour for associated agencies, and negotiating with the unions on how labour should be regulated in the implementation of the law's provisions.

The Development of Collective Bargaining

In effect, the first nationwide collective agreement for TAWs was already signed in 1998 (Paparella 1998); agency staff was instead to be covered by the agreement for workers in commerce. The TAW agreement fixed the maximum permissible duration of contracts with the same user firm, defined how the equal-pay principle was to be applied, and established the temps' union rights (the rights of assembly and to elect their representatives at the user firm). The 2002 second collective agreement marked the operational start-up of the sector's two bilateral bodies, aimed at furnishing TAWs with training and welfare provisions (see subsequent discussion). The third collective agreement of July 2008 took further steps towards the construction of a specific welfare system for temps. Besides extending information and trade union rights, and further specifying how the equal-pay principle was to be applied, the agreement provided for a number of benefits and support measures in regard to health and safety, workplace accidents, maternity, unemployment, personal loans, and transfers on long assignments. But the most innovative—and controversial—provision was a clause on the stabilization of workers, which stipulated their hiring on open-ended contracts by TWAs upon completion of a specified period of continued service with same agency.

This provision on stabilization had not been demanded by the unions but was proposed by Assolavoro in exchange for prolongation of the maximum duration of assignments at the same user firm, and to demonstrate that the agencies intended to shed their image as creators of precarious employment. However, it was opposed by a group of smaller agencies, which thereafter left Assolavoro and set up another association that signed a different collective agreement with minor trade unions. The main reason for the smaller agencies' dissent was their fear that they would be unable to bear the greater costs deriving from the agreement's implementation. However, it was also due to a more traditional interpretation of the role of TWAs; a role claimed to be that "of integrating workers into the labour market, with all legal and contractual protections, rather than replacing user firms as part of a misconceived welfare policy" (Lombardi 2008, 5).

In recent years, collective bargaining has mainly concerned measures to cope with the severe crisis that—amid the more general economic downturn—has hit the industry since 2008, in an effort to stabilize and add fidelity to the sector's human resources.

Therefore, an agreement to protect TAWs was reached among Assolavoro, the unions, and the Ministry of Labour in the spring of 2009, providing for a one-time payment to unemployed temps and the introduction of training vouchers intended to increase their employability. Another framework agreement to instead protect agency personnel was reached between Assolavoro and the national unions, which committed the parties to the greatest possible use of *job-security agreements*—that is, agreements negotiated locally to reduce, on solidarity principles, working hours to avoid dismissals.

In the same period, agency level collective bargaining began to spread. An example is the agreement signed by Adecco in 2009, which launched a plan to offer counselling, training, and outplacement based on an assessment of their skills to more than 3,000 temps who had not been ensured continuous employment. The intent was to stimulate workers to invest in their own employability while also maintaining relationships with the agency, within a framework of good trade union relations.

The Role of Bilateral Bodies

Attention to the needs of workers within a framework of good trade union relations also characterizes the activities of the two sector's bilateral bodies, Formatemp and Ebitemp, financed and managed jointly by the social partners.

The activity of Formatemp, devoted to the training of TAWs, stems from the provisions of the institutive 1997 law. As emphasized by a Ministry of Labour report, in Italy, concessions to the flexibility needs of firms have been offset by measures to promote the skills and employability of workers, and to support their incomes in periods of inactivity through the use of training (Ministero del Lavoro e delle Politiche Sociali 2006). How this principle of active labour policy is to be translated into practice has been defined by collective bargaining.

Currently, agencies set aside 4.5 per cent of the gross wages paid to temps for training purposes, and they must invest these sums in training schemes according to guidelines laid down by Formatemp and following a mechanism that encourages them to respond to the skill needs of local firms. It has consequently become a means by which demand and supply can be matched through training (Cecchi 2006, 8–9). This is all the more significant if one considers that in Italy active labour policies are still largely ineffectual.

This "micro system of tailor-made training for operators and users" (Caruso 2003, 1), on the one hand, adapts the skills of workers to the needs of firms; on the other hand, it enables individual workers to acquire versatile skills deriving from participation in formal training schemes, which increase their employability. At the same time, it is an instrument for the agencies to attract, enhance, and add fidelity to human resources.

The other bilateral body, Ebitemp, was established by the social partners in order "to reduce the hardships due to the discontinuity of service in temporary work," as observed by its first president, a former trade unionist and current vice president of an employment agency (Mattina 2009, 39). It furnishes benefits to workers not fully eligible for the protections available to permanent employees.

The measures envisaged include the creation of a fund for the issue of easy-term loans, payment of additional benefit in case of work-related injury, supplementary health coverage, allowances to support maternity and the use of day-care centres, one-time income support payment for unemployed workers, and a contribution for the expenses of transfers on long assignments. Finally, Fontemp—a fund financing supplementary pensions for workers in the sector—was created on the initiative of the social partners in 2011.

Overall, taking account of the features of the normative framework established in approximately 15 years by both legislation and the joint action of the social partners, today TAW is the most closely regulated and protected form of atypical work in Italy.

THE DEVELOPMENT OF THE SECTOR

Since its institution in 1997, the sector has undergone substantial development that exhibits distinctive features. This development is discussed here with reference to the characteristics assumed by agencies, trends in the use of TAW, and the profile and attitudes of agency workers.

The Agencies System

Compared with those of other European countries, the United States, and Japan, the Italian TAW sector is highly concentrated. Operating within it is a small number of agencies characterized by their large size in terms of turnover, number of branches, and employees per agency (Consiglio and Moschera 2008). In 2009, agencies in Italy still numbered only 85, and their branches 2,900, with a branch-to-agency ratio of fully 34.5, the highest in Western countries (Ciett 2011, 12–13). This close concentration is the outcome of strong barriers to entry and the demanding procedure to gain authorization established by the law.

Thus, the presence in this new market of mostly solid and reliable operators, able to undertake investments and commitments from a long-term perspective, has been favoured. Besides the large multinationals, Italian companies already operating in kindred sectors have also been entering the TAW sector. There have also been several cases of Italian agencies created for the occasion that are sometimes directly or indirectly supported by the unions (many of whose managers having been trade unionists).

Given these features (small number of agencies, large size, professionalism, high reliability of the largest agencies, and the presence of managers with connections to the labour movement), it is not surprising that one of the factors considered as fostering the sector's development has been the positive relationship of the agencies with the social partners (Consiglio and Moschera 2008, 14).

Over time, the system has consolidated through the opening of a widespread network of branches able to match supply and demand in a large part of the country, albeit with numerous differences. The diffusion process has, in fact, been driven by market perspectives as they have opened up, and the result has been a considerable concentration of agencies in the most developed areas of the country.

Trends in TAW

As regards business activity, the sector recorded sustained growth until 2008. The temps who had had at least one employment contract per year increased from approximately 25,000 (corresponding to 2,800 full-time equivalents) in 1998 to 582,000 (corresponding to 227,800 full-time equivalents) in 2008. The same period also saw an increased incidence of TAW on total dependent labour (rising from 0.1 per cent in 1999 to 1.2 per cent in 2008) and the incidence of TAW on total temporary employment (comprising also fixed-term contracts, seasonal work, and apprenticeships), which rose from 0.5 per cent in 1998 to 12.3 per cent in 2008. In other words, in 10 years, recourse to TAW grew in relative terms more than did total dependent employment and, in particular, more than other temporary forms of employment. There was a simultaneous growth in the average duration of assignments (47.6 paid days in 2008 compared with 41 days in 2003), although they still remained rather brief overall.

Between the end of 2008 and 2009, the market shrank by approximately one-quarter, mainly as a consequence of a dramatic decrease in demand by the manufacturing sectors that were most affected by the international economic crisis. However, as surveys by the Ebitemp observatory report show, the data for 2010 (and the estimates for 2011) indicate a substantial recovery, with the incidence on total employment returning to the levels of 2006–2007.

Even since the sharp downturn of 2008–2009, however, recourse to TAW remains concentrated on territorial and sectoral bases: More than two-thirds of temps are located in the northern regions, and approximately half in manufacturing. This signifies that the sector has considerable potential for development.

Profile and Attitudes of Agency Workers

On the supply side, the characteristics of temps have recently changed. Although temps continue to be predominantly Italian, male, and young, recent years have seen a substantial increase and stabilization in the incidence of foreign workers and female labour, and a continuously growing incidence of temporary workers over 40 years old.

Agency workers, therefore, constitute a growing pool of labour supply that has become more heterogeneous over time, and for which TAW offers diversified opportunities. Although it initially offered opportunities mainly for young people—and for males in particular—to enter the labour market, and especially the manufacturing sector, with time it has also become a means to re-enter the labour market or to retrain for transition to different service sectors by older workers, women, and foreign workers.

The data on training are significant. According to a Formatemp report (Ruda 2009), in 2008 courses were attended by more than 232,000 students—a large figure considering that the overall number of temps was approximately 582,000. The cost to the agencies was approximately €160 million, which accounted for just over 30 per cent of total spending on training by agencies in Europe. However, even more important is that (1) training was proportionally greater in the southern regions; (2) the type of training most frequently provided was vocational rather than basic and on the job; (3) a growing proportion of trainees were aged over 40; (4) the proportion of women (especially older women) and of foreign workers was expanding; and (5) the courses were mainly targeted for entry into the services sector.

Overall, the results are encouraging from the workers' point of view. According to the findings of a large survey conducted by the research institute of Cgil among workers who experienced TAW, whereas only 28 per cent of the interviewees had held a job six months before being hired by an agency, more than 55 per cent declared that they had a job after the temporary work episode. The authors state that "in the absence of efficient public services for employment, leased labour represents a useful mechanism of labour-market intermediation which increases mobility in the market and work opportunities, which [for many] can turn into stable employment" (Altieri, Dota, and Piersanti 2009, 10).

Not surprising, therefore, is the positive opinion expressed by the workers themselves: "Despite the temporariness of the contract," the authors write, "84 per cent declared themselves very or quite satisfied with the experience." Moreover, very few of them complained about the lack of protection, whereas this is an issue considered very critically by workers with other atypical forms of employment, especially freelance workers (Altieri, Dota, and Piersanti 2009, 10). An overall positive evaluation has been confirmed by the results of a recent European survey (Ciett 2011, 41–42).

In conclusion, the evolution of the sector has been characterized by a considerable expansion of recourse to TAW in the years prior to the crisis, and by a promising recovery in most recent years, as well as by greater differentiation of the reasons for, and modes of, its use.

Nevertheless, the extent to which recourse is made to this form of employment seems to fall short of its potential. This consideration prompts evaluation and discussion of the model's logic.

A SOMEWHAT UNCONVENTIONAL ASSESSMENT

In Italy, when TAW is discussed, the majority of observers stress its effects in terms of the uncertainty and future risks for workers due to the temporary nature and often brief duration of assignments. Thus, agency work is likened to other atypical forms of employment and considered another variant of precarious work. However, if account is taken of the normative frame of reference, TAW should not be viewed as simply a new form of employment introduced by legislators with a view to greater flexibility of the labour market, but as an opportunity that may contribute to improving the fluidity of the labour market, as well as to the security of TAWs. In fact, the legislative framework—which lays down stringent criteria for the accreditation of agencies; establishes clear norms to protect workers, delegating, however, their implementation to joint decision between the social partners; and leaves broad discretion to firms in the use of TAW—forms an institutional context that is particularly well suited to the coordinated and regulated growth of the market, to the advantage of both firms and workers.

For firms, besides the advantages of being able to cope with temporary needs or contingent necessities connected with production peaks, as well as with requirements of special skills to meet the evolution in the quality of product demand as highlighted by Bank of Italy surveys (Ebi-temp Osservatorio-Centro Studi 2008), there are the advantages that derive from the functions of supply/demand matching performed by the agencies, backed by their assignment to provide training for this purpose.

For workers, TAW may be a means to address, at least partially, the new risks that characterize work in a post-Fordist economy: risks connected with unemployment and job insecurity, but also risks of limited/inadequate development of human capital and of reductions in rights and deterioration in employment conditions (Regalia 2006, 2013). Indeed, as it is currently regulated, TAW offers workers the opportunity to enter/re-enter the labour market; to receive support in labour market transitions within a framework of rights and specific forms of protection; to develop their human capital by increasing their employability and, therefore, access to more stable positions in firms; and even to find new forms of stability within the system of tempo-rary work—this last point being connected with the norms on stabilization of employment by agencies as provided by the 2008 agreement.

From this perspective, the advantages for workers are potentially bet-ter than the advantages with other forms of temporary employment. What makes the difference is the role performed by the agencies (at least the larger and better-organized ones), which, within the institutional context described and in pursuit of their goals, are induced to invest in the enhancement of their principal form of capital—namely, the human resources to be made available to clients (Regalia 2013). Notwithstanding lack of empirical data, it is widely accepted that TAW is one of the main channels to enter the labour market in times of crisis, especially for the young. It is for this reason that one may ask why TAW has not developed to a greater extent. Answer-ing this question thoroughly would require adequate data, not so much on the attitudes of workers and trade unions as on the flexibility strategies pur-sued by firms. Such a study, to my knowledge, is not available. It is neverthe-less certain that for firms, recourse to TAW is one possibility that comprises not only fixed-term contracts but also (and especially) freelance contracts, labour furnished by cooperatives, and irregular or undeclared labour: forms of labour that are much less costly than regular TAW.

This reminds us that in 1997, in the aftermath of the law introducing TAW, well-informed observers of the Italian labour market had predicted that the new regulations would produce not the precarization of the labour market as foreseen by many, but instead its more transparent reorganization insofar as it would help bring to light irregular situations. At the same time, they expected the changes to be more qualitative than quantitative, owing to the distinctive characteristics of a labour market in which recourse to other forms of flexible employment relationships is standard practice (Carpo and Reyneri 1997).

It is highly likely that the continuing possibility for firms to rely on these other forms of employment hampers the more incisive development of TAW. Ironically, in the debate on precarization of the labour market, it is these forms of employment—less protected and regular, but widely used and that, for diverse reasons, enjoy broad social consensus—that have not been subject to thorough discussion (Mattina 2010).

More recently, however, things seem to be changing. It is significant that in the heated debate on the unsatisfactory functioning of the Italian labour market and its lack of universal protection, especially for the young—which intensified in early 2012 in view of its radical reform promoted by the technocratic Monti government—the way in which the TAW sector operates is perhaps the only point not being contested and implicitly viewed by all the parties involved (social partners and government) as good flexibility.

CONCLUSION

We may conclude by reprising, in more general terms, the main considerations suggested by the case analyzed. They concern the process of institutional innovation, the characteristics of the subsequent process of development and consolidation, and the problems that remain unsolved. As in other cases (Koene 2006), the introduction (or rather, the *legalization*) of TAW in Italy has been a process of institutional innovation in a socially hostile environment—and not only in the world of work—and within an adverse normative framework (prohibition imposed by law). If this process is to take place, it is not enough for the innovation to appear functionally useful (to firms that require more flexibility) and to have already been anticipated, to some extent, in practice (derogations from the law). Necessary for the purpose are new structural conditions that make it possible to break with the consolidated ways of framing the problem (positive and socially accepted management of the labour market) and institutional entrepreneurs who are able to draw advantage from the structural change, grasping the favourable occasion and intervening to present the change in a different and socially acceptable way (as an innovative means to create employment). This is what happened with the commitment to introducing TAW in the context of a more general agreement on reform of industrial relations in 1993, in a highly critical period experienced as an emergency by public opinion, and in which the initiative was taken by both a new (technocratic) government and by resourceful representatives of the social partners. But the agreement that change was possible was only a first breakthrough. A second step was necessary to move to the operational phase (also solicited by external pressures), in which the building of sufficient consensus on what to do resulted from a further agreement (the 1996 social pact for reform of the labour market). An opening was thus made for the first fundamental change to the law by a centre-left government and a pro-labour Minister of Labour. Other interventions specifying and readjusting the regulations (with a view to greater liberalization) followed in the next decade—on the initiative of centre-right governments.

In this case, therefore, the institutional innovation resulted from a prolonged process of institutional learning and consensus building, which required several breaches and subsequent action to readjust and soften the rules. Paradoxically, it was a centre-left government that promoted the creation of a private labour management market. In fact, it was the possibility to give guarantees, also symbolically, on the social sustainability of the change that made the innovation possible.

But this circumstance profoundly influenced the ways in which the new market could be regulated and consolidated. Both the law and interventions by the social partners contributed to establishing a new system, a system whose operation did not simply reflect market opportunities, but also aimed to strike a balance between the needs of firms and those of workers. This explains the scant restrictions imposed on the use of TAW by firms, on the one hand, and the attention paid to ensuring the protection of workers on the other, in a context of the responsibility of agencies and of the promotion of training and professional upgrading programs useful to both parties. In particular, TAW provides workers with an opportunity for flexible work of a regular kind, which increases their employability and opens up unexpected prospects of employment security, either as a stage in transition to stable contracts at the user firms or as an innovative route to stable employment at the TWAs themselves.

The system's main unsolved problems in the given institutional framework—and especially its limited diffusion—seem to depend on its strengths. It is precisely because TAW is intended to respond to the flexibility needs of firms while guaranteeing decent employment conditions for workers that it is more costly than other regular forms of temporary work. In fact, fixed-term contracts enable firms to save the fees charged by the agencies; by resorting to self-employed workers and freelance workers, firms can often impose employment conditions inferior to those of the corresponding dependent employees while also saving on social contributions (Berton, Richiardi, and Sacchi 2009). And TAW is evidently more costly than the less regulated forms of employment, which continue to be very widespread.

The shortcomings of the system, therefore, largely relate to the persistence of more unbalanced and perverse alternatives, resulting in unfair competition, but which in the short run can be convenient for many parties. And they perhaps also relate to a certain continuing cultural distrust in this form of employment. The issues to be addressed, therefore, are the characteristics of the Italian labour market, its dualism, and its insufficient transparency. And so too are the various factors (economic, but also political and cultural) that have enabled those characteristics to persist to date. To conclude, effective fulfilment of the virtuous opportunities furnished by the manner in which TAW has been introduced in Italy would require a structural reform of the labour market that modified its convenience to the actors, beginning with that of firms. When revising these conclusions, a major project of labour market reform, seemingly in the foreseen directions, has entered the political agenda. Were it successfully completed, new opportunities for the agency sector should open up.

NOTES

1. They had to be constituted as joint-stock companies or cooperatives engaged exclusively in the supply of TAW, suitably endowed with capital and organizational structures and operating with wide geographical coverage.
2. However, it seems that the labour courts often make restrictive interpretations of the reasons why TAW can be used, which the law leaves rather unspecified.

REFERENCES

Altieri, Giovanna, Francesca Dota, and Mariangela Piersanti. 2009. *Percorsi nel lavoro atipico: il caso dei lavoratori interinali.* Milan: FrancoAngeli.

Ballarino, Gabriele. 2006. "Between Institutionalized Concertation and Experimentation: The Regulation of New Forms of Employment in Lombardy." In *Regulating New Forms of Employment. Local Experiments and Social Innovation in Europe*, edited by Ida Regalia, 110–140. London: Routledge.

Berton, Fabio, Matteo Richiardi, and Stefano Sacchi. 2009. *Flex-insecurity. Perché in Italia la flessibilità diventa precarietà.* Bologna, Italy: Il Mulino.

Carinci, Maria, T. 2011. "Agency Work in Italy." Working Paper C.S.D.L.E. "Massimo d'Antona," 136/2011, University of Catania, Catania, Italy.

Carinci, Maria T. 2008. *Utilizzazione e acquisizione indiretta del lavoro: somministrazione e distacco, appalto e subappalto, trasferimento d'azienda e di ramo. Diritto del lavoro e nuove forme di organizzazione dell'impresa.* Turin, Italy: Giappichelli.

Carpo, Simonetta, and Emilio Reyneri. 1997. "Bill Introduces Temporary Agency Work into the Italian Labour Market." *Eironline*, IT9707308F. www.eurofound. europa.eu/eiro.

Caruso, Bruno. 2003. "Introduction." In *Formazione e Lavoro Temporaneo*, by Bruno Caruso, Giancarlo Ricci, and Loredana Zappalà. *I quaderni di Metis*, no. 4. Milan: Metis.

Ciett. 2011. *The Agency Work Industry around the World.* Economic Report. Brussels: Ciett.

Cecchi, Lisa. 2006. "Agenzie per il lavoro. Primo bilancio dopo la riforma." *Diario del lavoro*, 16 May. www.ildiariodellavoro.it/adon.pl?act=doc&doc=22821.

Consiglio, Stefano, and Luigi Moschera. 2008. *Dall'interinale ai servizi per il lavoro. Il comparto delle agenzie per il lavoro.* Milan: FrancoAngeli.

Ebitemp Osservatorio-Centro Studi. 2008. "Flessibilità interna, flessibilità esterna e lavoro interinale. I risultati delle indagini Banca d'Italia su Industria e Servizi." *News luglio 2008.* ebitemp.it/osservatorio-centro-studi/categorie-progetti -e-ricerche/ricerche-note-e-approfondimenti?page = 3.

Ferrera, Maurizio, and Elisabetta Gualmini. 2004. *Rescued by Europe? Social and Labour Market Reforms in Italy from Maastricht to Berlusconi.* Amsterdam: Amsterdam University Press.

Koene, Bas. 2006. "Situated Human Agency, Institutional Entrepreneurship and Institutional Change." *Journal of Organizational Change Management* 19 (3): 365–382.

Lombardi, Antonio. 2008. "Il rinnovo del Ccnl della somministrazione: un contratto che fa discutere." *Bollettino Adapt* 23. www.fmb.unimore.it.

Mattina, Enzo. 2010. *Elogio della precarietà. Il lavoro tra flessibilità, sussidiarietà e federalismo.* Rome: Rubbettino.

Mattina, Enzo. 2009. "Occupati a intermittenza: ecco il nuovo piano di welfare." *La Repubblica. Affari & Finanza* 4: 39.

Ministero del Lavoro e delle Politiche Sociali. 2006. *Rapporto 2005 sulla formazione continua.* Soveria Mannelli, Italy: Rubbettino.

Paparella, Domenico. 1998. "First National Collective Agreement Signed for Temporary Work Agencies." *Eironline*, IT9806170N. www.eurofound.europa.eu/eiro.

Parlamento Italiano. 2003. "Decreto legislativo 10 settembre 2003, n. 276." *Gazzetta Ufficiale. Supplemento Ordinario,* 235, 9 October. www.parlamento.it/parlam/leggi/deleghe/03276dl.htm

Regalia, Ida. 2003. "Decentralizing Employment Protection in Europe. Territorial Pacts and Beyond." In *Governing Work and Welfare in a New Economy. European and American Experiments,* edited by Jonathan Zeitlin and David M. Trubek, 158–187. Oxford: Oxford University Press.

Regalia, Ida. 2013. "Regional and Local Level Experiments for Labor Market Policy in Europe." In *Rethinking Workplace Regulation: Beyond the Standard Contract of Employment,* edited by Katherine V. W. Stone and Harry Arthurs, 155–173. New York: Russell Sage Foundation.

Regalia, Ida, ed. 2006. *Regulating New Forms of Employment. Local Experiments and Social Innovation in Europe.* London: Routledge.

Regini, Marino, and Sabrina Colombo. 2011. "Italy: The Rise and Decline of Social Pacts." In *Social Pacts in Europe. Emergence, Evolution and Institutionalization,* edited by Sabina Avdagic, Martin Rhodes, and Jelle Visser, 118–146. Oxford: Oxford University Press.

Ruda, Antonio. 2009. *Rapporto sintetico Forma. Temp 2008.* Rome: Osservatorio Nazionale Ebitemp.

11 Domesticating an Industry
The Swedish Case

Lars Walter

When publicly debated in Sweden, temporary work agencies (TWAs) are often described as a relatively new phenomenon on the Swedish labour market. However, a historical perspective reveals that they are not new: Private employment agencies and staffing agencies existed in Sweden as long ago as the end of the nineteenth century. They were banned in 1935, partly due to the dramatic events surrounding the labour disputes in Ådalen in 1931. Almost 60 years later, on 1 July 1993, a new law was enacted that deregulated the private employment agency industry and made TWAs legal again, long after the development of TWA industries in most other Organization for Economic Co-operation and Development (OECD) countries. Since then, there has been stable and continuous growth in the industry. In 2012, the penetration rate of this industry in Sweden was 1.3 per cent of the working population, an increase of more than 150 per cent since 1998 (Bemanningsföretagen 2013). During recent years, expansion has been more rapid in traditional blue-collar sectors, for example, the manufacturing and construction industries, making manufacturing the single largest sector for purchasing placement services at a rate of 22 per cent (Ciett 2013). According to Ciett (2013), about 60 per cent of the workers employed in the Swedish TWA industry are women, with more than 45 per cent of these being under 30 and close to 80 per cent under 45. More than 45 per cent of workers have a higher education, whereas 90 per cent have an educational level equivalent to secondary education or higher. More than 60 per cent of assignments have a duration of more than six months.[1] It is thus a fairly stable industry with a predominantly female workforce, which is, relatively speaking, well educated and young.

The purpose of this chapter is to describe the establishment of a Swedish TWA industry, as well as its business models and its managerial constraints. It also aims to show why this trend has not only managed to challenge the institutional framework of the Swedish labour market, but also given rise to relevant questions regarding the established understandings of the logic, functions, and effects of temporary agency work, and how these relate to the institutional conditions wherein they take place. The chapter will also show how different institutional conditions give rise to new business models and entail other types of managerial implications, related to the industries particular position in the labour market.

THE DEVELOPMENT OF THE INDUSTRY

In 1935, Sweden's private employment exchanges were outlawed. A new law gave the Swedish Labour Market Board a monopoly on all services matching supply and demand on the labour market. This board directed, coordinated, and developed labour market policy in Sweden; it also allocated government funding in the field. The reallocation of displaced labour to firms with higher productivity was the initial rationale of the extensive active labour policy that remains a key feature of Swedish economic policy. It is a key element of the so-called Swedish model (also known as the Rehn-Meidner model, named after two labour union economists who "invented" this model in the 1930s), a model aimed at promoting and accommodating structural change. The solidarity wage policy made pure wage competition unviable in the long term, acting to displace low-productivity firms (Edin and Topel 1997). The Swedish model made Sweden's unions generally cooperative towards productivity improvements, providing them with an important role to play as part of a system of industrial relations based on collective bargaining and collective agreements. For a long time, union membership has remained high in this country; by international standards, a large proportion of Sweden's workforce is unionized. Nowadays, approximately 70 per cent of all employees are trade union members (OECD).

The labour unions' strength, and their close connection with Sweden's Social Democratic Party, played a major part in underpinning the ban on private employment exchanges. Swedish legislation on private employment exchanges drew its content and legitimacy from an International Labour Organization (ILO) convention (no. 96). ILO Convention 96 was ratified by Sweden in 1950, reconfirming the ban on all private employment exchanges for profit-making purposes (SOU 2011). This had a particular impact on the companies that provided what was known as "ambulatory typewriting services"—that is, the provision of typewriting services by locating typewriters and typists in organizations requiring these services. Because Sweden's Labour Court interpreted these activities as a form of private employment exchange, a number of the companies providing the services were brought to court and declared guilty between 1957 and 1989 (Johnson 2010).

It is important to note that use of the terms "temporary work agency" and "temporary agency work" would be somewhat anachronistic in relation to events that took place in 1992. These notions did not form part of the vocabulary used when debating the issue publicly until the advent of initiatives to ease labour market legislation in the late 1980s and early 1990s. The debate centred on the definition of legitimate contracting and the distinction between providing placement services and other types of (consulting) services because companies had initiated activities on the fuzzy border between TWA services and subcontracting in the construction sector, particularly in shipbuilding (Fahlbeck 1978). In response to this development, new and more powerful legislation was implemented in 1971 (Lag 1970). In this new legislation, legal responsibility was extended to include not only the agency providing the staffing but also the client acquiring the services. It reinforced the interpretation of this type of "stretched" contracting activity in terms of being regarded as a placement activity and thus prohibited (Veldkamp and Raetsen 1972). Even during the period of deregulation of the legal framework in the 1990s, TWAs were not the centre of attention; instead, much of the debate centred on whether or not private employment services should be made legal as a way of increasing labour market efficiency and labour mobility (SOU 1997, 116).

In this context, Torbjörn and Ulla Murman, then the owners of Stockholms Stenografservice (later Teamwork, one of the first temporary staffing agencies to operate in Sweden following deregulation), established a trade association in the office work sector in 1967. The background to the creation of this association, Svenska Kontorsserviceförbundet (the Swedish Office Service Association), was the founding meeting of the international industry association Ciett (International Confederation of Private Employment Agencies). However, Svenska Kontorsserviceförbundet played a limited role within the industry, one important reason for this being the fact that it was a trade association—that is, a stakeholder group and not an employers' association. As such, Svenska Kontorsserviceförbundet (later renamed SPUR, Svenska Personaluthyrnings- och Rekryteringsförbundet) represented and lobbied on behalf of the interests of its members; however, it did not get involved in collective labour agreements, which had to be left to traditional employer associations and unions (Arhne, Brunsson, and Garsten 1998). This did not change until 2004 and the establishment of Bemanningsföretagen, an organization representing the TWA employers in the Swedish employers' federation Almega. In Sweden, having such an agreement was almost a *conditio sine qua non* for being active as an industry at all.[2]

The trade unions exerted a strong influence on the positioning of agency work in Sweden. From the trade unions' perspective, the companies involved in this particular type of contracting were teetering on the brink of, and even crossing the line into, lawlessness. Even after the 1993 deregulation had made TWA activities legal, the very powerful Swedish trade union confederation of blue-collar workers, LO, did not want to concern itself with the TWA industry at all. Their position did not change until 1998. The salaried employees union, Handelstjänstemannaförbundet (HTF), however, had already started to negotiate and sign collective agreements at an early stage. Because ambulatory typing bureaus constituted a kind of service activity, HTF, which organized white-collar workers in the service industries, started to sign agreements with three typing bureaus represented by the Employers

Association for Commercial and Service Organisations (Handelns Arbetsgivarorganisation, or HAO) in 1979. The 1979 agreement did not, however, cover temporary workers, only administrative staff within the agencies. In 1988, HTF and HAO entered into the first collective agreement concerning agency workers. Both agreements gave rise to a lot of conflict within the trade union movement. The HTF representatives were regarded as traitors by other unions, in particular by LO. The 1988 agreement included a guaranteed salary for agency workers who were not on an assignment. In congruity with all other industries, the TWA industry in Sweden thus started to become regulated via collective agreements. The principle of a guaranteed salary, laid down in the 1988 agreement, represented an important difference in relation to Dutch TWA practice because it entailed that the ambulatory workers would have a formal employment relationship, either by means of a limited duration or an open-ended contract with their agencies. However, an interpretation of the prejudicial importance of this agreement should not be overstated. At this point in time, Sweden was regarded as a country lacking an established TWA industry; activities that could be labelled as close to the fuzzy border with temporary agency work remained marginal and were not growing.[3] Formally, employment relationships other than those defined as limited duration or open-ended contracts remained illegal.

FORMAL ACCEPTANCE AND DEREGULATION (1991–1993)

Since the 1980s, the organization of the employment exchanges has been evaluated several times by the government, and several proposals have been put before the Swedish parliament to liberalize these activities. Eventually, deregulation was carried out in two stages. The first stage of liberalization was carried out by the Social Democratic government in 1991. A new law introduced several small exceptions to the ban on private employment exchanges. The focus of deregulation was private employment services but also included the legalizing of temporary agency work. However, TWAs were still subject to some important limitations, some of them similar to those imposed in the Dutch licensing system. The use of agency workers had to be preceded by a temporary need for additional labour, and workers could only be assigned to user companies via a TWA for a period of four months at most. Furthermore, there also had to be a written employment contract between the agency and the worker, a provision that formally aligned TWA practice with general labour practice.

By 1991, the TWA industry was still small and, according to Svenska Kontorsserviceförbundet, the placement of temporary workers at user organizations amounted to only approximately 500 man-years. Most of these workers were clerical staff. It was the 1993 deregulation that forcefully stimulated growth within the industry. This second stage of liberalization was introduced by the newly installed centre-right government in 1991; it announced that it was going to withdraw its allegiance to the ILO convention. In 1992, the government announced the formal abolition of the public employment exchange monopoly, something that was enforced on 1 July 1993. The purpose of this was to stimulate a better-functioning labour market. As there was no longer a ban on private employment exchanges, the new legislation meant, in principle, that there was no regulation of the TWA industry at all, with only a few important limitations. It was prohibited to charge individuals a fee and to prevent agency workers from taking a permanent job at user organizations. Thus, Sweden's regulation of TWAs was one of the most liberal in the world.

The decision to abolish the public employment exchange monopoly was criticized vociferously by the Social Democratic Party and the Left Party (Vänsterpartiet), which was afraid that an emerging TWA industry would lead to a more segregated labour market and the reduced matching of capacity on the labour market, in turn leading to increasing long-term unemployment. They argued that an increasing number of irresponsible businesses would enter the market, something that would lead to the destruction of the good labour relations characterizing the Swedish labour market. They were also critical of the way liberalization was being effected—in particular, the lack of a thorough investigation of the consequences that liberalization would entail.

The government pointed out that fears concerning irresponsible businesses and economic crime would be dealt with by the legal system and would not require any special regulation in law. In practice, however, two important labour market institutions limited the discretionary scope of the agency industry. Any disputes regarding working conditions would be handled via negotiations between social partners. Of special relevance here was the Co-determination Act (Lag 1976), which obligated the employers to negotiate with the trade unions when hiring subcontractors because, in principle, the trade unions would have the power to refuse the employers the use of temporary agency workers in the workplace. Furthermore, the unions could prevent an actual full deregulation of TWA practices through collective bargaining. In 1994, HTF renegotiated its agreement with HAO. A key condition of this was that employment through a TWA should take the form of an open-ended contract. The agreement also reconfirmed guaranteed salaries of 50 per cent of normal salaries when working in a placement.

Following the 1993 liberalization, several TWAs entered the market, both domestic ones, such as Proffice, and multinational firms—the latter mainly by means of acquiring Swedish TWAs, as Manpower did with Teamwork in 1996. The trade unions were worried about the expansion of TWAs on the Swedish labour market. They regarded agency work as bringing increased uncertainty to the labour market. They also expressed concerns about wage dumping and deteriorating working conditions for agency workers. Most importantly, it was regarded as ethically problematic for someone to profit from the victims of unemployment.

In 1997, an assessment and evaluation of the reform, which started in 1994, was completed (SOU 1997, 58). A committee appointed by the government suggested that the TWA industry should be subject to state authorization. It also proposed that all employment contracts with TWAs should be open ended. Successive limited-duration contracts were not regarded to be acceptable. However, the Social Democratic government did not follow the recommendations of the committee, instead being content to use authorization as a covert threat. This was surprising because, at this time, the Social Democratic Party had regained power, and the trade unions were expecting this left-wing government to reinstate the employment exchange monopoly or, at least, to re-enforce state authorization or other forms of regulating the industry. Given the government's rejection of the commission's proposals, the chairman of the latter encouraged social partners to set up their own regulation of the industry. Soon, the TWA industry's revived trade association took this task upon itself.

INCREASED LEGITIMACY AND SELF-REGULATION, AND THE SPREAD OF COLLECTIVE AGREEMENTS

Under the impulse of the four leading TWAs, Manpower in particular, Svenska Kontorsserviceförbundet had been revived in 1996 under a new name, Personaluthyrnings- och Rekryteringsförbundet (SPUR), and the organization was changed extensively. An important part of this change was to create a distinct profile. It was thus decided to change the designation of the industry from "the office and clerical services industry" to "*bemannings-branschen*" (the staffing services industry), which made a clearer distinction between it and other industries and gave it a more modern image. The main activity of SPUR was to enhance the legitimacy of the industry. Furthermore, this was mainly done as a sort of self-regulating endeavour aimed at escaping the very real threat of more government regulation. Members of the organization were required to comply with certain criteria: They had to have been active in the industry for at least 12 months, they had to have an annual turnover of at least SEK 3 M (€300,000), and management had to act responsibly and professionally. There should be an organizational framework in place to take care of the workers in a fair way and to manage human resources within the company in compliance with the statutes of the association and the ethical codes of conduct. The trade association also set up an ethical advisory board that would make sure its members followed the ethical codes of conduct (Bemanningsföretagen 2013).

Despite these activities and assurances, the trade association was regarded with suspicion by the trade unions. Several trade unions regarded state authorization as the only way to create order within the industry, and the demand for state authorization was used as an instrument to exert pressure and to bring about change in the industry. However, the trade unions could also see that membership of SPUR was putting some pressure on the members and that the attitudes of the companies within the industry was more businesslike and accommodating than previously.

The key actor in the revival of the trade association was Torbjörn Rindås, who became spokesman of SPUR in 1996. Before that, he had represented the TWAs' interests in the employers' association HAO; he was already involved in the collective labour agreement of 1988. However, even though the organization was located in the office of the Confederation of Swedish Employers, it was still defined as a trade association and not as an employers' organization. This entailed that collective labour agreements with unions were still being made by general employers' associations. It took until 2003 for SPUR to be transformed from a trade association into an employers' organization, thenceforth called Bemanningsföretagen (Bergström et al. 2007). Following this reorganization, Bemanningsföretagen took on the function of the negotiating party for the TWA industry. Since then, authorization has become mandatory for all companies that are members of Bemanningsföretagen (2007), the criteria for authorization have continually been changed and developed,[4] and new groups of workers have been covered by collective agreements, for example, the collective agreements covering physicians signed in 2009 (Bemanningsföretagen 2013).

The employers' application of the 1994 collective agreement negotiated by HTF became a disappointment for the trade unions. Unemployment benefit regulations at the time enabled employers to employ workers on limited-duration contracts and then leave them to receive unemployment benefits while not placed on assignments with clients. Thus, TWAs could transfer their labour costs to unemployment benefits, a possibility which they—according to HTF—used extensively. In response to this, HTF notified the media of this situation, whereupon the National Labour Market Board, from which the employers had withdrawn in 1991, decided, in 1996, to exclude temporary agency workers with limited-duration contracts from unemployment benefits. This decision made it even more important for employers in the TWA industry to sign collective agreements. In 1997, HTF and HAO signed a new agreement. Under this agreement, the guaranteed salary was raised to 75 per cent, entailing that it equalled the unemployment benefits level. This agreement also included the academic trade union and graduate engineers.

Because HTF was the first trade union to sign collective agreements covering temporarily placed workers in 1988 (Bergström et al. 2007), it played a particular role compared to other trade unions—that is, it legitimized the agency industry while at the same time critically monitoring its development. As the TWA industry continued to expand into more areas and new occupational groups, the collective agreements were extended to cover more and more trade unions. In 1999, turnover in the industry increased by 71 per cent. More than 400 companies were active within the industry. However, the share of agency workers of total employment (0.8 per cent) remained relatively low compared to the Netherlands, which had 4.0 per cent at that time (Storrie 2003, 232). The fact that TWAs were expanding into new occupational areas, and more and more workers were working as temps, caught the trade unions' attention. The unions found themselves in a new situation, and they had to do something about it. An important reason for the trade unions' change of policy in relation to the TWAs was that they could no longer block TWAs through government regulation. TWAs were here to stay. It was important to take the members' interests into consideration in a pragmatic way. It became evident that there were examples of agency workers who had acceptable working conditions that were sometimes better than those of permanent workers (e.g., higher salaries and more flexible working hours). The health care sector was one such example (Walter 2009). This meant that it was becoming increasingly difficult for the trade unions to carry on portraying the TWA industry as something completely negative. Although other trade unions had been sceptical, the health care workers' union had regarded TWAs as the kind of employer that created competition and change in an otherwise deadlocked situation for its workers.

Thus, although the trade unions' opinions about the TWAs during the 1990s remained differentiated, with LO in particular still considering them to be something that should not exist, collective agreements were spreading to more and more workplaces, companies, and trade unions. In 2000, an agreement was signed between the central employers' association Almega (Tjänsteföretagens arbetsgivarorganisation) and LO. This was regarded as a breakthrough for the establishment of the TWA industry on the Swedish labour market. From the TWA industry's perspective, it meant that the last pocket of resistance to the industry had been defeated. In consequence, the TWA industry may now be regarded as integral to the core of the Swedish model of industrial relations. At the same time, Swedish regulation of the TWA industry is remarkable in an international perspective given its distinct effect on the business model and operational logic of Swedish TWAs, which are unique in terms of employment security and the nature of the employment relationship.

THE SWEDISH TWA INDUSTRY AND
ITS BUSINESS MODEL

> Sweden has developed its own successful model for temporary agency work, a model that includes coverage of collective barging for workers employed in the industry and a high of proportion of highly qualified agency workers.
>
> (Bemanningsföretagen 2012)

The quote above is taken from the website of the Swedish employer association for the TWA industry (Bemanningsföretagen) where they describe themselves, their role in society, and what it means to be an employee in this industry using the services they provide. The quote is interesting in several ways. First, it provides very clear recognition of the importance of being regarded as a legitimate actor within the context of the Swedish labour market. The liberalized legislation, together with a lack of experience in understanding the particularities of the Swedish institutional context, initially led to a systematic underestimation of the importance of being a legitimate and responsible part of Sweden's labour market. It is interesting to note that none of the large multinationals now operating in the Swedish market initially managed to grow and expand in a way that firmly established their businesses in that market. They all tried, and they all failed. Despite their hard-earned experience of international operations, they only managed to establish themselves, adapt to Swedish conditions, and eventually start to grow by acquiring small domestic companies. This development, combined with the Swedish TWA industry continuing to strive towards becoming an established and legitimate actor in the Swedish labour market, made the industry adapt to Swedish conditions, often by describing itself and its services in terms of being a responsible provider of a type of privatized flex-security solution—a solution that, with time, would become institutionalized through collective bargaining and established business practices. Furthermore, in order to uphold this legitimate position, and to avoid further government regulation, the industry set up a system of voluntary authorization. However, in order for a company to be granted authorization, it needed to commit to the requirements stipulated in the industry's code of conduct, in addition to meeting criteria regarding financial stability and having the ability to display a track record of responsible practices over a period of at least a year. This meant that authorization not only regulated the behaviour of the involved TWA companies, but also created a barrier to new companies entering the market. This protectionist behaviour is likely to explain, at least partly, why the Swedish TWA industry, in 2005, was one of the most concentrated in Europe in terms of market share, with four companies accounting for more than 80 per cent of the market. By 2011, the criteria for gaining and maintaining authorization had changed. At the same time, the industry had become more diverse and was being less dominated by a few large companies; however, according to the Swedish employer association for the TWA industry, the six largest companies still held 75 per cent of the market share, with the largest company—Manpower—alone representing 21,3 per cent of the market (Bemanningsföretagen 2013). Furthermore, it is important to note that there might be a number of other equally important explanations of the way the industry has developed and matured.

Second, from the perspective of the industry, acceptance and legitimacy within the Swedish institutional setting were gained at the expense of what was regarded to be imposed constraints on business operations, constraints that could be summarized using the introduction of open-ended contracts for TWA workers and guaranteed salaries regulated through collective bargaining, both aspects aimed at strengthening employees' positions and rights at a level (almost) comparable with the conditions of any other Swedish employees holding open-ended contracts. Furthermore, the conditions stipulated in the collective agreements impact on the distribution of costs and risks connected with any employment of temporary agency workers in such a way that the conditions enabling TWAs to operate within a Swedish context become distinctively different from those of the outside world. The specific characteristics of the industry were shaped by the institutional conditions on the Swedish labour market. This, in turn, influenced the way that the Swedish TWA industry chose to organize its work, make sense of its operations, establish its legitimacy, and generate its profit. First, in a situation where TWAs need to offer their workers permanent contracts, the quality and skill applied by TWAs when recruiting workers increases in importance. The evaluation of potential recruitment candidates needs to be done not only with regard to specific placements or customers, but also with regard to potential future placements. This is done in order to avoid, or at least minimize, the risk of employees ending up without placements during shorter or longer periods, periods for which the TWA would then be liable to pay wages. As a result, the recruitment activity needs to be carried out more carefully in order to ensure that the company ends up employing "the right" candidates. Furthermore, this also suggests that the recruitment process needs to be focused on the more generic aspects and qualities of the candidates and their experience in order for them to be able to match a variety of job profiles. It is likely that, over time, most Swedish temporary agency workers will need to be able to fit into a number of different roles, functions, and workplaces. Second, in a situation where new customer requests for temporary placements continually needs to filled by permanent employees, recruitment will, most of the time, become separated, in time and space, from the actual placement of candidates. By separating the employment and recruitment processes from the placement itself, the TWAs are able to provide suitable candidates at greater speed than if the TWA had needed to go through the full process with every placement. However, this also complicates the matching activities because these are then limited to matching candidates who have suitable experience and skills with the requirements of the client; this also involves the coordination of employees and placements in order to avoid, or limit, time lags between placements. When the employment risk, together with an ambitious and time-consuming matching process, needs to be included in the price of its services, the TWA industry then finds itself in a disadvantaged position when competing with other labour-sourcing alternatives on the basis of (labour) costs. Instead, the price of their services needs to be accounted for, and motivated by, paying customers: By viewing themselves as professional labour market matchers, they are able to present themselves and what they do as providers of a high-quality matching service. "We are matchmakers and matching suitable employees with our clients' needs is what we do," was how one of the employees of a major TWA put it.

Assuming the position of a "matching industry" entails consequences. First, when providing matching services—rather than just flexibility or a cost-effective way of sourcing labour—there is an indication that this is an activity that requires skill, time, and resources in order to be performed and is, in consequence, a service worth paying for. Second, when an industry or a company positions itself as a professional matcher, it raises expectations regarding the service delivered, something that is mirrored not only in the sophistication of the matching activity developed at most of the major Swedish TWAs, but also in the choice of candidates to employ. Unlike in most other countries, the people employed by TWAs in Sweden have a higher degree of training and education than the labour force in general. In addition to formal qualifications like these, relevant experience is often a requirement for even being considered for a position with a TWA, suggesting that the potential of the Swedish TWA industry to function as a stepping stone into the labour market for marginal groups is limited, a function often attributed to the TWA industry in countries such as Holland and the United Kingdom. Furthermore, the penetration rates of the Swedish TWA industry are approximately 1 per cent of the working population, a level considerably lower than the other European countries that have a more liberal legislative framework for temporary agency work, for example Holland and the United Kingdom (Ciett 2013). This fact may partly be explained by the institutional conditions of the Swedish industry, primarily targeting the middle or upper end of the labour market and competing with high-quality services and well-qualified staff rather than price. Third, the development of the industry, and the industry's understanding of what it does as providing matching services in the labour market, suggests an extension of its operations into other areas, such as recruitment, restructuring services, and outplacement, which all are activities where the ability to match job candidates with open positions is crucial in order to deliver good, high-quality services.

MATCHMAKERS TO TRUST

To summarize, in comparison with most other OECD countries, a developed TWA industry is a fairly new phenomenon in Sweden, and, even though the legislative framework regulating temporary placement was eased in 1993, the development of a domestic TWA industry has very much been conditioned and shaped by the specific institutional framework of the Swedish labour market. A direct result of these conditions was the development of a distinct "Swedish" type of TWA industry, operating under conditions that, at the time, seemed not only to puzzle but also to challenge representatives of the established multinational TWA industry.

Furthermore, this specific Swedish version of a TWA industry comes with a set of managerial implications that is unique to the Swedish context. First, coordination between supply and demand of labour for placement not only becomes a more complicated managerial task, with a cadre of employees holding open-ended contracts, but also puts much more of a risk management perspective in focus during the production of placement services. Within such a framework, a company's ability to develop strategies that minimize, or avoid, exposure of its operations to employment risks is just as important as developing high-quality matching practices; risk management is thus likely to influence the design and implementation of every aspect of the company's operations.

Second, because the institutional framework in Sweden does not offer any obvious cost advantages when providing TWA services, compared to other types of staffing strategies (and more likely the opposite), it becomes essential to develop a business model that communicates some sort of value added to the company's in-house activities to clients. By framing the industry as a group of companies with expertise in the field of "matching and transition on the labour market," the industry indicates a focus on the quality of the services provided, as much as the result of their services. In other words, as illustrated by a quote from a manager at Manpower when asked to describe its operations: "We are matchmakers, matching is what we do." This is both a very typical description given by someone representing the industry in Sweden and an illuminating one because it highlights the importance ascribed to the internal process of providing high-quality matching services. Matchmaking becomes a professional capacity per se, and, as such, it is worth paying good money for.

Third, within a labour market framework that is largely shaped by collective agreements and comparatively strong unions, the issue of being regarded as a legitimate actor is a constant and crucial challenge facing any TWA operating in Sweden. So far, the industry has managed to achieve this mainly by adapting its operations in order to fit the Swedish conditions and institutional framework. However, the sector is continuously being challenged by unions and political parties that are calling for increased regulation, restriction in the use of temporary agency work and/or improved working and employment conditions in the industry. Being able to balance these particular characteristics of the Swedish operation is likely to be a constant and important managerial challenge within the Swedish context.

However, it is important to conclude that, even if the business model and the managerial challenges facing the TWA industry are somewhat different in Sweden than they are in most other OECD countries, the TWA industry today is in many ways a developed, well-integrated, growing, and frequently prosperous part of the Swedish business world.

NOTES

1. For further reading on workforce composition within the Swedish TWA industry, see Andersson and Wadensjö (2004, 2010).

2. For an elaborate description and analysis of the roles and functions of the Swedish employers' federation ALMEGA, see Fries (2011).
3. There are no statistics available regarding this group of workers; however, according to one of the ombudsmen at HTF who was involved in the negotiations in 1988, a few hundred people had this type of employment at that time.
4. One interesting addition to the requirements for authorization is the obligation for authorized companies to sign established collective agreements.

REFERENCES

Ahrne, Göran, Nils Brunsson, and Christina Garsten. 1998. "Standardisering genom organisering." In *Standardisering*, edited by Nils Brunsson and Bengt Jacobsson. Stockholm: Nerenius & Santérus Förlag.
Bemanningsföretagen. 2013. www.bemanningsforetagen.se.
Bergström, Ola, Kristina Håkansson, Tommy Isidorsson, and Lars Walter. 2007. *Den nya arbetsmarknaden: Bemanningsbranschens etablering i Sverige*. Lund: Akademia Adacta.
Ciett. 2013. *The Agency Work Industry around the World*. Economic Report. Brussels: Ciett.
Co-determination Act, Lag 1976: 580.
Edin, Per-Andersand, Robert H. Topel. 1997. "Wage Policy and Restructuring: The Swedish Labour Market since 1960." In *The Welfare State in Transition, Reforming the Swedish Model*, edited by Richard B. Freeman, Robert H. Topel, and Birgitta Swedenborg. London: University of Chicago Press.
Fahlbeck, Reinhold. 1978. "Sweden." In *Temporary Work in Modern Society*, vol. 1, edited by Willem Albeda, Roger Blanpain, and Gerard M. J. Veldkamp, 343–378. Dordrecht: Kluwer.
Johnson, Anders. 2010. *Hyrt går hem. Historien om den svenska bemanningsbranschen*. Stockholm: Informationsförlaget.
Lag 1970, 887
Lag 1976, 580
Statens Offentliga Utredningar (SOU). 2011. *Bemanningsdirektivets genomförande i Sverige*. ILO Convention No. 96.
Statens Offentliga Utredningar (SOU). 1997. *Personaluthyrning: slutbetänkande av Kommittén för utvärdering av avregleringen av arbetsförmedlingsmonopolet*.
Storrie, Daniel. 2003. "Conclusions: Contingent Employment in Europe and the Flexibility-Security Trade-Off." In *Contingent Employment in Europe and the United States*, edited by Olaand Bergström and Donald Storrie, 224–247. Cheltenham, Northampton, UK: Edward Elgar.
Veldkamp, Gerard M.J., and M.J. Raetsen. 1972. *The Provision of Labor in the Netherlands*. Chassiers of the IITT no. 2.
Walter, Lars. 2009. "Inhyrd omsorg." In *Mellan offentligt och privat*, edited by Kajsa Lindström and Maria Blomberg, 75–86. Uppsala, Sweden: Santérus Academic Press.

12 Alternative Staffing Organizations as Innovations in Labour Market Intermediation

Lessons from the United States

Françoise Carré, Joaquín Herranz Jr, and Silvia Dorado

In the United States, employment through the temporary staffing[1] industry increased five times more rapidly than employment economy-wide between 1972 and 2000. And, at their peak in 2000, temporary agencies accounted for almost 3 per cent of U.S. daily employment (Autor 2004). From 1972 to 2000, temporary agencies became the most widespread form of labour market intermediary, accounting for more workers than all other types of labour market intermediaries combined (Benner, Leete, and Pastor 2007). At the same time, temporary staffing agencies employed a disproportionate share of low-skilled and minority U.S. workers (U.S. Department of Labor, Bureau of Labor Statistics 2005). In the low-wage labour market, temp work (i.e., employment in the staffing industry) is especially prevalent among graduates of government- and philanthropy-financed employment and training programs. State-level government data show that 15 to 40 per cent of former public assistance recipients in employment following the 1996 U.S. welfare reform took temp jobs (Autor and Houseman 2010). A growing number of entry-level workers with low levels of formal education and skills turn to temp work to locate and evaluate job opportunities, represent their skills, and access jobs (Carré and Joshi 2000; Giloth 2004).

The relatively high proportion of low-skilled workers in temp work positions has generated a debate about the role of temporary staffing agencies in the low-wage labour market. Some research argues that temporary agencies make it possible for low-income individuals to navigate the volatile low-wage labour market and move towards economic self-sufficiency (Andersson, Holzer, and Lane 2005). Other research using state-level data about former welfare recipients with jobs after the 1996 U.S. welfare reform suggests that staffing agencies may help these individuals get a job within a few months; yet, after one to two years, these individuals are still very likely to have incomes below the poverty line (Autor and Houseman 2010). Underemphasized in this debate has been the emergence of a lesser-known innovation in the temporary staffing model, namely, alternative staffing organizations (ASOs). Similarly to the European worker integration social enterprises (WISEs), ASOs provide job placement and support services to low-income individuals facing job market barriers including few credentials, limited work history, homelessness, or disabilities. ASOs serve similar low-income populations as those placed in entry-level jobs by conventional temporary staffing agencies. In contrast to these agencies, ASOs provide services that may help job candidates overcome the employment barriers that hinder their ability to get and retain a job (Carré and Joshi 2000; Andersson, Holzer, and Lane 2005; Lane et al. 2003). Specifically, ASOs help individuals to access higher-quality employment and work to enhance their chance of good job performance. Also, they help them to develop a work history and—although not directly—acquire skills that increase their employability as well as connect them with supportive services, such as access to subsidized housing, food assistance, childcare, or health insurance.

ASOs were developed by community-based organizations and other types of non-profits (i.e., non-governmental organizations). ASOs charge a fee for their services to the customer businesses where they place workers and aim to finance their placement operations through these fees. They may reinvest net revenue to strengthen their operations and expand their services. The largest and most financially successful ASOs funnel these funds to other social programs (such as services to the homeless or to individuals with profound disabilities). They compete directly with for-profit staffing agencies in the temporary labour market. They are then, much like the European WISEs, a social enterprise or double bottom-line organization (Dorado 2006). The social equity bottom line involves helping individuals to overcome employment barriers. The financial bottom line involves providing commercially valuable staffing services to customer businesses for a fee—a per cent markup on the hourly wage of the position. However, in contrast to WISEs, ASOs are not created or instigated by the government/public sector; they are created within the extensive civil society network of community organizations and other non-profits. ASOs do not receive government support for their job placement activities per se, but they may receive funding for other activities (i.e., direct supports to workers). In a few and time-limited cases, they obtain a state subsidy on the wage paid if their temp worker fits a policy-designated category. Their parent organizations may receive government service contracts. In a few states (Texas, Oregon), ASOs receive preferred vendor treatment thanks to legislation that prioritizes the granting of government contracts to organizations that employ a preponderance of individuals with a qualifying disability. But even with this preferential treatment, the job placement success of ASOs is rooted in their ability to provide services valued by their customers, whether government agencies or businesses—that is, the ability to screen individuals with an adequate employment profile and their capacity to follow up on problems such as absenteeism or lack of adequate transportation to reach worksites.

In short, unlike both conventional for-profit temporary agencies, which prioritize fee-paying customer businesses and conventional government/donor-financed programs that prioritize the needs of jobseekers with barriers, ASOs aim to strike a delicate balance between the demands of fee-paying businesses and the needs of jobseekers. Some ASOs have operated for years, and a few for more than 25 years. Some have managed to remain competitive under conditions of severe competition, thereby offering an alternative to workers who otherwise would be at the mercy of some unscrupulous local operators or lost in the databases of the large ones. This chapter contributes to the literature on labour market intermediaries, particularly temporary staffing, by exploring the business model of ASOs and addressing a research gap in the field. We ask the following: What roles do ASOs play in the U.S. low-skill labour market? What are their key attributes, and what services do they provide? What types of workers and employers are served by ASOs? To answer these questions, we build on the empirical findings of a nationwide study in the United States conducted from 2001 to 2003[2] and enriched with insights from recent in-depth exploration of four established ASOs[3] (Carré et al. 2009; Carré , Holgate, and Levine 2011). The next section describes our methods and our analysis of the characteristics that define these organizations. We then describe the emergence and development of ASOs in the U.S. context. We finish the chapter with a discussion of the distinct characteristics of ASOs, their approach to serve disadvantaged workers' need for mediation in the job market, and the challenges they face in facilitating access to stable and quality employment.

METHODS

We examined ASOs in a study conducted between 2001 and 2003 and gathered data through three different sources: (1) a national search and screening for ASOs, (2) in-depth telephone interviews with the head of operations of 27 organizations, and (3) site visits with 8 organizations representing the full array of types of ASOs. Site visits included interviews with the head of the organization, staff engaged in job placement and support services, one or two worker focus groups, and customer businesses.

By design, random sampling was not implemented nor possible because the full range of types of alternative staffing services was not known ex ante. Instead, we identified broad types of organizations and patterns of activity, aiming to depict the full range of variation, rather than generating a frequency distribution of patterns. Our search process yielded organizations broadly arrayed in terms of the following: (1) the types of job placements they make, (2) the customer populations they serve, (3) the volume of their business, and (4) their geographical location. The survey includes most profiles of ASOs providing fee-based services that were fully operational in 2001 (and had been in business for one year or more). Out of 54 organizations, we surveyed 27 (Carré et al. 2003).

This information is augmented with insights from an in-depth monitoring study of four ASOs conducted between 2005 and 2009. Financial and payroll information complemented site visits (Carré et al. 2009).

ASOs: EMERGENCE AND EVOLUTION IN
THE U.S. CONTEXT

All ASOs were created by civil society organizations: community-based organizations or national non-profits. The first, Just Jobs Inc.—later named Harborquest—was founded in 1970 by Chicago social activists seeking to bring "justice to the temporary placement industry."[4] Other established ASOs include, among others, DePaul Industries in Oregon, Emerge Staffing in Minnesota, and Goodwill Staffing Services in Texas.

In many cases, their founders saw ASOs as a key part of a non-profit's mission to help workers facing employment barriers (Seavey 1998). From this perspective, temp work is seen as a "foot in the door," a chance for workers to prove themselves to employers and overcome employment barriers hindering them from getting permanent jobs. However, because it is most commonly structured by conventional companies, temp work frequently presents the risk of confining the worker to day labour pools or to low-quality, low-pay service jobs. ASOs are committed to alleviating these risks by finding better temp jobs—with employers that have further job opportunities—for the populations they serve. They seek to capitalize on the potential of temp work to facilitate access to jobs while alleviating barriers to employment and providing additional services that can help individuals access longer term employment opportunities.

The fee-based aspect of temp job brokering makes this activity substantially different from the activities usually pursued by ASO parent organizations, such as running a homeless shelter or family assistance program, which are usually funded through grants and contracts from government and philanthropy. Most commonly, the gross revenue generated by ASOs' job-brokering activities is used to pay the wage bill (including payroll taxes and insurance) of workers and to cover expenses most directly related to the brokering activities (i.e., staff and administrative expenses). The most financially successful ASOs use their income (minus administrative expenses), when available, to fund other programs that support employment. Thus, ASOs have two types of performance criteria for success: worker-level measures in terms of employment outcomes and financial measures.

There are currently about 50 ASOs in the United States. ASOs have one of three primary kinds of organizational affiliations: (1) affiliation to a local non-profit parent organization (e.g., EMERGE Staffing/New Unity Temps with EMERGE Community Development); (2) free-standing social enterprises, in some cases spawned off by a partnership of local non-profits; organizations (e.g., First Source Staffing); and (3) affiliates of two national non-profits, namely, Goodwill Industries and Experience Works.[5] Only five of the staffing services out of 27 in this study did not have a non-profit tax status in 2001.

The role of ASOs in the United States is partly the product of the thin social safety net available to individuals; there is no guaranteed minimum income and no mandated minimum health insurance, paid time off, or sick leave pay. Governmental resources for workforce development of low-skill individuals are limited and administered with contracts to non-profit organizations, scattered throughout the country, providing job-readiness training for individuals with little work experience and skill-training for people with limited education or skills. The federal and state governments have some vocational and apprenticeship programs, but they are small relative to the need, serving mostly those with secondary schooling. These workforce training systems are not comparable in scope and size to those available in some European countries.

Also, the staffing industry in the United States operates in a weak and fragmented regulatory environment. Regulation about terms of employment for temp workers (e.g., posted salary information and limits on worker transportation fees) varies greatly across states. Similar to their European counterparts, ASOs face a bipolar industry: a few multinational corporations on one end, and a large number of small, sometimes local, operators on the other end. After much consolidation in the industry, large operators operate in a manner in which it is easy for workers, particularly low-income ones, to get lost. Many local operators that employ low-income individuals, in turn, engage in rather problematic and abusive practices, such as charging low bill rates to customer businesses and turning a profit by siphoning it out from worker compensation; this is particularly common among day labour companies (Freeman and Gonos 2011). ASOs compete in such environments. Their existence offers an alternative venue for workers to escape the anonymity of the largest players and for the employers to hire temp workers without further contributing to the exploitative techniques of bottom-feeding temporary agencies.

FINDINGS

Types of Temp Job Placement Activities Conducted by ASOs

Almost 60 per cent of ASOs in our 2003 study had temporary placement as their primary activity (16 organizations). Of these, most (14 organizations) were also engaged in temp-to-perm staffing activities (providing services explicitly directed to turning temp jobs into permanent ones). Ten organizations did temp-to-perm assignments as a primary activity. Only 1 was engaged in day labour as a primary activity.

Characteristics of Workers Placed

The characteristics of workers served by ASOs are similar to those of the low-income or low-skill workers of conventional staffing agencies. ASO workers face a variety of employment barriers: economic "disadvantage" (fitting low-income or poverty policy criteria), lack of recent work history, physical or mental disabilities, ex-offender status, age (over 54 years old), and/or homelessness. Interestingly, the single largest group of workers placed by each ASO was not always the same as the one designated by the organization's core mission population. When asked about it, ASO managers explained that they had expanded their services over time to workers experiencing other disadvantages, in part because some workers fit more than one category of service need.

Not surprisingly, the services' locations determined, to a large extent, the race and ethnicity of the workers they placed. Operations in rural areas and the Midwest were more likely to serve primarily white workers, whereas those in inner city minority neighbourhoods drew from the local minority populations.

Twenty-six organizations reported on gender differences. Among them, 10 served mostly men, and 8 served men and women equally. We believe that the lower representation of women reflects the types of assignments that ASOs found, which tended to be in male-dominated industries such as manufacturing, landscaping, and manual labour.

In short, jobseekers served by ASOs have similar profiles as those who are sent in entry-level staffing assignments by conventional staffing companies. When ASOs are compared to traditional workforce development programs, however, their service population is more mixed. This is because programs must serve the population designated in their funding sources, whereas ASOs are less restricted in this regard and end up serving a mix of jobseekers with employment barriers in their geographical service area. The exceptions are those ASOs whose primary service population is a disability population and primary customers are state and local government agencies.

Jobs and Customer Businesses

ASOs, for the most part, and given the profile of their target populations, staffed entry-level positions as well as a few mid-level positions. Most ASOs surveyed (12 out of 26 providing data) primarily made placements in "semi-skilled/unskilled jobs," a varied classification that includes janitors, construction labourers, gardeners, and assembly line operators. A few (8 out of 26) primarily placed workers in clerical positions, and 5 primarily staffed service or personal care positions.

Although noting that they placed workers in a wide range of industries, ASOs reported that manufacturing (light manufacturing and assembly) and business services were the most common customer businesses. This preponderance mirrors patterns in the mainstream staffing industry, particularly as regards entry-level positions. Several ASOs also reported that they primarily served state governments, placing disabled workers through set-aside contracting programs.

ASOs reported that, with a few exceptions, the average hourly wage of their placements tended to be at, or a few dollars above, the prevailing minimum wage level (e.g., US$5.15 in 2001)

There was a correspondence between workers' genders and the jobs in which they were placed. ASOs placing semi-skilled/unskilled labour were more likely to serve either men or men and women equally. Finally, almost half of the ASOs (11) reported placing mostly workers with a high school diploma or equivalent, while a large number of ASOs (10) primarily placed workers with a high school diploma or less.

Total Revenue

By conventional staffing industry standards, alternative staffing services cluster at the lower end of the revenue range; they are small businesses. Most of the alternative staffing services interviewed for this study reported revenues for 2001 of less than US$1 million. ASOs, like conventional staffing agencies, use total revenue/billings and billable hours as measures of activity. Total revenue is the simplest measure of size; it is somewhat dependent on the wage level of placements (higher wages result in higher billing levels) but allows comparison across ASOs.

In comparison, a 2002 survey by the American Staffing Association of its members reported that only 10 per cent of respondents had billings below US$1 million (American Staffing Association 2002). ASOs with annual revenues of less than US$500,000 were usually in the start-up phase of operation. The majority (17 or 63 per cent) of ASOs in our sample had annual revenue/billings of more than US$500,000 in 2001; with this volume of revenues, they could begin to compete with conventional staffing companies for the business of large customers. Still, it is difficult for ASOs to compete under the tight profit margins and relentless competitive pressures faced by all operators (Theodore and Peck 2002). A survey conducted in 2007 by the Alternative Staffing Alliance (which associates most ASOs) indicates that ASOs have a higher cost structure (Alternative Staffing Alliance 2007). They incur higher costs because of direct services provision and staff time spent in assisting workers in areas such as job preparation, job performance monitoring, and customizing services to fit the needs of customer businesses.[6] Although these activities are within the purview of conventional companies, the latter frequently skip them in the context of entry-level positions, particularly when bill rates and markup are low and the volume of workers high. Other functions that increase costs for ASOs when compared with conventional companies are referrals to human services agencies, job-readiness workshops, transportation to the job site (in some ASOs), and occasional emergency cash assistance (see Carré et al. 2009 for details).

In addition, their higher cost structure is the product of the lack of economies of scale (less efficient administrative structures and information systems) because of their small size. Their capacity to compete with low prices is thus rather limited, particularly when faced with competition from operators who do not comply with all labour standards. ASOs do not compete with a high-volume, low-margin model due to the challenge of generating sales.

Most ASOs rely on grants and subsidies (private and public) to fund the mission-related costs of the operation (support to workers) and take advantage of their tax-free status to complement their business revenue; only a few are large enough to generate significant net revenue without grant funding (Carré et al. 2009). The business revenue covers the administrative costs of job brokering—that is, the costs that conventional companies incur (sales, candidate intake, job matching, and payroll). Another major challenge facing many ASOs is building the business acumen of their staff as well as identifying staff with the hybrid perspective of considering the business needs of customers (and the financial survival of the ASO itself) in parallel with the goal of opening doors for jobseekers—a changing, complex, and challenging balancing act that seasoned ASO staff manage day to day and to which newcomers must acclimate in order to succeed.

Discussion: A Third Venue for Temp Work

ASOs add value in that they strike a balance between the demands of employers and the need of workers. The middle ground created by these organizations provides an alternative for workers to avoid exploitative employment relationships with unscrupulous staffing agencies and for customer businesses who seek to hire temporary workers without contributing to this exploitation.

Value to Customer Businesses

For customer businesses, ASOs conduct the tasks connected with employment including background checks, drug testing, and worker preparation, as well as worker monitoring including follow-up on absences, problem solving, and occasional mediation. ASOs targeted customer businesses in their areas with above-average entry-level job quality for regular hires (e.g., with benefits) and stayed away from those prone to low-quality jobs. Assessing the quality of the customer business was a key priority for most ASOs sales personnel. Quality was usually interpreted to include a range of sought-after characteristics: wages above the minimum; employer reliability regarding bill paying; respect of health, safety, and labour standards; and potential for permanent hiring (e.g., anticipated job growth). Conversely, customer businesses were avoided that sought to bring the hourly bill rate (what the staffing service charges per worker hour) too low, thus barely accommodating the minimum wage and sometimes threatening contributions to mandatory workers' compensation insurance. Also avoided were potential employers that had dangerous work settings or a record of discriminatory practices (Carré et al. 2003).

ASOs also reported that being very responsive to the requirements placed by their customer businesses was a particularly high priority for them as a source of differentiation and competitive advantage in a highly competitive industry. It is a defensive strategy as well because they place workers facing barriers to employment. Post-placement customer services included quality checking (i.e., phone calls and visits) and replacing ill-matched workers promptly. Post-placement services to businesses also included mediation. Mediation was sometimes as simple as conveying the workplace rules and clearing up misunderstandings or arguing the workers' case and providing a replacement in case of absence. In its simplest form, mediation was ubiquitous among ASOs. In its most extensive form, mediation was provided only by a few ASOs, on occasion entailing direct on-site management. Some of the largest ASOs provided "vendor-on-premises" services, which were dedicated services for a single customer business. In addition to coaching, some ASOs provided customized recruiting and training as well as on-site payroll administration. In conventional staffing, vendor-on-premises services are a formula used with a large number of placements. ASOs, however, provided this service when a lower threshold of job assignments was involved.

Additional in-depth information about customers of four ASOs collected in recent years illustrates and further confirms these findings (Carré et al. 2009). The customer businesses interviewed reported that they used the ASO services particularly when they were "staffing up"—screening temps in view of possible hiring—and for gap filling (temporary need), or for staffing an entire function or shift.

Customer businesses reported valuing the ASO staff's knowledge of their business needs. The following comment is illustrative of what we heard: "[She] seems to know and care about our business" (Carré et al. 2009, 44). The ASO staff invests in acquiring knowledge about the production setting and job requirements to facilitate worker performance. Customers also found that, for the most part, candidates were well screened and matched to the jobs. For entry-level staffing, these customer businesses otherwise deal with operators that provide little customization of services and limited attention; their business model is a low-margin, high-volume model. Customers also noted the responsiveness of ASO staff to the difficulties that arose while workers were on assignment. The emphasis put by the ASO's staff on customer service is due to the need to maximize a worker's chance of staying on the assignment. Importantly, even customers who used a mainstream staffing vendor along with the ASO used the ASO services especially when they intended to screen temps in view of regular hiring because the ASO worker selection was more targeted to their needs. They did so even if the ASO hourly bill rate was higher.

Value to Workers

ASOs provide workers with an alternative to conventional staffing agencies. Through the ASO, jobseekers receive assistance in multiple areas prior, during, and post placement, including preparation for bidding to permanent (regular) jobs when the customer has a growing job base. ASOs engaged in most of these activities directly, except for training and some support services for which they frequently used referrals and other partnering mechanisms.

Pre-employment services include intake and screening job candidates, skills assessments, job counselling, and job-readiness training. They also encompass general job skills coaching such as interviewing and interacting with supervisors. The most common form of training was for job readiness; 11 of the interviewed organizations (41 per cent) provided such training. Job-readiness training is short term and covers basic rules of employment (being on time and courtesy). In addition, ASO workers receive job preparation such as information (schedules and dress codes) and cues about behaviour as well as workplace norms and expectations.

The study also identified the provision of, or referral to, support services as important to workers' ability to take a job assignment. Support services included social and human services, which ranged from help with gaining access (directly or through referrals) to housing or housing subsidies, food stamps, free work clothes, referrals for subsidized childcare or health care, substance abuse counselling and treatment, and legal assistance. Support services also included logistical services such as providing safety equipment for assignments and, frequently, providing subsidized or free transportation to job assignments. Lack of access to transportation was identified as a major hurdle for many low-income workers because many urban and rural areas lacked affordable public transportation systems geared to moving people from low-income residential areas to those where jobs were located. Educational support services included referrals to training providers. In cases where the ASO had a large number of job assignments with a handful of customer businesses, it occasionally customized safety training for these customers' production process.

ASOs use account representatives or job developers to perform the actual job-matching function—matching available workers to the available assignments. ASOs reported that accurately assessing the suitability of the match between worker and job assignment was a necessity because of the ASOs' aim to strike a balance between business demands and workers' needs. Although we did not conduct a representative survey, workers in focus groups consistently reported that they were not penalized by ASOs for reporting unsafe working conditions and requesting a different assignment when the current one was problematic. They commented that this practice contrasts with their experience with some conventional staffing companies, particularly "low-end" operators, which ask workers to remain on assignments and avoid giving assignments to workers who complain.

The job matching was complex in that it required ASOs to be able to generate placements to keep pace with jobseekers that were ready to work as well as meet ebbs and flows in customer demand for workers. It was also rendered more complex by the particular requirements of placing workers considered "disadvantaged" or hard to employ by customer businesses.

Finally, the peculiarity of the staffing relationship enabled ASOs to maintain contact with workers during the job assignment. The ASO remained the employer of record for the worker, responsible for all payroll administration, tax withholding, and proper insurance payments. But the study also showed that, in addition to these basic services provided by all staffing organizations, post-placement activity was an important part of the services provided by ASOs

All ASOs observed systematic follow-up practices such as checking with the job site supervisor and worker on the first day and regularly afterwards. Weekly paydays were a common way to have check-ins with workers. For example, ASO staff might find out about emerging difficulties at work and take the opportunity to address them early with the worker and the supervisor, as appropriate. In addition, a number of ASOs had dedicated job coaches whose duties of individual worker monitoring went beyond basic follow-up. Job coaching is a difficult job that requires staff skilled at motivating, providing short-term training, and ultimately supervising, even disciplining, workers while also being adept at delivering consistent service to the customer business. Job coaches shepherded workers through episodic difficulties, particularly during the early stages of a job assignment. They provided guidance and interventions geared at promoting job retention and performance. Many tried to address personal, behavioural, and other issues before they interfered with work performance. From workers' perspectives, coaching provided an optional buffer between themselves and the customer business.

In addition, social and human support services were often marshalled, through referrals, to address issues such as childcare breakdowns or housing crises. Thus, these services were not conceived exclusively as "getting a worker to employment" but as fostering retention. For customer businesses, these supportive services may not be visible. However, our later in-depth study of four organizations found customers that support services enabled the individuals brokered by ASOs into their jobs to perform more reliably and better than those brought in from conventional agencies (Carré et al. 2009).

CONCLUSION

We have addressed the role of ASOs in the U.S. low-skill labour market by presenting findings about the key attributes of these organizations, types of workers, and employers served, as well as the nature of the ASOs' relationships with workers and customer businesses. We found that ASOs provided key intermediation functions including finding job placements, assessing employer quality, and brokering workers into them. In some instances, the reputation of the ASO in the local labour market signalled to employers that these workers had received thorough job-readiness preparation and would be supported while in placement. Whenever opportunities existed to convert to regular hiring, many ASOs also prepared people in these types of assignments to bid for the jobs.

We found that these functions performed by ASOs were especially important for workers with barriers to gain access to employment and to build a record of work experience that was lacking due to barriers such as a recent spell out of the labour force or incarceration. Many workers in focus groups remarked that ASOs helped them with getting *and* keeping jobs. Importantly, the support provisions were also mentioned by customer businesses as a distinguishing and competitive characteristic of ASOs as compared to conventional staffing companies, particularly operators at the low end of the market.

This study reveals that many ASOs supported worker access to employment or re-employment, and movement across employers, thus helping workers build a work record, which enabled them to compete for and access more stable jobs. Access to a job is a crucial step in the road to better employment that is often overlooked in thinking about worker trajectories.

Nevertheless, ASOs encountered challenges related to the job structures within firms in some sectors. Although many ASOs preferred to look for opportunities for conversion from temporary to regular hiring, many reported that entry-level jobs were increasingly disconnected from job ladders within firms. Many entry-level positions were "revolving doors," filled either by rotating workers provided by staffing companies or by workers hired directly but in a highly casual arrangement. There were reports that in certain urban labour markets, light-manufacturing hiring practices had evolved in this direction. Several ASOs reported that they targeted better employers as part of their strategy to minimize the risk of "dead-end" temporary assignments. ASOs aimed to find customer businesses with significant use of temp workers but also with a growing regular workforce (e.g., a new shift opening), with a pay scale for regular jobs (and health coverage) that was better than what workers would typically earn if obtaining a job on their own, and whose entry-level positions were connected to other jobs.[7] Additionally, some ASOs counted on the fact that their staff was well acquainted with supervisors and the human resources department in steady customers, and had a track record of providing productive workers, to temper employer interest in implementing fully casual and externalized jobs. Through offering training and other supervisory support services, ASOs' staff actively promoted the added value of more stable arrangements for low-skill, entry-level hiring.

In conclusion, our findings add nuance to the ongoing debate about whether temporary staffing helps low-skill workers navigate the turbulent low-wage labour market out of poverty or whether such labour market attachment is short term and reverts these workers back to unemployment. Indeed, our study questions the notion that we should not expect too much from labour market intermediaries by highlighting ways in which some intermediaries—although clearly not all—may serve jobseekers who face barriers (Benner, Leete, and Pastor 2007). On one hand, we find that ASOs, like other intermediaries, face challenges associated with changing labour market structures. On the other hand, we argue that ASOs represent an adaptive innovation in labour market intermediation, developed to remedy some problems of the U.S. labour market and its mainstream for-profit temporary staffing industry. Although operating relatively quietly under the radar of most labour market researchers for several decades, ASOs have developed a relatively small, but growing, body of practice and experience in addressing some of the problems associated with the low-wage labour market.

Temporary employment need not necessarily result in chronic low-wage jobs or poor working conditions if the intermediary acts on behalf of the jobseeker as well as that of the customer business, meeting business performance and social-purpose goals. The experience of ASOs across the United States indicates that the temporary staffing model may be altered in ways that enhance the chances of vulnerable workers in the changing job market.

NOTES

1. Historically, the industry was named "temporary help" industry. It has since been renamed "temporary staffing" or "staffing." Jobs in the industry are commonly referred to as "temp jobs."
2. The study was sponsored by the Ford Foundation.
3. The study was sponsored by the C. S. Mott Foundation.
4. Harborquest website, www.harborquest.com/Vision_Mission_History.aspx (accessed 8 February 2012).
5. Experience Works closed its staffing services in 2004.
6. See Carré et al. (2009) for detailed analysis of four ASOs' cost structures.
7. Carré, Holgate, and Levine (2011) provides data on the employment status of former workers of four ASOs six to eight months after their job assignment with the ASO ended.

REFERENCES

Alternative Staffing Alliance. 2007. *Annual Performance Survey*. www.altstaffing. org/.
American Staffing Association. 2002. *Annual Economic Analysis of the Staffing Industry* (Alexandria, VA: ASA).
Andersson, Fredrik, Harry J. Holzer, and Julia I. Lane. 2005. *Moving Up or Moving On: Who Advances in the Low-Wage Labor Market?* New York: Russell Sage Foundation.
Autor, David H. 2004. "Labor Market Intermediation: What It Is, Why It Is Growing, and Where It Is Going." *NBER Reporter* (Fall): 7–10.

Autor, David H., and Susan N. Houseman. 2010. "Do Temporary Help Jobs Improve Labor Market Outcomes for Low-Skilled Workers? Evidence from 'Work First.'" *American Economic Journal: Applied Economics* 2 (3): 96–128.

Benner, Chris, Laura Leete, and Manuel Pastor. 2007. *Staircases or Treadmills? Labor Market Intermediaries and Economic Opportunity in a Changing Economy*. New York: Russell Sage Foundation.

Carré, Françoise, Joaquín Herranz Jr, Dorie Seavey, Carlha Vickers, Ashley Aull, and Rebecca Keegan. 2003. *Employment Brokering for Disadvantaged Job Seekers: Improving the Temp and Temp-to-Perm Job Experience and Enhancing Job Opportunities. Report to the Ford Foundation.* Boston: University of Massachusetts Boston by arrangement with the President and Fellows of Harvard College.

Carré, Françoise, Brandynn Holgate, and Helen Levine. 2011. *Finding the Right Fit: How Alternative Staffing Affects Worker Outcomes*. Boston: University of Massachusetts, Center for Social Policy.

Carré, Françoise, Brandynn Holgate, Helen Levine, and Mandira Kala. 2009. *Brokering Up: The Role of Temporary Staffing in Overcoming Labor Market Barriers*. Boston: University of Massachusetts, Center for Social Policy.

Carré, Françoise, and Pamela Joshi. 2000. "Looking for Leverage in a Fluid World: Innovative Responses to Temporary and Contract Work." In *Nonstandard Work: The Nature and Challenge of Changing Employment Arrangements (LERA Research Volumes)*, edited by Françoise Carré, Marianne A. Ferber, Lonnie Golden, and Stephen A. Herzenberg Champaign, IL: Industrial Relations Research Association, pp.313–339.

Dorado, Silvia. 2006. "Social Entrepreneurial Ventures: Different Values so Different Process of Creation, No?" *Journal of Developmental Entrepreneurship* 11 (4): 1–24.

Freeman, Harris, and George Gonos. 2011. "The Challenge of Temporary Work in Twenty-First Century Labor Markets: Flexibility with Fairness for the Low-Wage Temporary Workforce." Western New England University School of Law Legal Studies Research Paper 11-07, Labor Relations and Research Center, University of Massachusetts, Amherst. http://papers.ssrn.com/sol3/papers.cfm?abstract_id=1971222.

Giloth, Robert P. 2004. *Workforce Intermediaries for the 21st Century*. Philadelphia, PA: Temple University Press.

Lane, Julia, Kelly S. Mikelson, Pat Sharkey, and Doug Wissoker. 2003. "Pathways to Work for Low-Income Workers: The Effect of Work in the Temporary Help Industry." *Journal of Policy Analysis and Management* 22 (4): 581–598.

Seavey, Dorie. 1998. "New Avenues into Jobs: Early Lessons from Nonprofit Temp Agencies and Employment Brokers." Washington, DC: Center for Community Change. www.huduser.org/publications/pdf/ccc_avenues.pdf

Theodore, Nick, and Peck, Jamie. 2002. "The Temporary Staffing Industry: Growth Imperatives and Limits to Contingency." *Economic Geography* 4: 463–493.

U.S. Department of Labor, Bureau of Labor Statistics. 2005. *Contingent and Alternative Work Arrangements*. Washington, DC: U.S. Government Printing Office.

Contributors

CONTRIBUTING AUTHORS

Françoise Carré is Research Director of the Center for Social Policy, University of Massachusetts Boston J.W. McCormack Graduate School of Policy and Global Studies. She specializes in applied labour economics, comparative employment policy, and worker representation. She has written extensively about temporary and short-term work in the United States and in international perspective, low-wage employment, and worker representation. She co-authored "Working in Large Food Retailers: A France-United States Comparison" (with P. Askezazy, J. Berry, S. Prunier-Poulmaire, and C. Tilly; 2012) in *Work, Employment, and Society* (2013 Sage Prize of British Sociological Association); "Retail Jobs in Comparative Perspective" (with C. Tilly, M. Van Klaveren, and D. Voss-Dahm; 2010) in *Low-Wage Work in the Wealthy World,* ed. J. Gautié and J. Schmitt (Russell Sage Foundation); and "Nonstandard Work Arrangements in France and the United States" (2003) in *Non-standard Work Arrangements in Japan, Europe, and the United States,* ed. Susan Houseman and Machiko Osawa (Upjohn Institute). She co-edited *Are Bad Jobs Inevitable?* (Palgrave, 2012) and *Nonstandard Work: The Nature and Challenges of Changing Employment Arrangements* (Cornell University Press, 2000). She has chapters in books by Sage Publications, M. E. Sharpe, Presse de l'Université Laval, and Routledge. Other research is published in the *British Journal of Industrial Relations, Revue Interventions Economiques,* and *Women in Management Review.* Carré received a PhD in urban and regional studies from the Massachusetts Institute of Technology.

Maria José Chambel is Associate Professor at the Faculty of Psychology, University of Lisbon in Lisbon (Portugal). She has a PhD in social psychology and teaches in work and organizational psychology. She is member of the CIPUL (Research Centre in Psychology of the University of Lisbon) where she coordinates the group of Organizational Behavior and Development.

Her main research interests include subjects such as employment relations, temporary workers, and stress and well-being at work. She was
the responsible researcher for the project "Employment Relationships of
Temporary Workers: Human Resource Management Importance" (PTDC/
PSI-PTO/102046/2008–2009 to 2011; http://trabalhadorestemporarios
.fp.ul.pt). Currently, she is the responsible researcher for the project
"Temporary Agency Workers' Transitions: Motives, Experiences and Outcomes" (PTDC/MHC-PSO/4399/2012–2013 to 2015; http://taw.fp.ul.pt).

Catherine E. Connelly is Canada Research Chair and Associate Professor of Organizational Behaviour at the DeGroote School of Business
at McMaster University in Hamilton, Canada. She conducts research
on workers with non-standard employment arrangements (e.g., contingent workers, part-time employees, volunteers, board members, and
contractors). Her research has been published in several outlets including the *Journal of Management*, the *Journal of Applied Psychology*,
the *Journal of Organizational Behavior*, the *Journal of Management
Information Systems*, the *Journal of Vocational Behavior, Information &
Management*, the *Journal of Business Ethics*, and several others. She is
an associate editor for *Human Relations* and the *Canadian Journal of
Administrative Sciences.*

Dick de Gilder is Associate Professor at the Department of Organization
Sciences at VU University, Amsterdam. His research focuses on social
identity processes in organizations. One of his specific interests involves
the way temporary employees perceive their employment status, how it
affects their level of identification with their work group and organization, and how this relates to the level of positive and negative behaviour
towards their work group and organization. He has published on this
topic in *Personnel Review* and has published on social identity in journals
such as the *Academy of Management Review*, the *Journal of Applied
Psychology*, the *Personality and Social Psychology Bulletin*, the *Journal
of Experimental Social Psychology*, and the *European Journal of Social
Psychology.*

Ronald Dekker is Labour Economist at ReflecT: the Research Institute for
Flexicurity, Labour Market Dynamics, and Social Cohesion at Tilburg
University, an inter-faculty and multi-disciplinary research institute
initiated and coordinated by Tilburg Law School, in which Tilburg
School of Economics and Management and Tilburg School of Social
and Behavioural Sciences are involved as well. Dekker's research interests are in flexible labour, employment security and labour market
policy, and the relation between flexible labour and (social) innovation. Dekker has been involved in many research projects (European
Union, national governments), consultancy activities, and labour market punditry.

Jan de Leede is Assistant Professor of Human Resource Management, Faculty Management and Governance, University of Twente. Since the end of 2008, he has been the owner of ModernWorkx, a research and consultancy firm. Previously, he was employed as a senior researcher/consultant at TNO Work and Employment. He is focused on research and consultancy in the field of flexible labour, working times, and (virtual) team-based work. His work has been published in journals like *Ergonomics, Human Resource Management Journal, Personnel Review,* and *International Journal of Operations and Production Management.*

Silvia Dorado is Associate Professor of Management at the University of Rhode Island, United States, and Visiting Professor at the University of Waterloo, Ontario, Canada. Her research addresses topics such as the development of socio-economic hybrid organizations and institutional entrepreneurship. Silvia received her BA degree from Universidad Autónoma de Madrid, Spain; her MA from Massachusetts Institute of Technology; and her PhD from McGill University. She has published in some of the top journals in management, including *Academy of Management Journal, Journal of Business Venturing, Nonprofit and Voluntary Sector Quarterly,* and *Organization Studies.* Prior to her academic career, Dorado worked for Andersen Consulting, the Latino Economic Development Center (University of Massachusetts Boston), and the World Bank.

Bjørnar Fahle is Senior Personnel Coordinator at GE Oil & Gas. He holds a master's degree in change management from University of Stavanger, Norway. His main interests include organizational development, management development, and implementation of business strategy. He has conducted research on businesses in the oil and gas industry using highly skilled consultants in their core business. He has published the results of this research in his master's thesis, "The Use of External Consultants in the Oil and Gas Industry: Exploring Managerial Challenges."

Nathalie Galais is Senior Lecturer at the Department of Organizational and Social Psychology at the University of Erlangen-Nuremberg, Germany. Her main research interests include worker-organization relationship in non-standard work arrangements, effects of contingent work status on team climate, and workers' identity formation. She has conducted research on skill development and health outcomes of different groups of contingent workers for federal institutes such as the Federal Institute for Vocational Education and Training, the Federal Institute for Occupational Safety and Health, and the Ministry of Education and Research. She has published the results of this research in *Human Relations* and the *International Journal of Selection and Assessment.*

Daniel G. Gallagher is CSX Corporation Professor of Management at James Madison University, United States. He earned his PhD at the University of Illinois. He has been a member of the faculty at the University of Iowa, Michigan State University, the University of Pittsburgh, and Queen's University, Canada. Gallagher's research has focused on a range of topics, including impasse resolution procedures, union commitment and participation, non-standard employment arrangements, and the career challenges of independent contracting. He is also currently pursuing a research agenda in the areas of rule bending and negotiations. His work has been published in leading journals in the areas of management, labour relations, psychology, and organizational behaviour. He continues to serve as an editorial board member for a number of journals, including *Human Relations*, *Labour & Society*, and the *European Journal of Work and Organizational Psychology*.

Christina Garsten is Professor of Social Anthropology at Stockholm University and of Globalization and Organization at Copenhagen Business School. She is Chair of the Executive Board of Score (Stockholm Centre for Organizational Research, Stockholm University, and Stockholm School of Economics). Her research interests focus on flexible forms of employment, subjectivity, and identity (*Workplace Vagabonds*, Palgrave Macmillan). More recent research engages with transparency and accountability in global organizations (*Transparency in a New Global Order*, co-edited with M. Lindh de Montoya, Edward Elgar; *Organizing Transnational Accountability*, co-edited with M. Boström, Edward Elgar), corporate ethics (*Ethical Dilemmas in Management*, co-edited with T. Hernes, Routledge), and the role of think tanks in influencing policy agendas.

Anneke Goudswaard holds a professorship in New Employment Relations at Windesheim University of Applied Sciences. She is a Senior Research Scientist and consultant at TNO. She holds a PhD and is a specialist in the field of flexibility of work and organisation (flexible work processes, working time flexibility, organisational flexibility, and flexible contracts). As a consultant, she supports organizations in several branches (industry, government, health care, transport, and temporary work agencies). This practice is aimed at achieving sustainable flexibility: beneficial for both the organization and personnel. She is also an expert in the field of healthy working hours and self-rostering practices. Besides this, she has extensive experience in research, both quantitative and qualitative, on behalf of national and European governments.

Axel Haunschild is Professor of Work and Employment Studies at Leibniz University of Hanover, Germany. He held Visiting Professorships at Royal Holloway College, University of London, and at the University of Innsbruck, Austria. His research interests include changing forms of work and organization, creative industries, the institutional embeddedness of work and employment, corporate social responsibility from an industrial relations perspective, organizations and lifestyles, and organizational boundaries. He has published in journals such as *Human Relations, Journal of Organizational Behavior, British Journal of Industrial Relations, International Journal of Human Resource Management,* and *Creativity and Innovation Management.* He has co-edited *Work Less, Live More? Critical Analysis of the Work-Life Boundary* (Palgrave, 2008).

Joaquin Herranz Jr is Associate Professor of Public Affairs, Daniel J. Evans School of Public Affairs, University of Washington. Joaquín Herranz's research interests include strategic management of public and non-profit agencies, networks, and the intersections of community development and arts and culture. His research on the strategic management and performance of multi-sectoral networks is published in top public management journals. Herranz's research includes studies for the Urban Institute, the U.S. Department of Housing and Urban Development, the World Bank, and the International Labour Organization. His current research focuses on extending the triple bottom-line concept (i.e., economic, social, and environmental) to include a cultural bottom line. His published scholarship includes peer-reviewed articles in the *Journal of Public Administration Research and Theory, Public Performance and Management Review, International Public Management Journal, Public Management Review,* and the *Nonprofit and Voluntary Sector Quarterly.* He is currently writing a book about quadruple bottom-line organizational performance in which he adds cultural creativity as the fourth bottom line to the triple bottom lines of financial, social, and environmental performance. Herranz holds a PhD in urban political economy and policy from the Massachusetts Institute of Technology and a master of city planning from the University of California, Berkeley. He also holds a BA in urban political economy from Occidental College.

Bas Koene is Assistant Professor of Organization and Human Resource Management at Rotterdam School of Management, Erasmus University Rotterdam in the Netherlands. He studies human agency and leadership in processes of institutional change and organizational development, especially regarding the organization of work and the management of temporary employment. He is also director of the Rotterdam School of Management case development centre. He has published in journals such as *Leadership Quarterly, Human Resource Management Journal, Journal of Organizational Change Management, Personnel Review, Human Relations,* and *Accounting, Organizations and Society.*

Torstein Nesheim is Senior Researcher at the Institute for Research in Economics and Business Administration (Bergen, Norway) and Professor at the Department of Administration and Organization Theory at the University of Bergen. His main research interests are organization boundaries, non-standard employment arrangements, organizational structure, and knowledge sharing in organizations. Nesheim has published his research in journals such as *Human Resource Management, Scandinavian Journal of Management,* and *Personnel Review.*

François Pichault is Professor at HEC-Management School (University of Liège, Belgium). He is also Affiliated Professor in Human Resource Management at ESCP-Europe, Paris. He holds a PhD in sociology and chairs, at the University of Liège, an action-research centre (LENTIC) focused on human and organizational aspects of change and innovation processes. He has published numerous books and papers on organizational change and human resources management issues. He is currently in charge of a long-term interdisciplinary research programme on emergent flexicurity devices involving labour market intermediaries. He has published in journals such as *Organization Studies, Human Resource Management Journal, European Journal of Work Organizational Psychology, Applied Psychology: An International Review,* and *European Management Journal.*

Ida Regalia is Professor of Comparative Industrial Relations in the Department of Social and Political Sciences of the University of Milan. She has carried out research in the fields of comparative industrial relations, interest organizations, worker representation, labour policies, and the regulation of new forms of employment. Currently, she is the scientific coordinator of the three-year research programme "Old and New Paths of Labour Regulation in SMEs in European Countries: Trends and Challenges for Economic competitiveness and Social Sustainability." Her recent publications in English include the following: "Regional and Local-Level Experiments for Labor-Market Policy in Europe," in ed. K. Stone and H. Arthurs, *Rethinking Workplace Regulation: Beyond the Standard Contract of Employment* (Russell Sage, 2013); and the edited volume *Regulating New Forms of Employment: Local Experiments and Social Innovation in Europe* (Routledge, 2006).

Anita E. Tobiassen is Associate Professor at Oslo and Akershus University College of Applied Sciences, School of Business in Oslo, Norway. Her main research interests are knowledge sharing within and between firms, and internationalization and growth of small- and medium-sized firms. She has published in journals such as *International Small Business Journal, Journal of Knowledge Management, Journal of International Entrepreneurship,* and *Scandinavian Journal of Business Research.*

Lars Walter is Senior Lecturer at the School of Business, Economics and Law, University of Gothenburg, Sweden. His recent research focus has been on the organization and practices of labour markets and the intersection between labour markets and the organization of work and employment. Some of his recent publications include "Objects-in-Use and Organizing in Action Nets: A Case of an Infusion Pump," together with Kajsa Lindberg, in *Journal of Management Inquiry* (2013); and *Assembling Health Care Organizations: Practice, Materiality and Institutions* (Palgrave Macmillan, 2012), together with Kajsa Lindberg and Alexander Styhre.

Christa L. Wilkin is Assistant Professor in the School of Human Resource Management at York University in Toronto, Canada. She was a faculty member in the College of Business and Economics at California State University Northridge. She received her PhD from McMaster University in Hamilton, Canada. Her research interests can be broadly characterized as being in the area of employment relationships with two arching streams of research: (1) individual and team factors that influence work behaviour and (2) non-standard employment relationships. She studies factors such as the impact of emotions, personality, and organizational justice on task and contextual performance. Her research on non-standard work arrangements includes temporary workers and volunteers. Her work is published in the *Journal of Organizational Behavior*, *International Journal of Selection and Assessment*, and *International Journal of Human Resource Management*. She has also contributed chapters to several books, including *Underemployment: Psychological, Economic, and Social Challenges*; *The Role of Emotion and Emotion Regulation in Job Stress and Wellbeing*; and *Increasing Student Engagement and Retention Using Classroom Technologies*. She is also a certified human resources professional.

Ton Wilthagen is Chair in Institutional and Legal Aspects of the Labour Market at Tilburg University, the Netherlands. He is Director of ReflecT: the Research Institute for Flexicurity, Labour Market Dynamics, and Social Cohesion at Tilburg University, an inter-faculty and multi-disciplinary research institute initiated and coordinated by Tilburg Law School, in which Tilburg School of Economics and Management and Tilburg School of Social and Behavioural Sciences are involved as well. Wilthagen is also Chair of the Department of Labour Law and Social Policy at Tilburg University. Wilthagen's research interests are in employment regulation, industrial relations, and a variety of labour market issues. His main focus is on the themes of flexicurity, transitional labour markets, inclusive labour markets, and life-course approaches, on which he has published extensively. Wilthagen has been involved in many European-scale research projects, networks, and consultancy activities.

Virginie Xhauflair holds a master's degree in anthropology from the University of Liege and an MPhil in social sciences from the Catholic University of Louvain. She holds a PhD in management and economics from the Sorbonne

Graduate Business School (University Paris 1 Panthéon-Sorbonne) and from HEC-Management School of the University of Liege. After ten years of action research at LENTIC, a centre at HEC-Management School focusing on inter-organizational innovation processes, she joined the Centre for Social Economy in 2013. In 2011 and 2012, she was a visiting fellow at the Centre for Business research at the Judge Business School of the University of Cambridge. Her research work focuses on how innovative schemes emerging at the local level contribute to the transformation of social regulation, especially regarding labour market regulation. She is particularly interested in the reflexive role of third-party actors supporting and coaching these change processes.

Index

Printed in the United States
by Baker & Taylor Publisher Services